WHITE RACISM

WHITE RACISM

· A PSYCHOHISTORY ·

by JOEL KOVEL

VINTAGE BOOKS

A DIVISION OF RANDOM HOUSE

NEW YORK

To VIRGINIA, JONATHAN, and ERIN

Acknowledgments

SINCE I cannot hope to individually thank all the people whose personal influence is reflected in these pages, I must mention only those who have been directly involved in their preparation.

I am deeply grateful to Dr. Milton Rosenbaum for encouragement and advice, and to Dr. Joseph Cramer, who gave essential support; also to Dr. Heinz Hartmann, who gave counsel in psychoanalytic theory while I was trying to formulate some of my ideas; to Dr. Norman Reider, who kindly read and criticized an earlier draft; to Drs. Paul Nemetz and Joel Feiner, who each provided invaluable practical assistance in preparing the manuscript; and especially to Dr. Bennett Simon, who painstakingly read much of the manuscript and gave me the great benefit of many hours of fruitful discussion.

Further thanks are due to my brother, Alexander Kovel, and to Tom Cohen and Roy Jackson, for their moral and practical support throughout; to my secretary, Deborah DeMatteo, and to Carol Sudhalter, who worked long and well typing and retyping; to Martha Gillmor, whose support and editorial advice are deeply appreciated; and especially to Sara Blackburn, for her editing of the manuscript and counseling of its author.

My gratitude is also due to André Schiffrin, for his guidance through the toils of composition; and, last and most, to those to whom the book is dedicated, my wife and children, who sustained me and put up with my writing.

CONTENTS

And now, I think, the meaning of the evolution of civilization is no longer obscure to us. It must present the struggle between Eros and Death, between the instinct of life and the instinct of destruction, as it works itself out in the human species. This struggle is what all life essentially consists of, and the evolution of civilization may therefore be simply described as the struggle for life of the human species. And it is this battle of the giants that our nursemaids try to appease with their lullaby about Heaven.

Freud, *Civilization and Its Discontents*

WHITE RACISM

CHAPTER 1
INTRODUCTION

OUR RACIAL CRISIS has made us realize that white racism in America is no aberration, but an ingredient of our culture which cannot be fully understood apart from the rest of our total situation. In the pages that follow I shall consider our racial dilemma as the product of the historical unfolding of Western culture. The irrational power racism holds over us may then be seen as part of the larger unreason in which we live.

I am aware as I write that tons of paper and type have been devoted to racism in recent years. Why yet another study? What is needed, clearly, is positive action and not more words. But positive action does not come, or if it seems to come, brings another kind of disorder in its path. This predicament was the major stimulus to this work. By bringing a new approach to bear, I propose to delineate in depth what many know intuitively: that racism, far from being the simple delusion of a bigoted and ignorant minority, is a set of beliefs whose structure arises from the deepest levels of our lives—from the fabric of assumptions we make about the world, ourselves, and others, and from the patterns of our fundamental social activities. A program of action adequate to redress the wrongs of racism and to restore a just order to our society

3　•

will have to encompass a substantially more radical change than that envisioned currently.

The most difficult, because unpleasant, fact that we must face is that for all its malevolence, racism served a stabilizing function in American culture for many generations. Indeed it was a source of gratification to whites. It defined a social universe, absorbed aggression, and facilitated a sense of virtue in white America—a trait which contributed to America's material success. Racism was an integral part of a stable and productive cultural order. Because of the incompatibility of this old order with advanced industrial life, with our ideals, and with the will of black people, we must try to eradicate racism and to move away from its delusions. But this change of direction brings in its wake instability, and a set of anxieties and counterresponses which threaten the advances our culture has made.

If racism has had a stabilizing effect in our culture and helped sustain its "higher" elements by binding up the "lower," as I hope to demonstrate, then our culture is markedly less virtuous than ideology would have it. Our ideals are nourished by corrupt roots and survive by a continuously sustained act of self-deception.

In thinking through the hypotheses proposed in this work, I have reconsidered certain problems in the theory of culture and history. The result is a conceptual framework termed *psychohistory*, which is an approach involving a concept of culture as a *system of shared meanings,* an organized structure of symbols, made by men in order to define their world and regulate their mutual relations. Culture is both *organic*—in that it presents a coherent and self-evident view of human reality—and *synthetic*—in that it works upon and ties together elements of experience created by human activity. Human activity has no inherent order, aside from that imposed by culture and given by basic biological situations common to all men. Our activity is chiefly driven and unconscious. Accordingly, culture's work of synthetic integration must include relating all sorts of logically incompatible shreds of human experience. In this synthesis, culture distorts the actualities of our existence, placing intense emotional value on constructions of reality that are grossly absurd to an objective view. Nonetheless it proceeds, facilitated by the richness of the human symbolic apparatus and by man's instinctual urge to draw together with other men.

Men draw themselves together in a culture through the various structures upon which it rests: the institutions of society; church, state, systems of economics and work, systems of technology, systems of belief about other people, and so forth. Each institution has a distinct and differentiated structure, yet all are symbolically related in culture. Culture becomes an organism of meaningful symbols, which refer to "real" events and to institutional structures in society. To a certain extent, the institutions of civilization are given life because of the symbolic value they fulfill. Since that symbolic value is distorted in the interests of mental synthesis, the institutions and the activities they subserve are distorted in a corresponding way. All cultural institutions share a common symbolic ground, and all mean more to men than their manifest function suggests. Some cultural structures are heavily the creatures of symbolic distortion. Racism is perhaps the most glaring of this class. However, I am not suggesting that racism is merely a product of the symbolic foibles of the human mind. It is indeed a symbolic product, a set of fantasies, but only insofar as the *symbols and fantasies of racism have been themselves generated by the history of race relations and sustained by the rest of an organically related culture.*

This defines by implication the method of this study.

For we can see that racism (as well as any other aspect of culture) needs to be approached from the interaction of several lines of inquiry. Put simply, we must derive the symbolism and fantasies underlying racism, and study their historical emergence and transformations, simultaneously. The inner nature of a cultural phenomenon becomes understandable only when its historical substructure has been grasped. And so we must study racism both psychologically and historically, first as separate problems and then in integration. When we have integrated the two levels we may call the result *psychohistory*. Psychohistory, then, may be defined as the study of the *historical function of the changing meanings of things,* a theory of cultural change.[1]

This is no simple task, for we must dig into the structure of cultural symbolism without ignoring the surface of historical actuality. A failure to explore deeply would result in another rehash of what everyone already knows, while an ignorance of the surface would bring about a sterile reductionism comparable to a study of a living creature that proceeded by a chemical appraisal of its ashes. Our unit of study is racism; but behind racism is the totality of culture, an entity embedded within a deep and unconscious matrix of meanings. Racism also exists

[1] It should be emphasized that this is my personal definition of psychohistory. Others—such as Robert Jay Lifton—have also worked toward the integration of psychology and history, and have used the term *psychohistory* to describe their method. In each instance, though the over-all goal is roughly similar, the means of approach are different—and, ideally, different words should be used for each line of inquiry. But psychohistory is such a useful term that I am using it here.

I understand that the distinction between my method and Lifton's lies in the emphasis I place on the unconscious meaningfulness of culture as a synthetic organism. Lifton's studies have emphasized historical functions of national character. Clearly, culture and national character are closely related, and both are historical variables. Nonetheless, different vantage points are used to account for each phenomenon, and approaches to psychohistory will vary.

embedded in a matrix of culturally derived meanings, all of which change under the force of historical movement. Racism too changes and reflects in itself the over-all historical progression of our culture.

There are no independent variables in our study: everything in culture changes as a function of everything else; every symbol is tied to all others, and they all change their meanings. And yet there are common roots, historical continuities, certain basic patterns of meaning that inhere in symbols no matter how they are played upon by the changes of history, just as certain underlying biochemical and structural patterns hold true throughout biological evolution despite the endless changing and elaboration of organic forms. The search for continuity amidst change is the singular task of any historical or evolutionary study. We shall see that what is continuous in cultural symbolism reflects what is continuous in human life of whatever historical epoch. This continuity is grounded in the universal realities of the life of the body and the experiences of infancy, which are the reference points of human knowledge and the bedrock of the structures of culture.

No cultural study is complete without taking into account the immense repository of meanings that come from these sources. The symbolism of the infantile body invests everything else we do with enduring meaning. Though we are largely unaware of that meaning, it can be derived through application of psychoanalytic thought to the problems of culture. Therefore our study will rely heavily on the psychoanalytic calculus of meanings. No other approach seems to me as able to take into account the full range of human experience. I shall focus my discussion on the way psychoanalysis enables us to widen our semantic range, how it taps the unconscious meanings inherent in every thought or act, how it shows the imprint of past mental activity upon the present and explores the connections between the carnal and the sublime.

But this work is not an exercise in applied psychoanalysis. It requires another order of conceptualization derived from data on mass behavior and historical fact; and removed by a whole phase of organization from the data of individual psychology. From this order of conceptualization, connecting links can be drawn to the theories of psychoanalysis, and the tool of analysis can be used to elucidate cultural data. Culture is our ultimate subject: psychology is but a means of getting at the inner laws of cultural change. Consequently, the section devoted to an exposition of psychoanalytic theory is a highly selective one that pays considerable attention to certain aspects of analytic theory which are of special importance to our historical survey, and slights others. For example, the role of conflict, especially the inevitable conflicts along certain instinctual lines, has been stressed; while the role of healthy adaptation, or of what have been called autonomous functions of the ego, has only been touched upon. Clearly no individual can live off the harsh and painful situation I have described in the section on analytic theory. Yet such a situation exists and is a vital underlying element of historical change. Therefore I have described it fully, and largely ignored the "healthy" part of human psychology.

Implicit in this is a belief that human instinctual conflict, when projected onto culture, is one of the crucial determinants of historical power. And the power of one man or group of men over others—in our case, of white men over black—is the single most salient thread of history.

Let us grant that this approach to history is less than well-rounded, that it concentrates on the destructive, oppressive, and pathological rather than on the achievements of mankind. But what is racism if not destructive, oppressive, and pathological? And is not the pathology of culture in some ways the main stimulus to historical change? What is historical power but the ability of some to turn the destructiveness in culture to their own ends, and to thereby make those ends the direction toward which history moves? The power that invests history with so much dynamism is as much the product of the way people conceive of themselves, others, and the world, as it is the product of machines. The historical power we study as part of the problem of racism is in some way derived along with race symbols and fantasies—"along with" and not "from," for power is not derived from racism any more than racism is derived directly from power: it is often the least powerful who are the greatest bigots, while those at the top bask in tolerance and magnanimity. Yet both the mental attitudes necessary for power within our culture, and those that underly our variant of racism, are generated from a common ground. From this deeper level certain symbolic elements seep up to nourish and orient the mind as it acts within culture. Given these elementary ways of thinking about things, power can be generated upon the world, a power that will in turn reflect the symbolism that went into its creation. I hope to show that the power of which I write stems from a view of the universe that takes the symbols of *whiteness* and *blackness* with a deadly seriousness, spreads them out to the whole of human activity, and, from that point, onto the many-hued skins of men, thereby reducing them to the categories of race. And as a result of the many active lines of symbolism that radiate out from the ideas of race, both the relation of the white man with the black in America, and the struggle of blacks to achieve dignity, become a precipitate of our whole historical development and of all the discontents in its course.

Let me conclude this introduction with a plan of the work before us, along with some caveats.

I begin with a historical analysis of the course of white-black racism in America. It should be made clear that I will not discuss other styles of race prejudice and discrimination. This is not to deny their significance. I have focused on black-white racism for two reasons—because of its overriding importance, and because of my conviction that the pursuit of one phenomenon in depth can yield insight into the inner structure of culture.

Every fact in the historical presentation has been culled from a secondary source. I am responsible, of course, for the selection of data, and I have tried to make my interpretative position as explicit as possible by liberally weaving my notions in with the facts from which they were derived. My sources obviously cannot be held responsible for any errors in my presentation, nor for the opinions expressed, many of which I would expect them not to share.

Following the historical introduction is a section on psychology, the first part a theoretical discussion of some aspects of psychoanalysis (which is expanded in an appendix); the second, an examination of the fantasies of racism and a preliminary venture into the structure of racist belief.

From there we move into psychohistory proper. The basis for integration of the two levels of knowledge is discussed in the chapter on historical symbolism, which contains the nuclear methodological point of the entire study. Then we proceed into more substantive matters: two chapters on the general psychohistory of Western culture; a chapter, in some respects the culmination of the work, devoted to the special psychohistory of black-white racism in America; and an epilogue to round things off.

The ideas I present may arouse some controversy. If so,

one of my aims will be fulfilled: to stimulate thought and discussion about a situation so tragic and overwhelming as to demand the most remorseless examination. Having said this, I may note as well two aims that do *not* belong to the work. One is a presentation of the black situation. This is not a work in black history or psychology; it does not pretend to make an adequate analysis of the black response to Western culture. The "White Problem" is under consideration here: the problem of those children of history who created the situation of racism and therefore bear responsibility for it. Consequently, black sources, which would have to be studied closely in any full-scale assessment of the entire historical problem of racism, have been relatively unused in this work and appear only as they highlight the central theme of white experience.

Second, this book is not an attempt to formulate a comprehensive or even coherent program to resolve our dilemma—some "way out," some consolation. I have some notions, stated rather broadly, toward the conclusion of the book, as to the spirit in which relief should be sought and possibly achieved, but, given the general state of things, I suffer few illusions as to their possibility. Perhaps the pessimistic tone will not be borne out by the future. If so, no error could be more welcome.

CHAPTER 2
REFLECTIONS ON THE HISTORY OF AMERICAN RACISM

Those who live in a cold climate and in Europe are full of spirit, but wanting in intelligence and skill. [They] keep their freedom but have no political organization, and are incapable of ruling over others.

Aristotle, *Politics*

Historically, the non-white complexion has evoked and exposed the "devil" in the very nature of the white man.

What else but a controlling emotional "devil" so blinded American white intelligence that it couldn't foresee that millions of black slaves, "freed," then permitted even limited education, would one day rise up as a terrifying monster within white America's midst.

The Autobiography of Malcolm X

RACISM IS NOT a new phenomenon. Men have long tried to identify themselves not only as individuals but as members of social groups; and to set up viable social groups, they have thrust others out. These "others" have been differentiated in various ways, for instance, according to clan, tribe, nation, estate, or class. The forms change, but the process of self-definition is seemingly endless. And all these "others" have one feature in common: they are never quite as good as the self. Some mysterious tag of devaluation is attached to the other person as his essential point of distinction from the group of selves.

So much is common knowledge. Wars have been fought and nations sacked according to this odd way of thinking. History is littered with the corpses of selves and others who killed and died to defend their identity. And today, although we know a little better, the same source of destruction still hangs over our heads, poisons our societal life, and impedes in countless ways the long-awaited maturation of mankind.

Of all America's exclusions, none approaches in strength that of the black people by white people, the distinction of a self and an other according to the mysterious quality of race, especially as revealed in the mark of skin color. Nothing looms quite so large, both as an endless source of crisis and as the sign of a deep cultural malaise, as does racism.

Although the initial European reaction to the Negroid race was mixed and inconsistent, the "heathenism," nakedness, sexual libertarianism, and, above all, the blackness of Africans served to set them off as profoundly distinct men who were *ipso facto damned* and consequently quite suitable for enslavement. As Winthrop Jordan comments in his masterful study, *White over Black,* "In Africa these qualities had for Englishmen added up to savagery; they were major components in that sense of *difference* which provided the mental margin absolutely requisite for placing the European on the deck of the slave ship and the Negro in the hold."[2]

Even if we assume that race fantasies are to a degree immemorial and spring from the universal human situa-

---

[2] Winthrop Jordan, *White over Black* (Chapel Hill, University of North Carolina Press, 1968), p. 97.

tion, they have been greatly influenced by the actual historical use to which they have been put, not only in slavery, but in a host of closely related cultural activities. And so race fantasies were only a contributing cause to the phenomenon of American slavery; it was, like any culturally vital institution, a weaving together of many strands of innovation and tradition, necessities and contingencies. Let me mention briefly a few of those strands.

As Whitehead noted in *Adventures in Ideas*, slavery was an axiom of Western culture, and considered the bedrock of society. Not strictly an axiom—rather, a corollary to the even more basic idea of *domination*. Slavery flowed naturally from the virtually unquestioned assumption that something in human nature and culture led men to dominate one another. Where domination was extreme and direct, with one man forcibly wielding power over another, as it had been since humans broke out of their neolithic stagnation, slavery was the natural consequence. This was the case in Africa at the time of its first contact with Europe, just as it had been the case in Europe. However, the ideal of freedom would gradually take hold of Europeans. A curious aspect of the notion of slavery has been its dialectical relation to the notion of freedom: the rise in the West of one paralleled the rise of the other. This incompatible conglomerate of opposing tendencies grew most marked in the American offshoot of Western civilization, where it has persisted ever since.

The extreme form of slavery which underlies our racism took a long time to develop. The English were slow to seize upon it. When the opportunities presented by enslavement became manifest, however, the Anglo-Saxon's superior powers of expansion made more efficient and lucrative what his Hispanic cohorts had begun. Even the Spanish and Portuguese, who opened up the slave trade and used it to such advantage in the development of

Latin America, acquired but a secondary interest in the practice. Their ruling passion throughout, along with the English and all Europeans, was material and spiritual expansion. At first the slaves were a mixed lot, white and black alike suffering varying degrees of forced servitude. As time went on, however, the inner workings of the new North American culture inexorably forced the concepts of black men and slavery into complete one-to-one identity. Though to a certain degree this racial polarization was dictated by expediency (no other source of forced labor was quite so plentiful, cheap, and identifiable), two profoundly important aspects of the process deserve particular attention.

The first is that aspect of Western culture which has made it unique among peoples and has correspondingly made its brand of slavery unique: its attitude toward property. The most superficial glance at our civilization discloses the power of the concept of property, and a good deal of what is radically destructive to human potentiality in our culture derives from its well known preference for property rights over human rights. Well known indeed, and well attacked by generations of libertarians. Yet the preference remains; and it remains to a certain extent baffling. Why become so preoccupied with property that a world is laid waste in its pursuit? Only something thought to be profoundly important can deserve such interest. Property is made of "things." Why prefer things over humanity? What do these "things" mean to our culture?

Property is some portion of the external world that a man's self may call its own. Property means, therefore, that a man's self—the inner idea of his personage—is united with and enlarged by part of the "thing"-world. One part of the world ordinarily owned by every man's self is his own body. Indeed, the body is really all of the world that the self can own—ordinarily. But the West is extraordinary in that it has held for centuries that the *summum bonum* of life on earth is the expansion of the self through its acquisition of property.

On the other hand, the West, which was to convulse the globe in its search for material acquisitions, has never really been happy with its desire for property. Nowadays the whole process—desire for and horror of acquisition—has, without losing its basic force, been rationalized and made abstract: this has been the consistent direction of our history. But let us note, with Johan Huizinga, that the striving for material, concrete wealth grew in mounting proportion throughout the medieval era to a frantic preoccupation. Pride, the cardinal sin of the early medieval era, became supplanted by cupidity as time wore on; and at the close of the Middle Ages of Europe, preoccupation with wealth and anxiety about that preoccupation became one of the principal inner spurs to the changes which ushered in the modern era. We must postpone discussion of the transformations in culture that enabled Europe to master its impulses and dreads and at the same time mandated its conquest of the globe. Let us note, however, that despite the material success of what is called the bourgeois-Protestant alteration in European culture, the basic dilemmas centering about property were never resolved. Indeed, Europeans were giving the death sentence to petty thieves at the time they first encountered the allegedly barbaric African states, where the same crime warranted but a public shaming. In the eighteenth century, with the modern age well on its way, the machine about to take over the world, and Africa bled to the point of death by the slave trade, a child in England could still be executed for stealing a scrap of cloth —manufactured, of course, from slave-grown cotton. Nothing so demonstrates the oddity of the West's attitude toward property as the manner in which Western man enslaved black Africans. We noted earlier that property rationally begins and ends with the possession of one's own body. It was precisely this limit that the West breached with its slavery. For the American slaver did not simply own the *body* of his black slave—although even that may have been more extreme than some earlier variants of slavery, where the slave's freedom was but limited and only his work owned. The American slaver went one step further in cultural development: he first reduced the human self of his black slave to a body and then reduced the body to a *thing*; he dehumanized his slave, made him quantifiable, and thereby absorbed him into a rising world market of productive exchange. In the creation of this world market, the Westerner was changing his entire view of reality—and changing reality in accordance with his new conception of it. Thus, in the new culture of the West, the black human was reduced to a black thing, virtually the same in certain key respects as the rest of non-human nature—all of which could become property.

A particular master-slave relation developed under the specific circumstances of American history. Although there were points of similarity with other slave systems (much of which remains the subject of active investigation), a basic, and characteristically American, style emerged as black slavery hardened into an institution. The slaver in effect said to his slave, "While I own much, much more than my body, you own not even your body: your body shall be detached from your self and your self shall be thereby reduced to subhuman status. And being detached and kept alive, your body shall serve me in many ways: by work on my capitalist plantations to extract the most that can be taken from the land in the cheapest and therefore most rational manner; as a means to my bodily pleasure—both as nurse to my children and as female body for sexual use (for my own women are somehow deficient in this regard); and as medium of exchange, salable like any other commodity of exchange along with or separate from the bodies of your family. For in fact you have no family, since a family is a system that pertains to human beings, and you are not human. And since I, being a man of the West, value things which are owned above all else, I hold you—or, rather, the owned part of you, your body—in very high regard and wish to retain you as my property forever. On the other hand, since I have a certain horror of what I am doing, and since you are the living reminder of this horror and are subhuman to boot, I am horrified by you, disgusted by you, and wish to have nothing to do with you, wish, in fact, to be rid of you. And since this set of ideas is inconsistent and will stand neither the test of reason nor of my better values, I am going to distort it, split it up, and otherwise defend myself against the realization."

In practice this schema underwent endless variations. The distillation of this notion was the essence of the American slave system, however, and had a reality of its own: it became the basis in *culture* of the *idea* of the black man, and it has consequently become the historical nucleus of our present-day racism.

The reduction of the black person to a thing afforded the slaver much more than gratification. It also became necessary for his security. In order to safeguard the gains he was extracting with his new world view, and to protect himself from his inner reaction to what he was doing to other humans, he had to maintain *absolute control*. This was doubly necessary, for the blacks who survived their frightful passage to the New World were a selected lot of great hardiness. Moreover, they were by no means the Uncle Toms that later ideology made them; in fact we know they carried out, at first in the South and throughout Latin America, many serious rebellions. Thus, from the beginning, the slaver had to contend with real threats to his power.

But cultural evolution is a useful thing, and it eventually became apparent that the dehumanization which afforded the planters such satisfaction from their chattels also provided the best method of controlling the slaves' rebelliousness. Nothing domesticated the undesirable rage out of black people so much as consistent and prolonged "thingification." In time, a compact and coherent culture centering about plantation slavery grew up in the South; and since one function of culture is to determine what is to be considered reasonable and normal, the success of Southern culture made rational what seems bizarre to us today. As an example of this striking rationalization, consider the words of a South Carolina planter of 1682:

> A rational man will certainly enquire, "when I have land, what shall I do with it? What commodities shall I be able to produce, that will yield me money in other countries, that I may be enabled to buy Negro slaves (without which a planter can never do any great matter)?"[3]

Or those of a Virginia statute of 1669 that held it not to be a felony should a master kill a slave who resisted punishment:

> It cannot be presumed that prepensed malice (which alone makes murder felony) should induce any man to destroy his own estate.[4]

Slavery lost its rationalization only when the advance of a more diffused capitalism brought its weakness out into the open—in short, when it became unproductive. As long as slavery worked, it seemed perfectly sensible

[3] Quoted in Stanley M. Elkins, *Slavery* (Chicago, University of Chicago Press, 1959), pp. 47–48.
[4] Quoted in Elkins, *Slavery*, p. 59.

to most people. This reasonableness, this abstraction applied to what had previously been a straightforward philosophy of domination, constitutes one of the West's central contributions to cultural evolution. And in America, rationalization was applied right at the beginning to an extreme interest in dominated property—property that moreover became totally identified with people who happened to have black skin, the color that had always horrified the West. Here we strike the root of our racism.

Thus the first feature underlying our history of racism is the nexus of ideas about property. The second concerns the unification of the people who settled the North American continent into a national group with a national identity. Most historians tend to assume that this process is completed in the United States. They will cite the need for the formation of a national identity as one of the major and most complex problems for developing nations in Latin America and Africa. Yet in fact this process has never been completed in the United States; it has been blocked throughout by the race problem.

We cannot divorce this problem from that of property, for the two concepts, race and property, became linked at the beginnings of our culture. The connection was made official in the Constitution, which, as we know, wove the whole issue into the fabric of the nation by neatly quantifying black slaves into three-fifths of a person for purposes of representation. There are certain critical phases through which the historical forces in flux centering about race, property and national identity have played themselves out. Beginning with the establishment of slavery, these phases encompass many of the principal themes of our national history up to the present day— which is only to restate the centricity of race in American culture. I list the phases to provide points of reference for later discussion; it is presumed that the reader has fuller familiarity with their history.

1. *The Formalization of Slave Status.* Here the ideas of white and black races became coterminous with those of freedom and bondage. The early pattern, in which whites too could be held in some form of slavery, became rigidly redefined along racial lines. This occurred principally in the latter half of the seventeenth century, in the context of the bourgeois revolution which was sweeping Northern Europe. Henceforth the British colonies would be composed (in cultural ideal if not always in fact) of free, white, propertied bourgeois citizens, and black chattels.

2. *The Formation of the Nation.* A flurry of antislavery activity, spurred by the ideals of the Enlightenment, accompanied the War for Independence. When the time came to structure the new nation, however, propertied interests reasserted themselves and further etched the slave-race complex into our national culture. By this time some regional differentiation had set in, and slavery was disappearing from the North. Northerners put up little resistance to the institutionalization of racial slavery, largely because, despite having little direct use for slaves in their own economy, they were nevertheless accumulating fortunes from the slave trade and financial investments in plantation capitalism. A few years later, when the cotton gin and the dawn of the industrial age greatly magnified the profitability of our slave-centered economy, criticism died altogether, and black enslavement became a nationally accepted fact of life.

3. *Regional Struggle.* There were, however, regional variations in the mystique of property. The North (because of fear and lack of profit) eschewed direct ownership of black bodies and moved instead into a more general and fluid kind of economic transaction. The South

held on to what was in some respects capitalistic, but was fundamentally a means to a feudalistic order—held, that is, onto direct control of land and bodies of men, but tried to live within a larger bourgeois order. The North was vastly more successful as a subculture, and in the course of headlong growth there arose within it a group of influential intellectuals who urged the abolition of slavery. At first considered unworldly visionaries, the abolitionists gradually attracted support as regional expansion offered material grounds for opposing the extension of slavery.

For a host of reasons, detailed discussion of which would take us too far afield, intense pressures for growth were building up throughout the young nation under the ideological banner of "Manifest Destiny." However, vital distinctions in styles of expansionism were developing within the two regions. Expansionist tendencies grew along with productivity (and, in an obscure way, reformism) in the North; while in the South, expansion was, as Eugene Genovese noted in his *Political Economy of Slavery*, an increasingly desperate effort to compensate for a crippling economic stagnation. Southern torpor followed directly from dominant Southerners' insistence on holding onto a hopeless, unsuccessful and anachronistic style of life. They had their good reasons, including a real fear of black rebellion should their control slip. These regional differences gradually sharpened and hardened, and the struggle was played out in terms of the acquisition of new lands to the West. As new territory was finite, however, it was only a question of time before the differences led to the Civil War.

4. *White Reunification.* The War left one group of whites in power, another group in smoking ruin, and an indigestible mass of black so-called Freedmen. The next fifty years saw the reunion of the whites into a national culture with massive industrial powers, and the expulsion

of the blacks into a state of alienation which in some respects equaled slavery. Material success led to material expansion and the gradual gathering of all white Americans into a cult of productivity and ownership. Expansionism traveled beyond America's shores in an extraordinary flurry of imperial interest at the turn of the century; Manifest Destiny was reborn as white America joined hands.

Several complicating factors existed however, most notably the formation of proletarian classes which threatened revolution both on the farm and in the factory, and the presence of assorted non-Teutonic groups: poor European immigrants, newly annexed brown-skinned colonials and the ever-present mass of Southern ex-slaves. Clearly, these several factors could become one massive threat to the existing order of power. The threat was obviated however; and though many factors were at play, one of the most important was the intensification of racist attitudes—held by nearly all white Americans, no matter how sophisticated. Thus was class struggle thwarted and the unification of white America ensured. The sufferers were the non-Teutonic races—most notably the black, who fell victim to a system of segregation and expunged human rights which differed little from formal slavery in its continued dehumanization.

5. *Beyond Racism.* The height of racism was reached with the consolidation and expansion of white America. At the same time, a new historical entity had been created: the nation-state. The strong central government, eventually to become an active, and then the dominant, force in international affairs, directed its influence inward as well as outward. The nation-state began at the turn of the twentieth century to regulate and fuse with the productive activities of industrial capitalism. In contemporary times, with two thirds of the century behind us, this

fusion has proceeded to such a profound extent that one may, with John K. Galbraith, call the nation-state the Industrial State. A more immediate manifestation is the Leviathan we call the military-industrial complex, with all its implications for foreign and domestic policy.

Though the nation-state has been motivated in part by a concern for those people crushed beneath the unregulated machinery of capitalism, its basic function has been to rationalize and perfect the inner workings of the capitalist order. As such it strives to maintain underlying cultural assumptions about such fundamental ideas as property. And the State does its work by taking an active role in the regulation of culture, thus serving a function filled by the Church in previous centuries. The State has consequently entered the arena of racial struggle as a third party, along with the white and black peoples. But these two groups are also undergoing change in the modern world.

At the center of contemporary history is the rapid development of black people. Having survived centuries of systematic degredation, they have been taking vigorous measures to free themselves. The conditions of this freedom, the profound resistance offered to it by whites, and the resulting storms within our culture shall all concern us in some detail at many further points in this work.

Having introduced the *dramatis personae*, let us look a little more closely at the curious relationships between some of these phenomena. Bear in mind that the focus is on culture, and that culture is an evolving system of meaningful relations deriving from the sum total of the activities and institutions of a society. So we must look for relationships between elements of our history, even if at first glance these elements seem at best incidental to each other, or even contradictory.

In all phases described above, an existing institutional

arrangement was broken down and a new one was created to meet the needs of changing times. From the breaking down of loose domination and the formalization of racial slavery, to the breaking down of entrepreneurial capitalism and the formation of the Industrial State, each phase has involved some kind of major dislocation in American life. A general direction permeates all these dislocations: each dislocation, each set of new institutions and matching identities, has been of an expansive nature. Each has freed cultural energies and resulted in an increased size and potency of the cultural unit. The dislocations may be seen as a kind of molting, as a snake sheds its skin and assumes a new one when it passes a certain size. The metaphor is apt, for, just as a skin is a kind of boundary between an organism and the world, so too does racism provide boundaries within a culture. Therefore our racism can be considered a kind of bounding process that goes on in American culture as it grows. As we grew more powerful, complex, and variegated, so did we become more racist, the race fantasies serving to define and control what might otherwise have gotten out of hand. Racism belongs then, for all its destructive irrationality, to the regulative aspects of our culture.

But as such, racism is only a bizarre aspect of a much more general phenomenon. One of the conditions of the modern struggle against racism is that racism has become more threatening than useful as a regulator of culture. Indeed, the main force in contemporary culture, the State, attacks it precisely from this assumption and seeks to replace it with another regulating device more appropriate to its interests. All cultures include as perhaps their most vital element systems which regulate behavior. We are most familiar with these under the name of morality; yet morality is only the visible superstructure of a culture's devices to control behavior, the tenth of the iceberg above water.

Nonetheless, with the passage of time, and the drawing together of society into larger and more complex groups, normative functions tend to appear in increasing force within culture (and become increasingly represented, as we shall observe, within the individual psyche). The historical manifestations of these normative functions include efforts to reform institutions. Through reformism, culture seeks to adapt itself to changing realities.

It is in this light that we observe the two main historical surges toward reform of racial injustice: the abolition movement and the current effort to unseat the crippling force of racism. Note that this view automatically makes each of these movements ambiguously two-sided. For though the antiracist surges have been motivated by the desire of just-minded people to eliminate evil, they have also each become incorporated into a larger cultural system in which they serve as regulators—and hence as benefactors—of the underlying forces which have created the racial injustice in the first place. Just as racism has not been a simple matter of gratuitous evil, but rather has been an evil that has served a real use in maintaining the potency of American culture, so too may antiracism be directed both to the elimination of the evil and to the preservation of the potency of American culture. But it is precisely that culture which in its potency has generated the evils of racism. I am sorry to have to present the matter so ambiguously and in such a complex manner, but unhappily that is the way the situation presents itself. Culture is an organism, and nothing that goes on within it is without regulative effect on all else. Whatever exists within a culture has a function: we may heap ethical condemnation upon it, but the ethical condemnation has a function too, insofar as it is derived from the main sources of cultural power, and serves to regulate the evil, not to replace it. Hence artists and visionaries—those who see beyond culture—have always led the way; but their advice is taken only when it is in the interests of culture to use it. Culture, then, adapts only to maintain its potency; otherwise, it will not change.

As subtle as some of these relationships are in the abstract, the ambiguity of racial reform is glaring in its practice. From colonial times until the present, what has begun as a manifest effort to secure justice for the black race has ended in only another variant of racism: black oppression and white solidarity and power.

The prominent abolitionist Theodore Parker attacked slavery with the utmost fervor, wallowing all the while in a sense of grandiose guilt. This is how he presented the story of enslavement to his congregation: "America, where is your brother? . . . He was weak and I seized him; naked and I bound him; ignorant, poor and savage, and I overmastered him. I laid on his feebler shoulders my grievous yoke. . . . Askest thou for the African? I have made him a beast. Lo, there Thou hast what is thine." Here is a mixture of historical truth and moral flagellation which both appeases the guilt of the white and patronizes the black. In effect, it exhorts the white to purify himself for higher conquest. For, as Parker made clear on another occasion, "Of all races, the Caucasian has hitherto shown the most . . . instinct of progress." And how shall progress be made manifest? God has spoken: "Then by peaceful purchase, the Anglo-Saxon may acquire the rest of the North American continent . . . extending the area of freedom at every step. . . . America, the mother of a thousand Anglo-Saxon states, tropical and temperate, on both sides of the equator . . .; may count her children at last by the hundreds of millions—and among them all behold no tyrant and no slave."[5]

Parker's words have a familiar ring. From Manifest Destiny in the 1840's to Vietnam in the 1960's, we have heard a similar call: clean house, purify and expunge the evil (slavery, racism), and get on to virtuous (ergo, white) conquests. The action should be peaceful if possible; but if not—if others, usually of darker color, should resist—then the "terrible swift sword" of American armed justice would clear the way. Moralism became, with the antislavery movement and its later absorption into the Union cause in the Civil War, the necessary accoutrement of American power. Lincoln's genius was to some extent in letting this equation take full hold in the national culture. As he put it: "Let us have faith that right makes might, and in that faith, let us, to the end, dare to do our duty as we understand it."

But duty and right and faith all converged on one sure means to might: capitalism, driven by the mystique of property. And so abolitionism, which began with the courage of Transcendentalist visionaries, came into full cultural being under the aegis of the Republican Party, the party that was later to abandon the black objects of its reformism when it had consolidated itself and wearied of fruitless radicalism. From its inception, the ambiguity of the Republican party's assumptions about its fundamental activity was glossed over by classic American ideology: "Republicans," said Lincoln, "are both for the *man* and the *dollar*; but in cases of conflict, the man *before* the dollar." Indeed. This proposition had a certain truth only if the *meaning* of man were qualified with the adjectives *white bourgeois*. But meanings are the province

---

[5] Quoted in Elkins, *Slavery*, p. 175, and in Thomas F. Gossett, *Race: The History of an Idea in America* (New York, Schocken Books, 1965), p. 181.

of culture, and for American culture this formula has always worked. Not for the black man, however, for he was not considered a man, neither in Lincoln's formulation nor by the culture of the West. And so racial reform has always foundered in its goal of helping the black person, by and large ignoring him in his actuality and concentrating instead on the evils to which he has been exposed. In this way American culture has managed to expose the black to a succession of different evils by a succession of different reforms.

At times the attitude of reformers underwent a reversion to an extreme of race sadism, which opens onto a fathomless abyss in the American character. At other times the race reformer simply acted with remote and destructive coldness toward the alleged beneficiaries of his efforts.

One example of the first type, the throwback, is Tom Watson. Leader of the Southern Populists, and energetic supporter of the union of poor whites and blacks into a common class against their economic exploiters, Watson underwent a radical change in sentiment when the realignment of national forces at the turn of the century brought Jim Crow segregation to the South. He, who had been the black man's friend, could later say that the Negro simply had "no comprehension of virtue, honesty, truth, gratitude and principle." The South had to "lynch him occasionally, and flog him, now and then, to keep him from blaspheming the Almighty, by his conduct, on account of his smell and his color."[6]

Perhaps the most telling example of the other, remote, variant of reformer *cum* racist was Woodrow Wilson. The most morally pure of American leaders, certainly a far-

[6] Quoted in Gossett, *Race*, p. 271.

seeing advocate of principled reform, Wilson stated in 1912 that he wished to see "justice done to the colored people in every matter; and not mere grudging justice, but justice executed with liberality and cordial good feeling." Yet Wilson was in the American mainstream that equated white virtue with power. He did not hesitate to apply that power to America's black neighbors in this hemisphere; and at home, despite fine ideals, Wilson put the *coup de grâce* to the misfortunes of black Americans by issuing an executive order which racially segregated the eating and toilet facilities of federal civil service workers. His final blow was to give Southern federal officials the right to discharge or downgrade without due process any black employee on any ground they saw fit. Needless to add, it was an opportunity well seized. And when a group of black leaders protested to the President, he, offended, sent them summarily from his office.

These extremes offer examples of what we all should know: that racism springs from the most widespread and impenetrable level of American experience. But there is another point to be made. Although the conjunction of racism with reformism is in some ways remarkable and deserves special study, we must recall that by and large most racists have been uninterested in reform. Yet whatever the specific situation, most Americans seem to behave in a rough way like either Watson or Wilson. That is, although there is a broad overlap, and enormous individual variations exist, racists have been either of the type who wished to oppress the black directly—as did Tom Watson—or indirectly, through avoidance—as did Wilson. We may generalize here—for reasons that will become clear later—and define two broad types of racism in America, types in close relationship, indeed in a state of continuous transition. Let us call them the *dominative* and *aversive* types of racism. I shall return to their description in the chapter on race fantasies; and for now will simply point out a few basic relationships between them.

In general, the dominative type has been marked by heat and the aversive type by coldness. The former is clearly associated with the American South, where, of course, domination of blacks became the cornerstone of society; and the latter with the North, where blacks have so consistently come and found themselves out of place. The dominative racist, when threatened by the black, resorts to direct violence; the aversive racist, in the same situation, turns away and walls himself off.

A trace of each type is of course in every racist. But the dominative type is prior, and emerges under extreme threats, or in states of regression (as with Watson); whereas the aversive response belongs to those of higher principle and a more advanced stage of intellectual development, like Wilson. Consequently the passage of time has favored the appearance of the aversive type in America, while threats to the existing racist order favor a regression to domination. Thus in the South, segregation succeeded the intimacy of slavery (whereas in the "advanced" North, segregation appeared much earlier). Again in the South, disturbances in the formal social structure of white-black relations would in classic times bring out the lynch mob; while today, racial turmoil brings out a latent "white backlash" of domination in both regions, more "advanced" perhaps, than lynching, but part of the same pattern.

The dominative type usually has a personal tie (albeit destructive) with his black object—the extreme having been slavery, when the slaver allowed his black woman to suckle his child; the aversive type avoids this and treats the black person as though he were a thing. There is thus a kind of reciprocal relationship between domination and aversion, neatly summed up by an observation of a squeamish English lady who was visiting the antebellum South. She noted that in a stagecoach or railroad car, "A lady makes no objection to ride next to a fat Negro woman, even when the thermometer is at ninety degrees; provided always that her fellow travelers understand she is her property."[7] On the other hand, in Massachusetts, where the view of black by white had supposedly changed from that of dominated property to that of moralistic concern, the fugitive slave Frederick Douglass noted that he was "introduced as a 'chattel'—a 'thing'—a piece of Southern property—the chairman assuring the audience that *it* could speak."

This phenomenon is of the greatest significance, and its explanation will occupy the major part of this work. It underlies the difference between regions of America, and defines the historical development of racism and much else in our culture. Moreover, the relationship between the dominative and aversive forms of racism becomes even more intriguing when one considers that whites in the North developed a reaction of aversion, and even of horror, toward blacks without any personal experience with them. Racism, in other words, has come automatically to Americans: it is generated by their culture. And even more peculiar is the quantitative aspect. American aversive racists have been, if anything, more intense in their reaction than their dominative brethren. That most perspicacious of observers, Alexis de Tocqueville, put the matter clearly: "the prejudice of race," he wrote, "appears to be stronger in the states that have

[7] Quoted in Samuel Eliot Morison, *The Oxford History of the American People* (New York, Oxford University Press, 1965), p. 506.

abolished slavery than in those where it still exists; and nowhere is it so intolerant as in those states where servitude has never been known. . . ."[8]

We have come a long way from slavery, and still racism persists. People "know better" now: the social sciences have demolished the twaddle of racist ideology; education has created a large, informed elite capable of seeing through the old fables of racism; and the decent impulses of millions of people strive to get us beyond the racist nightmare. Yet other millions hold frankly to the officially discredited race prejudices; while the pressure for social change being mounted by militant, no longer docile blacks forces awareness upon even the enlightened that generous feelings and rational knowledge are in profound conflict with an irrational, obscure and yet immensely powerful current of underlying racist sentiment.

The racist sentiment which pervades the life of virtually all white Americans is, though real and potent, not the only obstacle to the achievement of racial justice. Equally important as a general psychological factor is the general apathy and remoteness, the nonspecific coldness that prevails in our time. By and large we do not care for one another; we can be momentarily aroused to compassion, fear, or even rage, but as a rule we soon slip back into the comfortable torpor that typifies our life.

Psychology alone does not nearly account for the scope of the racial problem. Even if white Americans really cared, and even if we could at last overcome the underground stream of race hatred and aversion that runs through our lives, it is doubtful whether racism could be eliminated in a period brief enough to satisfy the demands of simple justice. The problems of modern racism have to a great extent passed beyond the wills—destructive or

[8] *Democracy in America* (New York, Vintage Books, 1945), Vol. I, p. 373.

constructive—of individuals. It is a general direction of history for institutions to grow in power by absorbing human activity. And so in racism, as in much else that vexes us, corrective action proceeds against the inertia of the massed resistance of a set of impersonal factors that have become precipitates of all that is antihuman in the culture of the West. And the victims of these forces continue to include, among many, those who have always suffered most deeply from the West's crimes against humanity: the black people.

Therefore the story of racism in America today is the story of poverty and bureaucratic inhumanity. It is the story of the fate of millions of chronically oppressed sharecroppers who left their rural misery in the South for a promise of something better in the North and West, a promise of social progress and work made possible by the superabundant productivity of advanced industrial society, to find instead the wasteland of advanced society. For the machine age had "advanced" society to such a level of abstraction and technocratic skill that it had no use for the labor of the great majority of blacks; and in the wake of this profitable advance it had heaped up the stony shacks we call urban ghettos, which have become, through aversive racism, almost the exclusive territory of black people. Here oppression and aversion pass into invisibility and create a new revolutionary class.

The revolutionary situation of black Americans is a reaction to numerous related institutions of our national society. Some—such as the pervasive police brutality and inferior educational opportunities that follow from black poverty and white bigotry—operate directly against the black people. Other aspects act indirectly but no less tellingly, the most powerful of these being our need—one may with reason call it a religious mystique—to protect and enlarge material productivity at all costs. One cost is the well-being of the poor and the black. Our militarism is derived to a great extent from this need, for it serves our religion of productivity as a near-perfect means, though it also drains away the resources desperately needed for social amelioration. However, this draining away, and the human neglect it produces, is also a congruent part of our national culture.

All of these oppressive forces, which have together forced black Americans into their despair, rage and rebellion, have a common denominator. It has been hinted at from time to time in earlier pages and must receive our utmost attention in the rest of this work.

I am referring again to the advanced and general state of *dehumanization* which pervades so much of our culture, but which seems to have been focused in our racial situation. Dehumanization is a twofold process, involving first, the formation of an idea of another living person as less than a person, as a living or even inanimate *thing*; and second, an *action* upon that person so as to sustain one's dehumanized conception of him. Obviously these two aspects—the idea and the action—are utterly necessary to each other. We shall dissect this relationship in some detail later, but here let us note that slavery was at the first an extreme, yet focal, dehumanization, whereas industrial capitalism has created a slightly less extreme but more diffuse dehumanization. Both race prejudice and chronic poverty have followed from slavery and industrial capitalism, and to that degree have black people been more grossly dehumanized in the eyes of their white fellow citizens.

Today a new style of dehumanization has been added, more rationalized and vastly more diffused than previous forms. I refer to the omnipresent manipulation of taste, thought, style, and wants in the interests of stimulating demand and rationalizing activity—in short, with the aim of controlling and maintaining the material productivity of our society. Carried out by the communications media and the advertising industry (although they are effectively one and the same), this activity is part of the steady fusion of business and government into the Industrial State. People experience it, although often unconsciously, as a kind of general falseness, a bogus and synthetic quality that seems to permeate every aspect of life. It is crushing, squeezing and suffocating, a dry, cold force dressed in the guise of good cheer and objectivity; it is the concern for image over substance and for technique over truth, and it exists everywhere—in supermarkets, among politicians, on television shows. Certainly, lying is a given factor of the human situation, undoubtedly present throughout historical time. I would suspect that present-day *individuals*, more controlled, educated and sublimated than their counterparts in the past, are on the whole at least as truthful now as then. What we contend with today is *cultural* falsification: systematized, reasonable, pervasive mendacity, dished up with all the resources of electronic technology and used as a regulator of social activity. It is presented as an objective necessity and seems to be accepted with bland acquiescence. But it represents the cutting edge of all the antihuman forces in Western culture.

We cannot discuss what this development in culture has meant to black people to any substantial extent, until we have explored the fuller meaning of the changing styles of dehumanization. Aside from the usefulness of the technique of falsification in the interests of productivity, its role is in creating alienation, increasing remoteness, further distancing people from each other, and replacing their human ties—even the hostile ones—with a screen of cultural manipulation. In a broad sense, mass cultural falsification succeeded in pushing the black urban masses out of sight, and therefore completed (perhaps unwittingly) what early forms of racism began: the making of a person into a thing. But these non-persons are massed in the hearts of our cities; their presence now poses a threat to the order of industrial society. When blacks lived on the farm, scattered and demoralized, it was easy to control them; in the ghettos, living together in large numbers, exposed to the tantalizations of America's material bounty, they are a threat to the power system. The threat lies in rising expectations, rising alienation, and diminished control. The emptiness and sterile materialism that our culture offers to all becomes incendiary to these black poor, who experience only the manipulations without the possibility of the material rewards that pacify most other Americans.

Consequently, America is attempting once more to reform a racial attitude. The setting is in some respects vastly different from that of earlier reform movements, but certain basics remain the same: what had been invisible becomes visible when it threatens the order of things, and that order attempts to adapt to the threat so as to maintain its underlying assumptions about the world. The pattern of reform is also reminiscent of the past, including the antislavery movement: visionaries—people of courage, passion and good will—lead the way; the powers lurk behind, warily size up the force of the threat, begin to promise jobs, officially expel racism—*after* ghetto people begin to burn the cities and the factories where the power physically resides. And, just as the North and the Republicans eventually capitalized mightily on what had begun as antislavery reform, so today do corporations expect to expand as a result of racist reform; an antiracist-industrial complex to stand alongside of and fuse with—for such is the tendency—the military-industrial complex.

And all tend to fuse with the State, which has by now

erased a great deal of racist legislation from its books and regularly congratulates itself, for example, on the non-discriminatory policies of its Armed Forces. Here again is an ambiguous and conflicting pattern, for the work of eliminating racist institutions is so enormous that only the federal government can mobilize enough expertise, and combine it with enough economic power, to make reform effective. But the State also makes war and hires the talent that enforces our dehumanization. How is the State to resolve this final contradiction?

Consider the Moynihan Report of 1965, which was in some respects the apogee of America's recent efforts against racism. It proposed to restore the potency of the allegedly emasculated black male by using the State's full resources to strengthen his family life. "A new kind of national goal—the establishment of a stable Negro family structure," was postulated. Many of those who attacked the report saw in it the same patronization of the black that has characterized our culture for hundreds of years. But the Report also set a trend for federal intrusion into the very matrix of personality, the family—an idea that, freed of liberal rhetoric, seems totalitarian to a prudent mind. Beyond this, and perhaps more revealing, the Report exhorted the black man to use his State-granted virility for the greater glory of all in the service of our military. "Military service is disruptive in some respects," [but it is the only place in America a Negro can be equal, and is] "an utterly masculine world. Given the strains of the disorganized and matrifocal family life in which so many Negro youths come of age, the armed forces are a dramatic and desperately needed change: a world away from woman, a world run by strong men of unquestioned authority."

This enlightened document is a vivid prefiguration of one possible outcome of the current race crisis, and we must allow for its possibility. There are other grim potentials, the most troubling being the always-present threat of a reversion to the overt racism that has been layered over by the sublimations of recent history. Vaguely perceived in the so-called white backlash, this fascist trend was clearly and unequivocally articulated in the most recent Presidential election, and there is no way to forecast its future potential for growth.

Set against these ominous possibilities is the hope presented by the very disruptions of our times, and most evident in the degrees of liberation and organization which black people have so far achieved. The burst of black assertion in our times is an expression of cultural creativity of the first magnitude. The United States, increasingly strangled by technocratic banality and manipulation, badly needs such creativity—though whether it wants or is able to use it in a positive way is a doubtful matter, to be decided by an unpredictable future.

I am not calling upon the black people to "save" the white, just as we should never have imagined that the white could be called upon to "save" the black. Rather we must find a way to let growth occur, to let the forces of life inherent in all humans mold the forms of their activity. This is a profound and difficult task. Given the immense spread of forces opposing life and humanity in our culture, I have no blueprints to offer. But we can at least try to understand the plague-like pathology in some depth.

To this end, let us turn to psychological description, and to a theory of personality capable of understanding the phenomena of racism in all their bewildering complexity. Although, as I noted above, psychology is by no means a sufficient tool, it is a necessary one. For race prejudice—which is, whatever its roots, clearly a causal agent in racism—entails a certain kind of person in a certain kind of setting, holding onto some peculiar beliefs about another person who is designated as belonging to something called a different race. And so we will have to look into why. Indeed, psychology can carry us further yet. If we agree that dehumanization, the desire for property, and the need to dominate have all somehow contributed to the institutional forces that bind us in the chains of racism, it is clear that each of these pursuits requires a certain mental attitude toward the world, and therefore is to a certain extent a function of psychology. Indeed, it may turn out that the underlying attitudes necessary to build racist institutions are congruent with those involved in race prejudice.

Let us rest the matter at this point, then, and make a somewhat drastic shift into a study of the recesses of personality.

CHAPTER 3
ON HISTORY AND PSYCHOLOGY

Just as a planet revolves around a central body as well as rotating on its own axis, so the human individual takes part in the course of development of mankind at the same time as he pursues his own path in life. But to our dull eyes the play of forces in the heavens seems fixed in a never-changing order. . . .

Freud, *Civilization and Its Discontents*

THE ONE CERTAINTY about racism is that it has represented something of extreme importance to Americans. The racial turmoil in our time attests to this, as does the racist thread that is woven into virtually every aspect of American history. The very invisibility imposed for so long by white Americans upon black Americans was nothing less than an effort to defend white America against the realization of the meanings of racism.

Although each person in a society is unique in the detail and fine structure of his life, all share in certain common styles of action or forms of knowing—in this case, certain patterns of racist belief or action. To see culture as the organic total of these shared qualities is to give it a psychological definition. Another vantage point would be institutional: culture as the collection of economic, technical, political, etc. institutions—the set of structures through which men fulfill their social tasks.

Neither the psychological nor the institutional definition is sufficient to account for racism, or, for that matter, any other cultural phenomenon. Culture is multi-dimensional and must be seen as the integral of all of the separate points of view that enter into our understanding. Although in practice we are forced to treat each separately, in principle no aspect of culture operates independently of any other. Racist psychology is a prerequisite of racist institutions, and racist institutions engender a racist psychology. Put another way, we can say that just as men, with their knowledge and desire, ultimately make history, so too does history make men. The psychology of a culture is to a great extent a symbolic precipitate of the kinds of experience forced upon a group of people by their history. Thus what we call personality is a historically evolving system, and personality and culture may be considered congruent.

It is clear, and the preceding historical study tacitly took this into account, that insofar as any phenomenon can be raised to the level of a cultural institution, it must satisfy at least one condition: it must affect and be meaningful to large numbers of people within a social organization. Being meaningful implies a congruency with the personalities of the people within society; there must be something within personalities that responds in a mass way to the effect of the institution.

The most reliable guide to the psychological importance of any institution is simply its importance as an element in culture. This importance in turn can be measured in one clear way: through its role in history. What is culturally and psychologically negligible will disappear and be forgotten; what is important will endure and matter, will influence other elements of culture and persistently recur in human consciousness. The most important psychocultural strands are identical, then, with those that have been the subject of histories—religion, the state, and economic systems, for example—those systems that men have invented to provide for the satisfaction and regulation of their vital interests, those to which all men must respond. On the other hand, the tree that falls unbeknownst in the forest is not a cultural phenomenon in itself (although the idea of this tree is, insofar as it is used as an example of a non-cultural phenomenon); just as the sparrow that falls in the desert is non-cultural except as it becomes an image in the eye of God who is represented within the mind of men. The schizophrenic's particular vision of God is non-cultural, for he does not share it directly with anyone. By contrast, the general idea of God is deeply cultural, for it existed in and was assimilated from the culture by the schizophrenic before he elaborated it into his private hallucination.

But by and large we do not study psychohistory through the behavior of mentally disturbed individuals. It is the average man, with his "normal" racism and fantasies, whose behavior will give the key to the deeper meanings of racism. For, if personality and culture are congruent, then it is the "normal" man's personality which most accurately mirrors the psychohistory of his culture.

Given this assumption, as well as the proposition that the most historically significant events and institutions are also those of the greatest psychological significance, it should be possible to look to the record of what was historically decisive within culture, and to induce from these phenomena the underlying themes of psychohistory. The behavior of men as they pursued and still pursue their economic activities, as they participated in a process of dehumanization by selling slaves or institutionalizing property in the formation of American society, will provide a pattern of clues that may be inductively woven into an underlying fabric of symbols and fantasies. Just so will the activity of the Industrial State provide clues about the present nature of these fantasies. More can be derived about psychohistory from a study of the content of advertising, for example, than from the behavior of a neurotic on the analyst's couch. And beyond content, the *form* and style of cultural activities, of media and advertising and technology and warfare, will provide deeply important material for the understanding of psychohistory.

Finally, there is one aspect of culture, hitherto neglected in our study, that provides the most direct access to the innermost working of psychohistory: art. Art is a means of expressing a historically conditioned yet enduring truth in a shared way. As such it meets most accurately the demand of psychohistorical understanding: that it comprehend simultaneously what moves both the individual and the mass. The artist—especially the novelist, for the novel is the most explicitly historical of art forms—is only worthwhile to the extent that he can see beyond and beneath the immediate surface of culture, and so seeing, can create a new organic order of vision to be shared with other men. Thus, as we proceed, art, and especially literature, will be drawn upon to illuminate the deeper unities of history.

I asserted at the close of the preceding chapter that an understanding of the phenomenon of racial prejudice was vital to the understanding of the history of racism, and that race prejudice was a phenomenon that takes place in the mind of an individual whom we call a racist. I am asserting, of course, that racist belief is based on fantasy rather than fact; that the essential belief of the racist is indifferent to its truth value. It is irrelevant whether a bigoted statement such as "Negroes are smelly, lazy," etc., is true: the racist believes it because of "inner" reasons and not as a matter of scientific objectivity. To be sure, we—or his culture—may then see to it that the prejudiced-against person lives up to the stereotype with which he has been labeled. This kind of secondary action is of great historical importance and will be studied at length. Furthermore, once the world is restructured to make racist beliefs come true, the fantasy itself becomes nourished and perpetuated. Without such reciprocity, nothing cultural would endure, and the very structure of personality would be dismantled. At this stage of our inquiry though, we must focus our attention upon *fantasy*, which shall be defined as a *form of knowing based upon wish and desire*—i.e., upon the internal mental state of a person.

In the next chapter I shall dissect the various fantasies and personality traits that coalesce into race prejudice. Let us realize, however, that the kinds of fantasies which appear in racism are not unique to race relations. Rather, racism is a specific historical situation in which some elemental aspects of human experience are turned toward the classification (and oppression) of people with different ethnic traits. Race fantasies are applied only at second hand to races; they are actually generated in the universal human setting of childhood, and used by culture to handle its historical problems.

The full range of meanings involved in race fantasies cannot be understood unless their infantile root is taken into account. I feel that this task is essential for this study. However, because it is somewhat off the mainstream of our inquiry, I have presented a detailed discussion in an appendix, and confine myself here to some brief introductory remarks.

The presentation is, as noted before, along psychoanalytical lines. Accordingly, fantasies are to be seen as remnants of infantile wishes; they are the products of developing human drives and forms of thought. Our drives are twofold: sexual and aggressive. The drive is what charges a fantasy. Each drive is biologically given; each is exceedingly plastic and undergoes a specific plan of change as the child develops from a helpless infant to a relatively autonomous person living among other people. The drives provide the impetus and valence for the nature of attachment between the self and other people. As the child develops, the drives become associated with certain bodily zones and tasks. Thus the child passes through the well-known phases of oral, anal, phallic and oedipal organization.

The nature of each phase is greatly variable between individuals and across cultures, but some such broad progression appears to be universal. And from each level of development, certain universal fantasies arise, each to be combined in the development of personality and put to use by culture alongside its more rational pursuits.

Our study of racism will bring us into contact with several of these phase-related fantasies, and the more general discussion which follows will widen the scope. Let us note some of the infantile constructions which will appear.

1. *Oral Phase.* Here arise wishes to incorporate, to take into the self, and corresponding fears of being incorporated.

2. *Anal Phase.* This stage is of the greatest significance to our study. Certain nuclear ideas, such as those revolving about the concepts of *dirt* and *property*, take hold of the personality during this stage of development, and remain throughout life associatively linked to the idea of excrement. Thus, to the child, dirt corresponds to that which is hated in his excremental activities. This becomes symbolically generalized to include anything which can be associated with what comes out of the body, and which hence should not return back into the body. On the other hand, property is considered to be the loved

part of his excrement, the part he wishes to take back into himself or to give to those he loves. Excrement becomes the unconscious link in later life between these notions; hence *filthy lucre.*

The anal phase is so important in discussing racism because anality is the form of drive behavior which predominates during that time when a child is painfully detaching himself from his mother and establishing himself as a separate person. In this light, excrement—what is expelled from the body—becomes symbolically associated with the ambivalent feelings a child has about his separation from his mother and the establishment of himself as an autonomous person. Dirt becomes, then, the recipient of his anger at separation; while the love of possessions becomes the substitute for the love of what has been separated from him. Since racism involves the separateness of people, so must it become invested with anal fantasies.

3. *Phallic-Oedipal Phase.* In this stage the fantasies are about genital sexual activity, in particular with forbidden people and in the setting of competition and envy. The central theme is castration, as the specific form of aggression directed toward sexual rivals and feared from them. The most superficial glance at racial behavior will provide abundant examples of such fantasies. But they are involved in a much wider way too, for the oedipus complex provides the fantasy substratum for the entire historical progression of patriarchal power.

At another level, the resolution of the oedipus complex condenses all the previous stages of development—oral, anal, phallic—under one mental organization, the superego. The superego is the controlling portion of the ego, which is, roughly speaking, the functional part of the personality. Ego is set against id, a repressed and unconscious body of repudiated infantile strivings. The superego turns back onto the self the aggression that had been directed outward, and so brings about inner control. It also provides a mental structure through which the individual can ground himself in culture and obey its morality and normative regulation. By adjusting his superego to the set of cultural controls, a person adapts and becomes "normal." If he is a white American, it is likely that he will then find an outlet for some of his infantile fantasies about dirt, property, power and sexuality, in his culture's racism.

CHAPTER 4
THE FANTASIES OF RACE

All I have to say now is that the woman was white and that she gave our odor as an excuse for fleeing me, because she didn't dare chase me away. Ah, the great days when they used to hunt the Negro and the antelope. . . .

Jean Genet, *The Blacks*

Both authorized and anecdotal literature have created too many stories about Negroes to be suppressed. But putting them all together does not help us in our real task, which is to disclose their mechanics. What matters for us is not to collect facts and behavior, but to find their meaning. Here we can refer to Jaspers, when he wrote: "Comprehension in depth of a single instance will often enable us, phenomenologically, to apply this understanding in general to innumerable cases. Often what one has once grasped is soon met again. What is important in phenomenology is less the study of a large number of instances than the intuitive and deep understanding of a few individual cases." The question that arises is this: Can the white man behave healthily toward the black man and can the black man behave healthily toward the white man?

Frantz Fanon, *Black Skin, White Masks*

I PROPOSE in this chapter to isolate and study some of the fantasies with which white men have clothed black men. The problem shall be to analyze within a historical framework the elementary notions which characterize racial thinking. Hopefully the discussion in the preceding chapter will have prepared the way for the comprehension of racial prejudice in its psychohistorical role.

A large body of recent scholarship has laid bare that aspect of racism called *prejudice*. This was of primary importance both conceptually and realistically, for race prejudice—against Negroes, Jews, or any other group—is the most gross and immediately destructive of the guises of racism.

After all, the bigot is the man who applies the blow that society prepares for the racially oppressed. Emboldened by his belief, it is the bigot who burns a cross or plants a bomb in a Negro church; who strikes, jeers, excludes, or merely offers the cutting slight that, when multiplied by the similar acts of his millions of cohorts, brings racial prejudice into direct expression.

Who are these bigots; what do they share? How can one equate the paranoid ravings of an American Nazi, the murderous plotting of a Ku Klux Klanner, the rantings of a Senator Bilbo (or the more genteel equivalents of his congressional heirs), the insensate rage of a lynch mob, with the polite distaste and coldness of a Northern suburbanite? As we know, at the less prejudiced end of the spectrum, there is a fine grading, a shading off into the most imperceptible of twinges; at the far end of normality the bigot may present himself as tolerant and rational, and may hold his racist belief in a remote attic-room of his consciousness; may have, under the impetus of moral censure, driven it from consciousness into a latent zone that is not activated until a black attempts to move in next door or pays attention to his daughter. It may even take a riot to activate the racial stereotype —"You see, *they* can't be trusted; *we*'d better arm ourselves." It may even be that, in sharp distinction to his frontier ancestors, who could never have tolerated any such insurrectionary behavior without violent reprisals, the white clings to his liberal conscience and refuses to yield to the facile certainties of bigotry even in the face of "civil disturbance." Yet this same man (who could be any of us who take pride in having at least moved from the Dark Ages of racial intolerance to the Enlightenment of democratic liberalism) might in his dream life dredge forth fantasies markedly similar to those that, in conscious form, propel the most blatant and murderous of racists. Indeed, since we all live in one culture, whose fantasies we at least partly share, and since this culture is obsessed with white-black racism, it would be hard to conceive of any American, no matter what his conviction or social role, who lived free from racial fantasy. And yet there are patterns: where does one draw the line?

Two practical guidelines emerge from the above spectrum. The first would divide people according to whether or not they actually believed such fantasies; the second, according to whether they acted upon those beliefs, or held them in check by restraints of conscience. Obviously these are matters of definition, and so they lead to the imposition of a simple schema upon an endlessly varying reality. There are in fact many gradations of overt racist action, from lynching to very subtle types of job discrimination. And racists hold all degrees of intensity of racist beliefs: some never move into action; others may, when provoked, reject the voice of conscience and pass entirely into the arena of open racial hostility. Finally, individuals themselves are alterable, like the man described by the analyst Terry Rodgers.[9] He wrote of a white Southerner who, under the emotional pressure of the self-realization of psychoanalysis, moved from a stance of nonracist, liberal support for the Negro cause, to membership in the

[9] "The Evolution of an Active Anti-Negro Racist," *The Psychoanalytic Study of Society*, Vol. I (1960), pp. 237–43.

local White Citizen's Council. We are all scarred by the
same society, and most of us at least feel impulses, in
varying combinations and at varying times, toward some
part of racist behavior. The varieties of racist experience
are mixed in the real individual. No one behaves simply;
he is the amalgamated product of a host of historical, cultural and personal influences.

Nonetheless, Ideal Types (in Weber's sense) can be
discerned, and their consideration will prove fruitful. For
these ideal types represent the nodal fusion of history in
the individual. Their combination and progression will reveal the inner workings of historical change, and will
enable us to see more clearly the traces of the past on
the present and their possibilities for the future. We have
already noted their historical occurrence. Let us reintro-
duce them.

1. The type who acts out bigoted beliefs. Whether a
Night Rider in the South or a member of a mob protesting
open housing in Chicago, he represents the open flame
of race hatred. The true white bigot expresses a definitive
ambition through all his activity: he openly seeks to keep
the black man down, and he is willing to use force to
further his ends; let us call him the *dominative racist*.

2. The type who believes in white race superiority and
is more or less aware of it, but does nothing overt about
it. An intrapsychic battle goes on between these sentiments and a conscience which seeks to repudiate them,
or at least to prevent the person from acting wrongly
upon them. This often means not to act at all, and such
inaction serves as the only resolution of the inner conflict.
Because of this, the person tends to behave in ways that
avoid the issue: he tries to ignore the existence of black
people, tries to avoid contact with them, and at most to
be polite, correct and cold in whatever dealings are necessary between the races. We call this complex type the

aversive racist, in accord with his most characteristic style of handling the race problem. Within this type we find at one extreme those individuals who, upon threat—such as when a black gets "too close"—lapse into dominative racism; and at the other, those who, impelled by a strong social conscience, consider themselves liberals and, despite their sense of aversion (which may not even be admitted inwardly), do their best within the given structure of society to ameliorate the conditions of the Negro. Aversion in these variants is revealed in a pronounced willingness to undertake social reform via remote, impersonal means, and by a corresponding reluctance to engage in any kind of intimacy with black people. The range of aversive racism reveals it to be a transitional type between dominative racism and our third type.

3. He who does not reveal racist tendencies at all—except as the unconscious persistence of what may be considered mass fantasies. He belongs to the advancing edge of history and is considerably less defined than the first two.

The three types of racism represent different formal organization, different styles of expression. They all float on the same pool of fantasies, but organize them in different combinations, differing relative intensities, and different modes of realization.

Only the first type, dominative racism, includes what we ordinarily think of as the racially prejudiced person. What is outstanding about this type is not that it is composed of persons who have racist fantasies, but that, out of their personality structure, they transform their racist fantasies into a personal reality that can lead to action.

The time when racist belief and action were morally sanctioned and formed the intimate fabric of American society is passing, although prejudiced people still cling to it. Anachronisms all, their persistence in holding on derives from a peculiar rigidity of personality which forces them to find objects of intolerance in their lives.

The bigots of this country have been systematically described by Adorno, Frenkel-Brunswik, *et al.*, in their study of the authoritarian personality. Almost invariably in a subordinate position in society, the bigot worships power. He generally comes from the lower middle class; he is the "little man" who lives off the scraps of bourgeois culture. His life revolves about an ideal of external power. A level below the worship of his masters, however, lies the hatred that derives from his terror of submission. This mixed love and hate fix him in his social orbit at a respectful distance from authority: if he is too far, he loses his security; if too close, he risks penetration, destruction. He is safe only if he keeps his place. His hatred of the masters is kept out of consciousness by his projecting it onto someone he can see as lower than himself. His rigidity of character forces him to see things as unalterably true; he perceives the external world as if he were forced to peer through a sequence of lenses made to focus on one section of a slide. The exquisite tension between his need for and fear of submission reduces him to extreme dependence upon external stability; hence his worship of the past—the more remote the better—when everything had its place, and authority was secure. Hence his frantic rage at disturbances or the slightest changes in the social order. When his son grows up and seeks to move into a higher class; when mass changes, induced, say, by war or a depression, alter the social climate; and, most of all, when the object of his prejudice begins to reject his debased role—whenever the fabric of stable authority tears, the bigot rises up, casts off his veneer of conformism, and takes to the streets.

Every study of authoritarian prejudice reveals a common truth: the dominative racist is irrationally and profoundly dependent upon the object of his prejudice. He cannot leave him alone. Hate implies a kind of love, or at least an inability to rid the mind of obsessions with the hated other. And these obsessions are invariably tinged with sexuality: a preoccupation with, a deadly curiosity about, the sexual excesses of the hated group, etched in the imagination by the acid of a harsh moralism. The dominative racist must not only keep the needed object of his hatred oppressed; he must also ensure that this other person enact those very traits that the bigot needs to see in him, needs to enjoy vicariously and needs to punish. The anti-Semite must create his Jew; the white bigot, his nigger. As Archibald says in Genet's *The Blacks*: "Bear one thing in mind: we must deserve their reprobation and get them to deliver the judgment that will condemn us. I repeat, they know about our crime. . . ."

There is no fruit like forbidden fruit; there is nothing more delicious to enjoy and punish freely than the crimes of sex and aggression which authoritarian repression has forbidden. Nor are there lives more dull, more deprived of erotic joy than those of the people who exist in the gray recesses of a dominative culture. The acting out of racist fantasies can be the only stimulation to enliven such existences.

The essence of the bigot's world is to forbid and punish in the interests of exteriorizing an inner guilt. A good psychoanalytic discussion of the personality structure which leads to prejudiced behavior may be found in Brian Bird's essay "A Consideration of the Etiology of Prejudice."[10] Bird emphasizes the positioning of the prejudiced person between a higher class he envies, and a lower one he must despise as he fears the higher class will despise him for his envious strivings. The situation is

---

[10] *Journal of the American Psychoanalytic Association*, Vol. V (1957), pp. 490–513.

analogous to the attack on a younger sibling in place of an attack upon a more desired and feared parent. Thus prejudice controls aggression by discharging it on a safe object—one who must be kept safe. Bird also emphasized the role of guilt: not all dissatisfied people are prejudiced, only those who are guilty as well and who cannot tolerate self-criticism—i.e., those with a harsh and maladaptive superego. The superego is harsh: it contains an unneutralized aggression affixed to a parental image in whose life one cannot share for fear of sexual mutilation. The distance from power is also characteristic. The bigot is generally something of a failure, unable to adapt his superego smoothly to institutional sources of power, and therefore unable to sublimate enough aggression to do well in the world. He is frequently the most faithful of employees, but the attachment is brittle; it is based on an overcompliance that prevents true identification. The dominative racist of today is thus "maladjusted"—a defect that applies as much to the inner workings of his personality as to his relationship to society. There are, so to speak, gaps in his superego: instead of smoothly regulating all aspects of ego function, it permits an overly close awareness of sadistic impulses. Harsh moralism can hold these in check only if external reality is rigidly structured: when disturbances of that reality occur, the fantasies of race become actualities.

Beset with sadistic impulses he cannot acknowledge, except through their fantasied presence in the object of his prejudice, and hobbled by an equally sadistic conscience which keeps his life pinned to a dreary and joyless mold, the bigot would be a pathetic figure if his menace were not so real. It is real because today, the dominative racist's fantasies take the form of a need to use direct force to keep the other inferior. In general, he fails at effecting this, because modern culture has replaced direct domination with an indirect, rationalized version of it. In earlier forms of social organization—slave society being the nuclear example—direct domination of one race over another was the elementary relationship. Thus dominative racists in these systems—i.e., those who had the basic conviction that the Negro had to know his place and stay there, or else—did not have the rigid and maladaptive personality structure of today's bigot. Their superegos worked smoothly to adapt social norms to infantile wishes; they were spared the guilt that threatens the bigot unless he keeps up his bigotry; and, most significantly, they were free to act intimately with black people and to sexually enjoy the bodies of black women. Being satisfied on so many counts, the culture of dominative racism in the antebellum South retained that spontaneous and graceful quality that has endeared it to American mythology. It is toward this mythic past of unquestioned authority that today's bigots look for the stabilization of their inner life; and it is the disparity between these halcyon days of dominative racism and the real situation of modern bourgeois society that parallels the maladjustment, the failure and the joylessness of the little men who today represent the historical type of dominative racism.

What had been directly acted upon in those simpler days of domination becomes the fantasy of today. The actual behavior of the dominative racists who enslaved the bodies of black people, who raped black women and emasculated black men, now returns in the projected fantasies of contemporary bigots. The sins of the father are punished by the sons—but the punishment is not directed against the fathers, for they must be venerated and their fantasied power retained. Rather, their sins become ascribed, in one of those amazing twists the human mind can perform, to the sons of the victims of the fathers—those whom the bigot would like to claim as victims for himself. Thus would he at once express his rage at his father and his identification with him—if only culture would allow it.

But culture can no longer afford such luxuries. Just as the patriarchal Southerner who practiced direct domination over blacks failed as a result of the changing social pattern, so today the dominative racist fails in the bourgeois society that supplanted slaveholding society. His failure was another's success. The *aversive racist* made the compromise; he abandoned the wish for directly dominative racist activity in exchange for material gain. In this he has succeeded in being truer to the deepest levels of race fantasies. At the same time he has retained his sense of superiority over blacks, but it has become a moral superiority. The aversive racist keeps his distance, both physically and morally. He does not concretely touch those black bodies so coveted by dominative racists. In his dealings he is fair, remote, logical—for this is the way his life at large is conducted. He is motivated by the rational search for gain; he is the true descendant of the Puritan strain that flourished on American soil.

The major difference between these styles of racist experience can be seen in the structure of the superego. In the dominative racist (of today) the superego is incomplete and harsh, taxed with the suppression of vivid fantasies and hobbling adaptive action, whereas the superego of the aversive racist functions in a smoother and more unified way. The self of the aversive racist is realized as a more socially coherent system within bourgeois culture, and such articulation may result in exceedingly principled activity. The aversive racist may behave in the most apparently constructive way, even to the extent of giving money and support to the cause of bettering the lives of Negroes, yet retain the characteristic aversion. As we have observed earlier, many respected Americans, men of character and principle, have belonged to this category, which from colonial days has included the moral vanguard of our civilization.

Even the Quakers, who, alone among early reformers, devoted themselves not only to the attack on slavery but to the welfare of the individual black man, retained the sense of aversion as part of their inextricable root in culture: Quaker burial grounds usually contained a separate plot for Negroes; and Quaker societies, the most egalitarian of American cultural strands, avoided the potential dilemmas of miscegenation and racial intimacy by displaying a notable lack of interest in including Negroes within their membership.[11] For the Quaker, as for the masses of American aversive racists, distance becomes a singularly effective mode of defensive adaptation. As a consequence, the active entertainment of race fantasies is suppressed. The fantasies become weaker, neutral; they are sublimated. The sublimation takes the form of a general rationalization of the personality, a diffuse coolness in sensibility and functioning. The aversion toward black people becomes but an aspect of the general personality change—perhaps the most sensitive and most easily disturbed aspect, but nonetheless a part of the larger whole. This larger whole, the sublimative rationalization of the personality, has a symbolic significance of its own.

It is clear now that a certain group of elementary beliefs about race has become organized into enormously complex patterns of cultural response. Now let us look

[11] Jordan, *White over Black,* pp. 132, 419–22.

at the fantasies themselves. What is it in the biological-historical fact of the Negro that has so bedeviled America and the West?

Bedeviled is indeed the word. The devil was a construct in Western thought before the Westerner encountered black people. Eventually, black people themselves came to represent this construct. The devil is black; and so, Europeans noticed, were Africans—if not absolutely black, at least mightily dark. Blackness was the nuclear fantasy, and joined with its polar cognate, whiteness, the two being symbolic abstractions of a human vision of a world that in reality has no such absolutes.

One can find in the *Oxford English Dictionary* the meanings the symbol blackness held *before* the sixteenth century—before the Negro peoples came into Western historical view. These included, "Deeply stained with dirt; soiled, dirty, foul. . . . Having dark or deadly purposes, malignant; pertaining to or involving death, deadly; baneful, disastrous, sinister. . . . Foul, iniquitous, atrocious, horrible, wicked . . . indicating disgrace, censure, liability to punishment, etc." Whatever objects the human could conceptualize as bad, the abstract idea of badness itself, became coordinated with blackness.

When dark-skinned men were observed on African shores, and when their first members came or were brought to Europe, they provided an immediate shock to mentalities that had arrived independently at such a vision of reality. When it was further discovered that these black people pursued a different way of life, that they did not cover themselves and in general behaved more freely toward their bodies, the fantasy of blackness became greatly intensified. It was not at first organized into a schema of race—that was a later product of historical development. Rather blackness seemed to confirm a

sense of radical difference between peoples, a difference
that, combined with the African's evident heathenism, gave
the Europeans[12] a sense of awe. The fantasy of blackness
immediately became elaborated: these people were black;
they were naked; they were unchristian: ergo, they were
the damned. As an observer put it, Negroes "in colour so
in condition are little other than Devils incarnate."[13]

Another fantasy or, more exactly, myth (which is a
complex cultural story rooted in fantasy and given conscious value) was called upon to account for the existence
of dark-skinned Africans. They were descendants of Ham,
the son of Noah. The Bible had described how Ham had
looked upon his father naked, and had not, as had his
more obedient brothers, covered the old man. In punishment for this indiscretion, God willed that Ham's son
Chus (or Canaan) and all his descendants would be
black, and would be banished from his sight. The crime
of Ham was of course more than the act of looking at
his father, and, as Hebraic commentators of the early
Christian era emphasized, more than disrespect. It was
the castration of the father—the violent rejection of paternal authority and the acquisition of the father's sexual
choice. The blackening and banishing of Ham's offspring
represents, then, the retaliatory castration by the higher
Father. What is black and banished cannot be seen (as
King Oedipus blinded and banished himself for learning
of [seeing] what he had done). By punishing one of their
number, the other sons of Noah (and by identification
with them, the children of Israel) gained the approval
and protection of their paternal God. That was an aspect

---

[12] We speak mainly of the English here. Similar sentiments existed
among the Spanish and Portuguese, but without the same radical sense
of distinction. This was undoubtedly related to the Moorish influence
on the Iberian Peninsula.

[13] Jordan, *White over Black*, p. 24.

of *their* cultural absorption of superego; and it represents perhaps the earliest recorded instance of aversive racism. The bad son, marked with the sign of the black curse, was forever banished—at least until the European descendants of the white sons of Noah found him again.

The first explanation advanced to account in a scientific way for the pigmentation of black skin—that the Southern sun had, through aeons, scorched the Africans black—could not stand the most elementary tests of reason, especially when relatively fair Indians were encountered at a similar latitude in the Americas. So the myth of Ham was reactivated to account for this pigmentation. Soon, however, it combined with the more immediate feelings of Europeans to cement the view that the bodies of the dark peoples of Africa were the objects of the most ancient of curses. To punish Ham, a commentator wrote in the 1570's, God willed that "a sonne should bee born whose name was Chus, who not onely it selfe, but all his posteritie after him should bee so blacke and lothsome, that it might remain a spectacle of disobedience to all the worlde. And of this blacke and cursed Chus came all these blacke Moores which are in Africa."[14]

Such views contained in elementary form many of the fantasies of race; but they were not yet applied to an abstract concept of Race itself. They did serve, however, both to stimulate and to justify the enslavement of these seemingly accursed blacks. Once the blacks were enslaved, the fantasies grew in intensity and elaboration until they flowered into the myth of Race.

It began in this form in the West, and it persists in this form. In essence the Fantasy of Blackness underlies all, and invests its historical elaborations with its mark of badness and dirtiness. Frantz Fanon, in some respects the

[14] *Ibid.,* p. 41.

most powerful voice to have articulated the emerging consciousness of black peoples across the world, said it most clearly:

> Will this statement be susceptible of understanding? *In Europe, the black man is the symbol of Evil* [italics Fanon's]. . . . The torturer is the black man, Satan is black, one talks of shadows, when one is dirty one is black—whether one is thinking of physical dirtiness or of moral dirtiness. It would be astonishing, if the trouble were taken to bring them all together, to see the vast number of expressions that make the black man the equivalent of sin. In Europe, whether concretely or symbolically, the black man stands for the bad side of the character. As long as one cannot understand this fact, one is doomed to talk in circles about the "black problem." Blackness, darkness, shadow, shades, night, the labyrinths of the earth, abysmal depths, blacken someone's reputation; and, on the other side, the bright look of innocence, the white dove of peace, magical, heavenly light. A magnificent blond child—how much peace there is in that phrase, how much joy, and above all how much hope! There is no comparison with a magnificent black child: literally such a thing is unwonted . . . in Europe, that is to say, in every civilized and civilizing country, the Negro is the symbol of sin.[15]

Or, as Blake wrote,

> My mother bore me in the southern wild,
> And I am black, but O! my soul is white;
> White as an angel is the English child,
> But I am black, as if bereav'd of light.
> (*Songs of Innocence*)

Whatever a white man experiences as bad in himself, as springing from what Fanon described as "an inordinately black hollow" in "the remotest depth of the European consciousness,"[16] whatever is forbidden and horrifying in human nature, may be designated as black and

[15] Frantz Fanon, *Black Skin, White Masks* (New York, Grove Press, 1967), p. 188.
[16] *Ibid.*, p. 190.

projected onto a man whose dark skin and oppressed past
fit him to receive the symbol.

There is more about this, and I shall return later to a
discussion of how the choice of blackness and whiteness as
cardinal symbols came about. At this level we may understand that, spurred by the superego, the ego designates
the id, which is unseen, as having the quality that comes
from darkness; as being black. The id, then, is the referent
of blackness within the personality; and the various partial trends within the id, all repressed, make themselves
symbolically realized in the world as the forms of blackness embodied in the fantasies of race.

The fantasies express certain more or less distinct forbidden instinctual trends—not the trend in itself, but the
trend as actualized in some form of historical reality. To
choose an obscene example: scarcely anyone grows up
without exposure to the myth of African cannibalism:
grinning black devils with bones stuck through their nos-
trils dancing about the simmering pot containing the hap-
less missionary. What child has not contemplated this
scene in one form or another? Now, we know that cannibalism is both a universal infantile wish arising in the
oral sadistic phase of development (by virtue of which
it becomes an element of the mass unconscious), and a
well-defined cultural custom in some aboriginal groups.
Both of these truths are being represented here, but are
combined with a third one: that the culture of the West
is representing by projection what it has done to the culture and peoples of Africa, namely eaten them up. The
missionaries have always been burdened with being the
direct representatives of the culture which has destroyed
African civilization and brought it to that kind of feral
state which requires the assistance of missionaries. Their
ambiguous role makes them the fitting sacrifice, in the
myth, to the more primitive state to which they minister.

It is doubtful that such representation would have attained nearly the degree of forcefulness it has, if the West had not committed upon the black people, in a mass historical form, precisely what it accuses the blacks of having perpetuated in their savage state—and which foible is moreover one of the repertoire of rationalizations for the "white man's burden."

The same forces are at work, in more systematic ways, within the issue of sexuality. A mountain of evidence has accumulated to document the basically sexualized nature of racist psychology. Yet it is doubtful whether the majority of educated people have any idea of the extent, organization, or intensity of such fantasies. Allegations as to the Negro's sexual prowess, or the heroic proportions of his genitalia are a widely known legend. And it need scarcely be emphasized that discussions and speculations about Negro sexuality are neither casual and dispassionate, nor uncharged. The utmost passion has been devoted to the topic throughout our history. We know that the archetypal lynching in the old South was for the archetypal crime of having a black man rape (= touch, approach, look at, be imagined to have looked at, talk back to, etc.) a white lady. Moreover, the archetypal lynching often included a castration of the black malefactor; and even when it didn't, the idea of castration was immanent in the entire procedure. Before there were lynchings in the South, there were laws to do what mobs took upon themselves to perform after the Civil War, and these same laws often punished Negro infractions of all kinds with castration.

Throughout our history, even in these progressive days when the wish to actually punish sexual crimes by castration has been repressed out of the consciousness of all but a few psychotics, sexuality remains a widely acknowledged core of the race problem. Miscegenation is indeed the most forbidden of inter-racial practices—a taboo only now cracking as the media seek to remake the American mentality—and so sexuality and racism must be indeed intertwined.

Even from the few facts presented above, however, it is clear that sexuality in racism is not an isolated phenomenon but is most intimately connected with issues of power and dominance. The fullest versions of the sexual fantasies have sprung forth from the American South, the land of direct domination. Northerners, right from the start, were more secretive and guilty about all aspects of their sexual behavior toward blacks, and locked within the darktowns of their minds what was openly acted upon in the South.

In the classic South—and, as the fantasies generated there were diffused, throughout America—the sex fantasy has been incorporated into the white assumption of superiority and the demand for black submission. Whenever a black man bowed and scraped, whenever a white man called a black man "boy," or in other ways infantilized him, just below the surface of the white man's consciousness, a sexual fantasy woul be found yoked to the symbol of power and status. These sex fantasies erupted whenever the power relationships were threatened. In the colonies, the slightest rumor of a slave revolt was accompanied by wild stories of blacks wreaking their ultimate revenge in wholesale rape of white women. Nor should anyone think that, below the surface of reasonable concern, the fears aroused in whites by the current black rebellion are different. The specter of omnipotent black sexuality has obsessed whites from their first glimpse of an African until this very day. And, as with all such fantasies, the truth it represents is of secondary importance, and may itself be caused by belief and wish, rather than the converse. The key to this is not in the content of the fantasy so much as in the fascination it has held for white minds.

In classical Southern society, alongside the white man's obsessive fear of black male sexuality was his preoccupation with the bodies of black females. Black women were supposed to be more passionate than white women; and they doubtless were, since the whole of Southern culture converged to force the white woman into being the most worshipped, the purest, the least vital, and certainly the least sexual of females. The evidence for this is perhaps too well known to need documentation.

Such extraordinary fantasies as those cited by Cash in *The Mind of the South* spring from deep in the Western tradition [17]; but they reached such a staggering intensity *only in a society that held black slaves*. Though the myth is in some disarray, elements continue to endure in White America, as anyone who witnesses the Tournament of Roses or a beauty queen contest can readily verify. Even now it has a most profound influence upon our culture. Lillian Smith writes with great sensitivity of this aspect of Southern life in *Killers of the Dream*, in which she describes what a bitter lot it ironically became for the white woman, how much rage between the sexes was concealed within the marmoreal idealization of the Southern belle, and what crippling results ensued. To perpetuate the idea of her icelike purity, the Southern white woman had to give up, at least in principle and often in fact, the two major erotic joys of a woman's life: the passion of her husband's desire, and the nursing of her infants. Both these prizes went to Negro women (who were of course also denied, by custom and status, the full enjoyment of even the natural vitality that accrued to

[17] Cf. Jordan, *White over Black*, p. 8, for a discussion of how whiteness was the especial epitome of female perfection in Elizabethan England.

them by this default), who were held to be the infinite
inferiors of the white lady. And, writes Smith, "of all the
humiliating experiences which Southern white women
have endured, the least easy to accept ... was that of a
mother who had no choice but to take the husk of a love
which her son in his earliest years had given to another
woman."

Now consider the complications this dual maternity implied for the white Southern male: to forever split his af-
fection between a warm impure black "mammy" among
whose kind he would later seek free sexual pleasure, and
a cold, "pure" white mother whom he would idealize [18]
and for whose virtue he could later, as a man with power
in a patriarchal society, kill and castrate any black who
could be imagined to entertain sexual wishes toward
white women. Consider further that these same black
men, so debased and humiliated in actual life, should be
invested in white men's fantasy life with the most pruri-
ent of wishes and the most prodigious of sexual capacities,
and should be in fact the subject of profound envy by
those who dominated them. These despised men also became the object of a desire so secret that it could be admitted only by way of projection or from the underside
of culture: whatever black men may have wished of white
women, the true source of the desire was often those
"pure," repressed white bodies who were held as an asexual ideal by the men in power. If we bear these remarkable contradictions in mind, we will be able to realize,

[18] In degrading the women they enjoyed and idolizing the ones they
didn't, Southern white men were carrying to an extreme one of mankind's oldest practices, the same that has been the root of such disparate
forms as prostitution and chivalric love. Cf. Freud's paper, *On the
Universal Tendency to Debasement in the Sphere of Love*, in *The
Standard Edition of the Complete Psychological Works of Sigmund
Freud*, ed. and trans. James Strachey (London, the Hogarth Press,
1964), Vol. XI, p. 179.

as John Dollard wrote in his classical study, *Caste and Class in a Southern Town,* "What a peculiar state of affairs is to be explained and how bizarre the white attitude toward the rape problem seems; and we grant that some potent, but not very obvious explanation is required." The reader will have no doubt surmised from the context of this work the kind of explanation to be offered. Only the theory of the Oedipus complex—enlarged into a cultural apparatus that defines and binds real roles even as it apportions fantasies amongst the players of these roles—will account for this variety of phenomena. And in these cultural fantasies, the symbolic freedom of the human mind is allowed full sway. Black man, white man, black woman, white woman—each realizes some aspect of the oedipal situation; and in this realization, the infantile impossibilities of the oedipal conflicts attain their perverted resolution by being projected onto split elements— elements split into black and white—of culture.

We have seen the pattern: blackness is bad, what goes on in the dark comes from the dark: therefore, make the black man represent *both* father and son in their destructive aspects. There is evidence for this in the structure of his social role: he is the bad father who possesses the black mammy (who is herself impure), and he has the genital power which forever excites the child's envy; he is also the bad child who lusts after the pure and utterly forbidden white mother (made sexless, in reality). By making the rape fantasy the cornerstone of his culture, the white male only repeats in adulthood the central incest taboo of his childhood. And here Southern culture makes its unique contribution to an ageless human problem: the Southern white male simultaneously resolves both sides of the conflict by keeping the black man submissive, and by castrating him when submission fails. In both these situations—in the one symbolically, in the other directly—he is castrating the father, as he once wished to do, and also identifying with the father by castrating the son, as he once feared for himself. All that he has to do to maintain this delectable situation is to structure his society so that he directly dominates black men.

During the Detroit race riots of 1943, the analyst Richard Sterba [19] observed in the dreams of his white male patients the emergence of fantasies of the Negro male as the cruel, powerful father who had to be hunted down in a mythic recapitulation of the primitive hunt for the totemic animal. These occurred, of course, under riot conditions, when blacks were, to say the least, asserting themselves. Ordinarily, Sterba observed, the fantasies of whites represented Negroes as younger siblings—that is, as manageable rivals for parental attention and acceptable recipients of one's own guilt for the wish to overthrow father. This, it will be recalled, is precisely the nuclear dynamic of prejudiced thinking.

Similarly, Rodgers' patient, mentioned earlier—who in the course of analysis reverted from a liberal pacifist to a white supremacist—began to express murderous fantasies toward blacks at precisely the time of mobilization of his own incestuous conflicts: he began to say that capital punishment was necessary to keep Negroes in line, approved of the Emmett Till murder, and, most revealingly, became concerned lest a Negro rape his mother (to whom he was inordinately close) during his analytic appointments. The *coup de grâce*—and a moment so charged with anxiety that it marked the turning point away from analysis and toward the White Citizen's Councils—was his dream that a bull with black horns was raping his mother. In the dream, he ripped the horns off the bull, and during

[19] Some Psychological Factors in Negro Race Hatred and in Anti-Negro Riots," *Psychoanalysis and the Social Sciences,* Vol. I (1947), pp. 411–27.

the analytic session, Rodgers interpreted the castration theme, whereupon the patient said spontaneously that all Negroes should be castrated, for the danger of rape by them was a real one.

This man was virtually psychotic, and with the clarity of psychosis he expressed the fantasy shared and actualized by a whole culture: keep the black man down, and he becomes the debased son who suffers for all, whose punishment frees all other sons to hold power free from guilt; let him rise up, or be imagined to rise up, and he becames the image of the father who, being weak in reality against the massed strength of white culture, is fit to be lynched and castrated. In the first version, he is once again Ham; in the second, the totem animal. But the two versions are at base aspects of one, for each son is a potential father-to-be, and each father was a son; does not each man retain in his mind the eternal duality of father and son?

There is then a reality to the sex legend, if only a partial reality: the black man keeps the sexuality but loses the power. White society, especially in the South, at least covertly and often overtly, eggs the Negro on in his promiscuity, removes, with the power, the superego structures that come from identification with power, and frees the black to act out what the white cannot. Whites also encourage the other side of black "bestiality": naked aggression—discharged, to be sure, only against their own kind. Recall the boxing match that the hero of Ralph Ellison's *Invisible Man* engages in for the entertainment of whites.

Besides providing whites with vicarious thrills, these displays of black aggression and sexuality have helped greatly to maintain race oppression. By discharging their sadism upon each other, black people bled off aggression that could otherwise be sublimated (not to mention, directed against whites); perceiving the contempt of the culture at large for this, they only translated it rawly into self-hatred, which in turn can only be discharged among the Negro group, and so the cycle has been perpetuated. In their classical role relative to the white master, their lot has been to, shuffle and grin and play stupid, and so to satisfy the need of the white to see them as both emasculated father and chastened child. Even if there was revenge in this—as when the slaves behaved so inefficiently as to wreck farm implements and hobble the Southern system into ruin—and even though there was mockery behind the slaves' masks and vital pleasure to be retained in their own subculture, it was the most self-destructive of pleasures, the most Pyrrhic of victories. There is a kind of awful symmetry to the differentiations in American culture (in pure form in the South; as remnants, often entirely intrapsychic, elsewhere) by which the fantasies of the oedipus complex are represented. It can even be diagrammed. (See Figure 1.)

The only winners in this process are the white males. But their victory has been ruinously expensive. Note that guilt is placed in their position on the chart. Guilt is indeed the specific oedipal emotion. In reality, however, guilt was not a conscious aspect of the white Southern mentality. Their élan, their very appeal to the mythology of the nation, followed from the lack of restraint, the aristocratic self-assurance of these men. Yet the term was placed in the chart for a reason, for, as Lillian Smith wrote: "guilt was then and is today the biggest crop raised in Dixie."[20] Except that the guilt was not conscious. This was the triumph of the South, the principal defensive task of all its institutions—to keep the minds of the masters unaware of guilt. Their guilt was unconscious, but it was realized elsewhere—in the sterile frustrations of idealized

[20] Lillian Smith, *Killers of the Dream* (New York, Anchor Books, 1963), p. 87.

(For each category the social role and symbolism are noted above the dotted line, and psychological qualities mentioned below. Arrows indicate psychosexual relationships between categories that are permitted or tabooed according to the oedipal structure.)

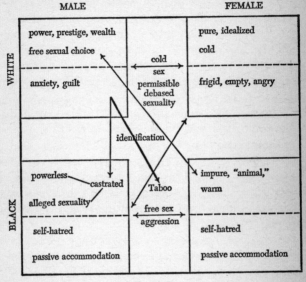

Figure 1

white women; in the patient suffering of black women; in the brutalization of black men; and, principally, in the failure of the whole society, which they visited headlong upon themselves and raced toward with a desperate energy. Everybody had to pay the penalty for the crime of Oedipus; and in the endless cycle of crime and retribution, the black man had to be continually re-created out of the body of the white culture.

In Faulkner's *Light In August*, Joe Christmas, the protagonist, is said to be a Negro, and believes it himself. But he looks white and may not be a Negro at all—it cannot be known. He was designated as black because of the presumed negritude of his father, with whom his mother had illicit intercourse in violation of her own paranoid father's incest taboo. In penalty for this, both of Christmas' parents were killed by his grandfather—the father slain in the dark (never seen); the mother allowed to die in childbirth. Christmas is taken from his orphanage by a white farmer, McEachern, and is raised with all the sadistic moralism of which rural white Calvinist culture is capable. He reaches adolescence, takes a white woman, and is discovered by his adopted father, who threatens vengeance. Christmas turns upon him with all the rage imprinted over a lifetime of harsh repression, and slays McEachern. He becomes a vagabond, and at the same time he begins to actively assume the identity of a Negro. After twenty years of wandering he comes upon a white spinster, Joanna Burden, whose lonely life has been spent in philanthropic aid to Negro colleges. Beneath this sublimation are hidden all her own repressed incestuous wishes toward the father who raised her after her mother's death. She and Christmas begin an affair, in the course of which these repressions dissolve and drain away. She enacts wild fantasies of unrestrained license, meeting Christmas naked in the garden of her home, shouting in exultation "Negro! Negro! Negro!" at the height of her corrupting passion. But Christmas has only made manifest what has long been within her. He, white to the eye, is black as a symbol, and arouses in her the "black abyss of its own creating."[21] Conscience follows desire, and perverts what has been allowed outward expression. She withdraws sexually from him, begins to moralize, tries to "uplift" him, tries to make him pray. This, which arouses his own guilt, he refuses to do. Matters deteriorate, and Joanna turns outward the sadism her conscience sought to contain. She tries to kill him; he kills her instead, and becomes a fugitive once more.

[21] William Faulkner, *Light in August* (New York, Modern Library, 1932), p. 246.

Once the townspeople learn that Christmas, whom they had thought peculiar but white, is Negro and has been living with the white woman, the presumption of his guilt becomes automatic. That he actually committed the crime is both profoundly important—for to him it was the living out of his black destiny—and profoundly immaterial—for to them his alleged negritude meant certain guilt. And certain guilt means, in terms of the myth which becomes culture, certain retribution. Christmas, who is able to escape, knows this. In the act of escaping, having obtained the shoe of a *bona fide* Negro, whose different scent enables him to frustrate the bloodhounds on his trail, Christmas pauses to muse. "It seemed to him," writes Faulkner, "that he could see himself being hunted by white men at last into the black abyss which had been waiting, trying, for thirty years to drain him and into which now and at last he had actually entered, bearing now upon his ankles the definite and ineradicable gauge of its upward moving."[22]

He marches fatalistically into town and is arrested. The white authorities, after their fashion, attempt to safeguard due process, although the verdict is known in advance. However, a young man, Percy Grimm, representing the night-rider vigilante spirit of the little man made fascist— representing indeed the unrepressed wish of repressive culture—sets himself up as executioner/protector. Christmas, bearing the faint hope (aroused by his grandmother, who had at last reclaimed him) that a defrocked and despised minister, Gail Hightower, could save him, escapes and runs to Hightower's house. He is followed there by Grimm, shot, and then castrated.

With the "black blast" of blood issuing from his groin, Christmas dies, and "seemed to rise soaring into their

22 *Ibid.*, p. 313.

memories forever and ever."[23] This nightmare passage suggests the death and resurrection of Christ. The presence of this theme cannot be doubted in a book whose main character bears the name Christmas, is born under uncertain circumstances, becomes a wanderer, lives to his early thirties, is betrayed by a man he benefacted, and dies a martyr's death. Even Hightower ("a man's name," it is state, ". . . can be somehow an augur of what he will do, if other men can only read the meaning in time"[24]) can be seen as a decrepit symbol of Godhead. He is a central pivot of the book's action, the only character who relates to all the others; and he is midwife to the two births which occur in the book. His very degradation and failure is Faulkner's comment on the decline of the South and of its degenerate patriarchal religion.

The presence of the Christ myth in *Light in August* has been generally admitted, and also generally regarded as an artistic flaw, as the laboring of a theme that does not organically relate to the rest of the novel. But consider: Christ became the universalized Son of the universalized Father, through whose suffering all men's sins, and especially the parricidal sins which have tormented history, may be borne. Being such, He rose and spread His subliminatory cloak over Western culture, allowing men to identify with Him and, through His mediation, with the Father they fear and need in the struggles of their lives. He included them all within His dematerialized Body, and provided for Christianity its universalist sentiment within which the earth became contained. But other workings out of the patriarchal myth have arisen to express the truth that men, for all their Christian aspirations, have never been able to contain themselves equally within the body of society. This paradox between the urge for universal

[23] *Ibid.*, p. 440.
[24] *Ibid.*, p. 29.

inclusion and the real need for keeping some men both down and out of the social structure of the rest has, from the first days of white Christian encounter with black men, been the single greatest inconsistency between the ideals and the reality of Western civilization. The Negro has always been both out and down, because, in the last analysis, he represents a form of symbolic guilt that cannot be assimilated, neither in the superego of the individual nor in the myth of Christianity. He represents instead the object upon whom white men have projected their guilt; and the figure who, so designated by the fantasies of culture, has been so treated by the historical realities of culture. He represents, in short, for we round the circle, that other parricidal myth, the myth of Ham, the son who looked on his father's shame and who was thereby excluded by a less charitable, but more realistic, variety of Godhead. And *Light in August* presents the impossible tension between these two mythic solutions of the same theme: the Christ myth of inclusion, the Ham myth of expulsion; and in so presenting, it does what all good novels do: it reveals the underlying impossible truth of the culture in which the novel is grounded, the truth realized in the manifold sufferings of the South and in the larger dilemma of Western culture.

Now we have surveyed the history and presented some of the psychology of racism, but have not clarified or even grasped their deep relationship. By tracing the most ancient sexual and power conflicts in the unfolding of American race relations, we have only shown again, as all history shows, the persistence of the past in the present. But what has been shown is principally the *recurrence* of themes. Nothing has been said of why and how they have progressed; nothing has been shown of their specific importance to the particular historical development of the

West and of the intimate relationship between historical
and regional shifts in racial attitudes on the one hand, and
the course of American history on the other; nothing has
been learned about why the fantasies about black people
became elaborated into the mythic structure of Race, or
of how this myth differs from others, such as that of Ham,
which contain the same elements. And nothing has been
grasped of why this ancient fantasy about blackness
should have assumed the fantastic proportions it did and
still does in our culture. And finally, nothing has been
learned of aversion, of why and how dominative racism
passed into aversive racism—and beyond this, of the problem of passing beyond racism altogether.

The key issues in all these questions may be found in the
development of aversive racism. For what is psychohistorically crucial emerges from what is historically crucial;
and though the full-blown racial situation surged to life
in the South, the same situation became historically powerful only when it appeared in muted form in the North.
The Civil War settled that question, showed that the
South's racial structure was a tissue of destructive fantasies, while the North's contained within it the germ of
whatever it is that has kept the West alive as the dominant
world culture.

All these problems amount, then, to the understanding
of one puzzling historical fact: how do we account for
the fact confirmed at numerous stages of our history, that
the avoidance of black people was *greatest* in those areas
that were the most materially successful and the least
tainted with slavery or the kind of direct domination that
became the hallmark of the Deep South? How can we
understand this irony, so painful to black people who fled
the South for the imagined justice and prosperity of the
North and found, standing between them and those goals,
coldness and disgust? This is indeed the central problem

of our racism. It reveals an aspect of our culture that not only contributed to the original enslavement of blacks and to the elaboration of the system of dominative racism itself, but also has today, when dominative racism is the province of maladapted bigots, become of central importance in the misery of the urban black masses within advanced industrial society.

Now, the fantasies so far elaborated do not account in themselves for aversive behavior. The oedipal fantasies of whites, in fact, seem to be associated with the need for intimate, if grossly unequal, relations with black people. Only direct domination can ensure this. But there is another set of fantasies, touched upon in the previous chapter, which enters directly into aversive behavior and directly into the overriding fantasy of blackness. These are the fantasies pertaining to that peculiar abstraction called dirt—and they belong to a deeper level of our experience than that ordinarily thought of as sexual, and to a deeper aspect of historical power than that studied to this point.

Every group which has been the object of prejudice has at some time been designated by the prejudiced group as dirty or smelly or both: thus have the Irish been regarded by the English, the Jews by the Poles, the Poles by Anglo-Saxon Americans (consider the rash of "Polish jokes" popular in Chicago and elsewhere). The sentiment extends far beyond the ethnic: Communists and capitalists are to one another "filthy Capitalists" and "dirty Commies"; the English upper classes regarded the English middle and lower classes as dirty; the middle classes felt the same way about the lower classes; and if the lower classes had "Untouchables," as in India, they would have doubtless exercised the same privilege over their lowliest as did the various castes within Indian culture. Indeed, lowest in social scale connotes the idea of dirtiest and smelliest, and untouchability sums up all these concepts in the framework of aversion. Once again, as with the fancies concerning the penises of Negro men, the reality of the situation does not directly affect the underlying belief. No matter how a prejudiced-against person scrubs himself, he will always smell dirty to the true bigot.

Although the reality of the situation does not directly affect the prejudiced belief, *aspects* of this reality are indeed of great importance, especially those which might form the basis for fixed perceptual cues. Such cues, which have little to do with the belief, can nonetheless supply the mind of the believer with symbolic nutrient. They may provide that one link with reality which, if it be enduring and clear enough, will enable the entire complex of prejudiced fantasies to attain the certification of belief. When it is held by an isolated individual, such a false belief is called delusion; but when it is shared in a meaningful way by great numbers of people, the delusion becomes a part of culture.

Of all prejudiced-against people, none have suffered the appellation of filthiness so much as Negroes, and this peculiar fate has had something to do with the natural melanotic pigmentation of their skin. The random clustering of assortments of genes that are the human evolutionary heritage has led to certain easily perceived differences among groups of men. Science has convincingly shown that, whatever the unsolved biological problems of race, these external differences have little or nothing to do with the kinds of inner constitutional variations that may in fact be of significance in determining innate endowment. Although there are differing innate capacities, these have had nothing to do with the fantasies of race which have determined the history of racism. What counts to men is what their symbolic apparatus can seize upon; and nothing is more evident than the blackness of black skin (even if it is really brown). Just as the natural prognathism of Negroes, combined with their dark skin and tropical habitat, fixed for many generations the delusion that they were half ape and half men,[25] so has the skin color itself, that all-important yet trivial biological accident, contributed to their being fixed in the minds of whites as an *essentially* dirty and smelly people.

The idea of the allegedly distinct smell of black people has fused with their unmistakable skin color into this potent white fantasy. No matter that empirical study fails to show that any conclusive difference between the races exists. Each of us has a unique and distinct, biologically determined smell pattern, which dogs and police laboratories can sort out quite well. Perhaps there is even a racial assortment of such smells. The question of immense importance is this: why should whites blow up what is at all odds one of the most objectively insignificant qualities of a human being into a massive and axiomatically justified fantasy, the very condition of human disgust?

Aversion is the cardinal manifestation of modern American racism. (By contrast, it is relatively lacking in more primitive forms of race prejudice.) A sample of quotes from a *Newsweek* magazine survey of racial attitudes will illustrate some familiar responses:

> In cafeterias here you go around and collect your food, then niggers paw over it and then you have to give them a tip to carry your tray. Big, old, dirty black paws pawing over your food and then you've got to eat it.
>
> It's the idea of rubbing up against them. It won't rub off but it doesn't feel right either.
>
> I don't like to touch them. It just makes me squeamish. I know I shouldn't be that way but it still bothers me.[26]

[25] Cf. Jordan, *Black over White*, for a discussion of these fantasies as they blossomed in the early years of European contact with black people.
[26] *Newsweek*, October 21, 1963. Pp. 48–50.

We observe here some of the basic aspects of aversive racism. There is the sense of conflict, both against better knowledge and against moral judgment: "It won't rub off." . . . "I shouldn't be that way." And there is the sense of something so urgent and immediate and existentially valid that it overrides these scruples and forces the white person away. This something is the fantasy of dirt.

Recall that dirt is at symbolic root anything that can pass *out* of the body, and that hence should not pass back *into* the body, nor even touch it. Thus the common theme of the three quotes: contact with black hands contaminates food and makes it unfit to enter the body; contact with a black body will result in the blackness rubbing off on one's own precious body and thereby befouling it.

Yet these people are, by their very frankness, not pure aversive racist types. Their willingness to experience and express this fantasy sets them halfway between aversive and dominative racists; in the normal course of affairs, they would very likely practice overt discrimination. A more typical aversive racist would be too scrupulous to admit these beliefs openly; while the purest kind of aversive racist would hold these beliefs but not admit it even to himself. He would practice a double aversion: aversion from the black body, followed by a mental aversion from his own experience. The nuclear experience of the aversive racist is a sense of disgust about the body of the black person based upon a very primitive fantasy: that it contains an essence—dirt—that smells and may rub off onto the body of the racist. Hence the need for distance and the prohibition against touching.

Millions of whites have used this prohibition to buttress defenses against sexual contact with blacks. These defenses become necessary whenever the system of direct domination breaks down: with this breakdown, which is, of course, the supposed goal of a democratic society, the sexual threat which had been held in check becomes real and forces the mobilization of the sense of aversion. And the sense of aversion now operates as a potent inner barrier to the experiencing of forbidden feeling.

We see that the two main forms of racism, dominative and aversive, merge in the issue of sexual contact. Within this problem, the historically more advanced fantasies of aversion serve to protect the racist against acting upon his dominative urges. After all, one is not supposed to directly dominate another to this degree in an advanced democratic society. It should also be observed, however, that, in contrast to their historical order of progression, the fantasies of aversion belong to a more *primitive* level of mental organization than those of dominative racism. Modern aversion stems from anal sadism, while domination is phallic and oedipal in origin.

Although the fantasy of dirt, and its projection onto the black man, attained its full force at a late stage in our history, it was present from the beginning as an element of the white man's reaction to the black. As Jordan comments when he introduces the theme of anal fantasies in his study of early American racial attitudes: "One sort of stress arose from emotional turmoil within individuals, and here it is possible to gain an occasional glimpse into the deepest, least rational *meaning* [italics his] of human blackness for white men . . . the Negro's appearance, his blackness, seems to have served certain deep-seated unconscious needs of at least some white men. There are sufficient indications of this fact in colonial America to make ignoring it difficult. Sexual intermixture was frequently referred to as 'staining' the white population. . . ."[27]

Gross elements of these aversive fantasies still persist in our culture and wherever racism is found. The idea of

[27] Jordan, *Black over White*, p. 255.

"staining" the blood lives on in the "mongrelization" fantasies cherished by all racists, and especially in America where, as Jordan points out, the belief emerged that the Negro's blood shared in the general filthiness illustrated by his skin, and that this same "blood" would be directly transmitted through the generations should intermarriage occur. Then there is the coarse racist epithet "boogie," a word applied both to the black human being and to specimens of mucus that, because they come from the body, automatically become a symbol of dirt. The list of dirt fantasies which whites apply to the Negro could be extended indefinitely.

Just as the basic dirt fantasy emerges early in human development, so does its application to black people. This point has been subjected to empirical proof in an outstanding example of social anthropological work by Mary Ellen Goodman. As reported in her book,[28] a sample of 104 small children, both Negro and Caucasian, revealed the uniform fantasy that a), Negroes differed from whites in being dirty and that b), this implied a sense of basic inferiority. These beliefs set in during the pre-school years and had become quite well developed by the age of four. The author writes perceptively of how the sense of inferiority so engendered enters into the minds of the black children to produce the nuclei of a lifelong low self-image; and of how the reverse conviction settles into the personalities of the whites. In this study, we can sense the depth of the irrationality inherent in the problems of race. As Goodman comments, "the fact is that mere intellectual awareness of the physical signs of race is not all of the story. There is another part which is not merely startling but quite shocking to liberal-humanitarian sensibilities. It is shocking to find that four-year-olds, particularly white

[28] Mary Ellen Goodman, *Race Awareness in Young Children* (New York, Collier Books, 1964).

ones, show unmistakable signs of the onset of racial bigotry."[29]

We have been talking of dirt, which represents a set of peculiar fantasies based upon bodily experience. The central aspect of bodily experience upon which this tissue of daydreams rests is, of course, the act of defecation, and the central symbol of dirt throughout the world is feces, known by that profane word with which the emotion of disgust is expressed: shit. Furthermore, when contrasted with the light color of the body of the Caucasian person, the dark color of feces reinforces, from the infancy of the individual in the culture of the West, the connotation of blackness with badness. And since this dark brown color is derived from blood pigments, since in fact blood is the only internal bodily substance which is dark, the absurd beliefs about "staining" the blood through intermarriage with "inferior" races gain an ironic verification—one which, however, the proponents of these beliefs would be loath to accept.

Thus the root symbol between the idea of dirt and the blackness of certain people is that highly colored, strongly odored, dispensable and despised substance which the human body produces so regularly. How strange that this substance—which, after all, knows the body on the most intimate terms, and which is, aside from the pathogenic bacteria occasionally associated with it (another piece of reality immaterial to the life of fantasy), certainly innocuous enough—should have received the brunt of such contempt and rage! Almost as peculiar is the general reluctance to come to realistic grips with those distortions of the world which so clearly derive in part from their symbolic association with feces. This reluctance is evident even in those who study racism, as shown by the fact that only two articles were found in a survey of the psychiatric

[29] *Ibid.*, p. 245.

literature on prejudice that dealt with this theme in an explicit way[29a]: a paper by Lawrence Kubie, in which the idea of the fantasy of dirt which he had proposed in 1938 was developed into a theory of prejudice roughly similar to our dynamic schema of aversive racism,[30] and James Hamilton's essay "Some Dynamics of Anti-Negro Prejudice."[31] A review article on prejudice in the presumably compendious *American Handbook of Psychiatry* failed to even mention the theme.

By and large, connections between feces and the various symbolic organizations with which it is associated remain deeply repressed. The substance itself is abhorred, although the word, shit, is used freely enough; but for the rest the connection is mediated through the more remote, and hence less threatening, symbols of dirt. However, as we have observed in the case of castrative wishes, the deeper meaning becomes more explicit when the social structure within which these fantasies are realized becomes strained. Just as when a Negro became "uppity," he could expect a kind of brutal reprisal that might culminate in a castrative lynching, so when blacks today "move too fast" for the taste of whites one may expect certain raw manifestations of anal fantasies. Hamilton's article lists some amusing examples of these, especially as stimulated in the course of an open-housing movement in Ann Arbor, Michigan. He noted misprints in the ordinarily scrupulous local paper: the substitution of "demoncracy" for "democracy"; or, in a bridge column, of "in that shit" for "in that suit." And in a letter to the

---

[29a] Since the preparation of this manuscript, Charles Tinderhughes has taken up some of these themes. See his "Understanding Black Power: Processes and Proposals," *American Journal of Psychiatry*, Vol. CXXV, pp. 1552–7.

[30] "The Ontogeny of Racial Prejudice," *Journal of Nervous and Mental Disease*, Vol. CXLI (1965), p. 265.

[31] *Psychoanalytic Review*, Vol. LIII (1966–1967), pp. 5–15.

editor the author, doubtless unawares, clearly linked the open-housing movement (for which he professed support) with what he considered the outrageous habit of having dogs defecate on lawns. From another, more historically potent context, Hamilton recalls the fate of certain white students who, because of their friendship with James Meredith during his hotly contested entry into the University of Mississippi, returned one day to their rooms to find the walls smeared with excrement.

Finally, we may mention another bit of evidence Hamilton gleaned from the Ann Arbor incident. Immediately following the civil rights drive, the white citizens became intensely interested in cleaning up their town: a crackdown was ordered on homosexuals, and an anti-litter ordinance was frantically passed. The threat had been met with an outburst of moralism and reaction formation: purer and cleaner, the community was able to settle down to business as usual.

In this response, moreover, we can see our way to wider ground, for it maps the repressive transformation of a bodily fantasy into a whole style of behavior. The fantasies are indeed vitally important, but they enter history mainly through their influence upon styles of action. In the style of response chosen by the citizens of Ann Arbor —morality, cleanliness, and efficiency welded together; the hallowed wedding of cleanliness and godliness; Puritanism itself—we observe that singular transformation of body into spirit and spirit into action that is the hallmark of our civilization and the distinguishing, historically crucial aspect of its racism. These transformations, then, which will concern us for the remainder of this work, are grounded somehow in a bodily fantasy about dirt, which rests in turn upon the equation of dirt with excrement: the inside of the body turned out and threatening to return within. And within this nuclear fantasy, black people have come to be represented as the personification of dirt, an equation that stays locked in the deeper recesses of the unconscious, and so pervades the course of social action between the races beyond any need of awareness. Whatever the individual variations of this fantasy—and there can be no question that it exists in widely varying degrees of intensity and consciousness—it exists as a distinct, unpleasant but real element in our culture, and so needs to be understood.

It is not difficult to anticipate the kind of protest which may be raised against this assertion. Human beings, it will be argued, are too complex to be so reduced, or to reduce others, to such an elementary concept—to this fantasy at once oversimple and excessively degrading, to this epitome of disgust. It is, the argument might continue, as if the humanity of the black man were completely removed, as if he had no standing at all, not even the standing of the debased and castrated shadow attributed to him within the oedipal myth, as if he were only an element of filth to be worked over within the white mind! People, and especially Americans, the one people for whom freedom and humanity became the integral cornerstones of society, are not that simple, nor can they be such monsters, capable of regarding another human as a piece of excrement.

It is true that human beings, in their extreme complexity, do not reduce the world to any one element, nor see themselves or others as bearers of one simple trait. Quite the opposite; men are creatures of conflicts, of seams and splits and dialectically opposed beliefs: creatures of impossible contradictions, of whom it might be said that the higher one part of them reaches, the lower another part must stoop for anchorage. Men are, as Freud observed, both far more moral and far more immoral than they realize. It is the very impossibility of reconciliation between incompatible trends that drives them into ever widening splits. And so it might be that the purer a man becomes in one respect, the less pure he becomes in another; and if he cannot bear the coexistence of these two trends within himself, he may assign the hated one to another man, and then despise and shun him to yet further remove his own self from the source of its pain. It is precisely this process of purification that creates the need to see another as the exemplar of impurity and to treat him as if he were exactly that. And the task is lightened if the other is both recognizably and enduringly physically distinct from the self; and if this distinction seems, to the delusional mind, to be those very aspects of the self that need expulsion in the ritual of purification, then the task is lighter still. And finally, as to the *thing*ification, the radical loss of humanity implied in application of the repulsive fantasy of dirt: how have black people been treated if not as dirt, if not as things, commodities to be abstracted and extracted from each other and other human beings? The generations of American slavery, with its unique dehumanization, were no accident; and slavery's effect upon the cultural psychology of all America throughout its historical course has been no accident either.

Through this process of radical dehumanization, we can see the tracings of the more primitive fantasy of dirt upon the more advanced fantasy of Ham/Oedipus. This latter mythic structure, which has energized human culture since the first kings strode forth in Mesopotamia, reached a new intensification in the domination of slavery and then, under the influence of the excremental fantasy, receded and faded away into darkness, thus:

black man as father ———→ as child ———→ as body ———→ as penis ———→ as feces ———→ as inanimate thing ———→ as nothing, invisibility.

We observe that with debasement goes *abstraction,* until the final point of nothingness is reached. And this too is blackness, perhaps the fantasy of blackness most familiar to everyone: the blackness of Night, the gentle bringer of rest as well as the condition of darkness and the fears thereof—fears of death, fears of the return of projected monsters, fears about the return of what has been repressed.

Accordingly, no matter to what extent whites dehumanized blacks, the fears persisted, and remained affixed to that concrete, trivial and profound badge of dark pigment. This is not to say that white Americans did not try to ignore the threats from those they had so denigrated. But one basic maneuver was required to render these underlying fears and fantasies manageable: simply not to consider the Negro a human being. And for a while the whites congratulated themselves on a seeming success . . . as when Huck Finn accounted for his lateness to Aunt Sally by inventing an accident aboard a river-boat:

> "It warn't the grounding—that didn't keep us back but a little. We blowed out a cylinder head."
> "Good gracious! Anybody hurt?"
> "No'm. Killed a nigger."
> "Well, it's lucky; because sometimes people do get hurt."

CHAPTER 5
THE SYMBOLIC MATRIX

> *Successful high-grade organisms are only possible, on the condition that their symbolic functionings are usually justified so far as important issues are concerned. But the errors of mankind equally spring from symbolism. It is the task of reason to understand and purge the symbols on which humanity depends.*
>
> Alfred North Whitehead, *Symbolism, Its Meaning and Effect*

OUR INVESTIGATIONS to this point have shown that although racism has been an integral part of American life since the earliest colonial days, the passage of time has brought about certain changes in racist styles. What began as domination was in time overlaid and then replaced by aversion. Aversive responses were present right from the beginning, but in rudimentary form; with the triumph of the Northern way of life over the Southern, aversion gradually became the preponderant style of American racism. Therefore, the key to the psychohistory of our racism lies in aversion and the fantasies of dirt which underly it.

Since aversive responses occurred (and still occur) with such irrational intensity, and moreover occurred in people who had little directly to do with the Negro objects of the fantasy of dirt, then it follows that these fantasies pervaded the lives of white Americans and are not limited to racism. If such an infantile response can maintain such intensity in the most mature and "normal" of adults, then there must be something at large in culture to sustain it. The normal person is one who lives effectively within his culture; his normality is grounded in a congruence between his ego and his culture. Therefore, the best-adjusted, most productive, and most typical of Americans who respond aversively to black people they have not personally oppressed or even known, are no more than vehicles for the larger and axiomatic ideas of their times. This implies that the Negro is not actually the basic object of the fantasy, but a substitute, a surrogate. By virtue of the way he has been treated historically, he continues to represent in a concrete way something which persists actively in white American culture at an unconscious level, and which rises, as in racism, to find certain objects in the given world. As whites continue to treat blacks in such a way as to sustain their debased position within society, this in turn maintains the black's suitability to represent the white's fantasy. This *secondary* activity is of great importance in the actual workings of history. But it is secondary: it does not sustain itself but is sustained by a *primary* activity that must reveal itself in the most varied aspects of culture. This primary activity must be widespread—else the phenomenon of aversion would not be widespread; it must be intense—else such an irrational, infantile fantasy would not be able to endure amidst so many strong and mature minds; and it must be deep—else an awareness of it would not be so defended against.

It is by reason of this hypothesis of a primary activity that we insist that racism is not synonymous with race prejudice. The prejudice against race is a special psychological issue in which specific people may handle their specific problems by drawing on the nuclear racist fantasies. Racism includes this, but also the more fundamental phenomenon of the generation and sustaining of these fantasies. Prejudice is the surfacing of racism. Racism is the activity within history and culture through which races may be created, oppressed, and fantasied about without the aid of bigots. And it must be present in more than the dealings of people of one color with those of another: it pervades the history of our culture at that deepest of levels at which the *primary* fantasies are generated. The problem of racism is part of the problem of Western culture. And thus, its central aspect is not that blackness whose many meanings we touched upon in the previous chapter, but its cognate, whiteness. For the world is neither black nor white, but hued. A lightly-hued people —aided perhaps by fantasies derived from their skin color —came to dominate the entire world, and in the process defined themselves as white. The process that generated this white power also generated the fear and dread of black.

People of all cultures have always been afraid of darkness.[32] Children certainly are, and doubtless they have been since Paleolithic times. What has distinguished the West from other cultures is that these elementary issues, without losing their infantile core, have taken on a fantastic elaboration: They have been employed systematically and organically in the generation of *power*. No other culture has so drawn upon these primitive beliefs to superordinate itself to others; and if a culture has done so at all —as did Japanese culture—then the activity has clearly been an emulation of the West, and another proof of the viability of the Western system.

In the generation of power, the various meanings of white and black converge into a historically potent system. History, since the beginning of civilization, has been

[32] Cf. the issue of *Daedalus* (Spring 1967) devoted to *Race and Color*.

driven predominantly by the mysterious issue we call power, and the record of history is basically of the successions of that power. All the complexities of culture are harmonics about this basic theme. One might wish it otherwise; reality will not have it so.

Therefore, the questions posed at the beginning of the chapter take another form: how have the meaningful presentation of the world and the meaningful styles of historical action become harmonized with the themes of white and black in the culture of the West, so as to permit the generation of power by the nations of the West, most particularly the United States? When we have grasped this, it will be possible to see the full extent of the racial problem that has grown in concert with Western power.

Psychohistory is the study of the changing meanings of things. But meaning itself means but one thing: symbolization. All meanings are but symbols, for a symbol is an element of experience that is used to represent another element of experience. We must put the matter abstractly and risk the aridity of theorization. Otherwise we will get lost in an overly narrow conception of symbols and will miss the cardinal point: that both the culture without and the ego within operate through the creation of an immense variety of symbolic differentiations, and the simultaneous binding of those differentiations into a synthetic whole. This is a very broad notion of symbolism. It extends far beyond the customary idea of a symbol as a fixed representational image, such as the cross, the swastika or a religious icon. And it extends beyond the idea that a symbol need have only a one-to-one connection with its referent. Concepts are simply partial aspects of symbolic activity. The activity as a whole is nothing less than the mind's apprehension of reality, including the reality of itself. Whenever an organism passes from the immediate sense perception of an object in the world to some action based upon the functional use of that object, it is engaging in an elementary symbolic process.

Symbols arise in the course of differentiation, and there is no inherent limit evident in the degree to which the mind can differentiate and sort out reality. Furthermore, as any dictionary reveals, even the relatively discrete symbols called words cannot—by the very nature of human mentality—rest at a single level of meaning but are continually changing their signification, acquiring new layers of meaning and new emphases for their old meanings. New proper nouns and technical words continue to appear, assigning unique and precise meanings to things, but the ceaseless progression of history gradually washes these formations into the shared sea of symbolism.

Just as each dream can be endlessly analyzed, until it comprises an individual's entire mental history, so does each symbol—whether it be word-symbol, image-symbol, or abstract-idea symbol—spread out and eventually touch upon the entire range of shared human experience. And this experience passes beyond the surface of verbal cognition.

Thus each symbol stands at the center of an immense network of meanings extending from the most far-flung operations of culture to the deepest recesses of the individual mind. The richer such meanings, the more dynamically charged and the closer to historically important events, the greater the psychohistorical import.

Within the ramification of human symbols, there occurs a basic polarity across the dividing line of consciousness. The process of repression forces certain instinctual fantasies out of awareness, through the establishment of an inner unconscious counterforce created by the ego. When the ego's work negates the forbidden fantasy by drawing upon it, stealing its thunder, as it were, and taming that thunder to its own sublimated aims, the repressed urge persists in the unconscious id. And the ego, even in the process of defense, draws off that which it represses; thus what is repressed endures. Awareness is gone; the style of action changes from a direct and immediate urge to a sublimated, delayable one. Still, an active portion of the original fantasy persists. If the ego is to hold itself together—and this synthesis is absolutely necessary—then a further modification is required. This is carried out automatically by a change in the perception and understanding of the outer world. The knowledge of part of reality becomes distorted to suit the persistence within both ego and id of the original instinctual wish. These distortions then become a special class of symbols.

Let us summarize this schematically:

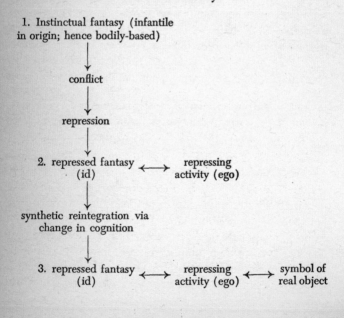

1. Instinctual fantasy (infantile in origin; hence bodily-based)

    ↓

conflict

    ↓

repression

    ↓

2. repressed fantasy ⟷ repressing
  (id)   activity (ego)

    ↓

synthetic reintegration via change in cognition

    ↓

3. repressed fantasy ⟷ repressing ⟷ symbol of
  (id)   activity (ego)   real object

Recall that the symbol may have more than a single referent. That is, it need not represent simply the repressed fantasy, but may also stand for the repressing activity of the ego (these two being in turn congruent). Some symbols may, for all practical purposes, represent only an element of the repressed wish. Such symbolic elements are, for example, kinds of images that appear in dreams, or in conscious daydreaming. These images may be quite vivid and exciting, but their appearance lacks one decisive component: action. The instinctual drive embedded in the fantasy impels the organism to action. If the fantasy is repressed, then a partial awareness, at times quite a vivid one, may be allowed as long as the person does nothing about it. This is in fact the condition of sleep: deprived of mobility and adaptive response, the organism is free to engage in the wildness of its dreams. But dreaming is not enough: humans exist through activity. And since the repressed wish continually strives for expression, the unconscious continually seeks a form of this activity within the world which will express its will free from awareness. Thus the decisive symbolic elements will be those that represent not only repressed content, but ego activity as well.

Symbolic forms are created, then, by the ego to relate the content of the repressed wish, the congruent form of the repressing activity, and the realization of this activity in the external world. These are the symbols that become culturally important: culture itself is established to maintain the world in a shape that conforms to the symbolic needs of the ego's activity. It is one thing to daydream and conjure up wishful images of the way things ought to be in order that one's instinctually-based fantasies may come true. It is quite another matter, and a more important one in cultural terms (for daydreaming in excess is the province of the neurotic), to restructure the world symbolically and to *act* upon it to achieve discharge and mastery—to actually apply symbolic vision to the alteration of reality itself. The symbols so employed will be more remote from the original wish than those in dream activity, because they represent, not the original fantasy itself, but the fantasy as altered through the interposition of the ego. But what is lost in vividness is gained in safety, for the ego now assumes active control over what had been threatening to the person, when, as a helpless child, he suffered the full brunt of his impossible wishes. And what is gained in safety becomes multiplied in power.

Although the basic trends represented in the id are not very numerous, their elaboration in reality is endless—such is man's symbolic gift. A whole array of symbols may represent a given fantasy and its ego-expression, each relating to the other and expressing part of the original wish. The more widely such spread occurs, the more potent is the ego's operation.

Thus the symbolic apparatus of culture includes a host of representations by which the people within it sustain the inner balance of their personalities. Once established by the repressive activity of the ego, such symbols become especially important in history. They are each rooted in a timeless biological striving which, no matter how realized, is never realized as its original desire. Yet the original urge persists, never frees men of its demands, and continually goads mankind onward. Furthermore, the root of the symbol, based in the id, is handled according to the intensely mobile and free form of thought characteristic of the id. This is how the symbol becomes permanently related to all those other instinctual fantasies which swim about in the inner sea of the unconscious mind. Even as the ego works without to perfect the symbol into a unique representation of its will, the id works within to maintain the endless connections with the rest of the unconscious and primordial mind. No matter how divided, the unconscious mind never lets go of anything of dynamic significance, but continually seeks to reshape everything into its timeless mold.

Closer inspection of the immense aggregation of potential symbols reveals two classes, divided according to whether the symbol is closer to inner fantasy or to outer realities. This division is to a certain extent arbitrary, and not at all absolute, but it will be useful to our understanding.

The first class we shall term *primary* symbols. These include any symbol that refers to a feeling, thought, action, value, etc. and which is, correspondingly, free of reference to an external object. Blackness and whiteness are two such symbols, as is any abstract and general idea—such as the idea of progress, or even that of material substance. The goals of cleanliness, efficiency or rationality, and the idea of holding power over another, are all primary symbols. Primary symbols are related to each other: thus, blackness may symbolize evil, gloom, and dirtiness, all primary symbols. Dirt, in the abstract, is a primary symbol, since such an entity exists only in the peculiar fantasy by which men consider anything that represents what comes out of the body to be dirty. Primary symbols do not long remain free of objective reference, however; and when applied to objects in the world, they become fixed in a different form. In the process of this passage they become *secondary* symbols.

These secondary symbols, then, are the symbolic value of any external object. Property in the abstract may be a primary symbol; a particular piece of property may be a secondary symbol. Dirt as such is primary; *this* piece of dirt is a secondary symbol. Bodily products themselves, insofar as they are considered dirty, are to be counted as secondary symbols. The object of the bigot's prejudice is a secondary symbol: greedy Jew, smelly Negro, dirty Red, etc. The person who holds power, and the one over whom power is held, are secondary symbols.

Insofar as the ego can act upon the world, it has to affix to it a primary symbol, deriving from the inner strivings of the mind. In its action the ego creates secondary symbols, and if such symbols prove particularly fruitful for the representation of primary symbols, they will become enduring parts of culture. In practice this usually means that the secondary symbol serves to represent several primary symbols; the better it works as such, the more tenaciously culture will hold onto it, and the more historically important it will become. Black people, for example, became symbols of blackness, of dirt, of being dominated, etc., and so became a basic part of the symbol system of Western culture.

The secondary symbols can at times no longer suitably represent those several primary meanings which gave them their cultural validity. Considering the basic impossibility of many of the infantile trends represented, the incompatibility of one trend with another, the conflicts arising when people do not wish to be represented in the way culture wants them to be, or wish to supplant those in power—considering all these contingencies, it is almost certain that the set of secondary symbols that comprises a culture will eventually fail to function. There is a part of us that is timeless; and another part which, by its historical activity, generates the passage of things, the sense of time. The two parts cannot remain out of conflict for long. When this inevitability occurs, the symbolic system has to be adjusted to a more or less radical extent. If it is not so changed, then the vital functions it fulfilled will fail. The harmonious integration of repressed trend and repressing force depends upon the external activity, applied to those symbols which the ego created out of the world to match its needs. When the symbols no longer work, neither does the inner defensive stabilization. Sublimated activity will break down, resulting in massive anxiety and/or forms of regression incompatible with civilized life. Major instances of such breakdowns are the substance of historical change; in dramatic form they become cataclysmic, as in the breakdown of German culture and the rise of Nazism. The passage of epochs, as at the end of the Middle Ages, is marked by the failure of very basic secondary symbols, and the need to find new ones—not just individual symbols, but whole new systems and forms of symbols.

Any historical event may contain some such process. The dislodging of outmoded secondary symbols from primary meaning is never spontaneous, for they are held with all the synthetic force of the ego and are underlined by the timeless urges of the id. This timeless id does not care that the symbol is useless; it does not care for reality at all, but wishes instead to retain for itself the symbol of satisfaction. There is an inertia in culture then, a resistance that implies the need for an energetic struggle within each historical event. The struggle is generally between opposed sets of people, who represent different interests, and compete for power. At times this struggle leads to war; sometimes it can be carried on peacefully; at times a group may even, by an inner upheaval, change its symbolic structure to match new realities. In the course of the event, there is a freeing of primary symbolic activity and a corresponding loosening of inner restraints. Such times are characterized by increased anxiety, uncertainty, and doubt. Within each event, primary symbols may be reorganized under this momentary freedom; and from each event emerges a new secondary symbol. Each secondary symbol, since it arises basically from human activity in the world, is thus the heir to a historical occurrence. Each historical occurrence will add, to a degree

proportionate to its actual historical importance, new symbolic structure to human experience; and so will change
the human ego. Personality is therefore a historically
evolving system.

The ego we are discussing is not that of an individual,
however, but rather the egos of a mass of personalities as
they present themselves in a historical situation. Let us
call it a Cultural Ego; just as we could refer to a Cultural
Superego, or even a Cultural Id. Within these structures,
there exists then a Cultural Unconscious. This is more or
less synonymous with what is loosely called the mass
unconscious, which exists, not as some kind of mysterious
ethereal or genetically endowed substance, but as the
summation, on a mass level, of the unconscious mental
processes of the people in a social group. It is thus no
more mysterious in principle than the individual unconscious, which is to say, it is a mental system of *meanings
without awareness*. The existence of both the individual
and cultural unconscious is demonstrated in the same way:
by the assumption of causality and the inference of meanings from a pattern of symbolic forms. In the individual,
these forms are found in the meaningful details of his
behavior and in free association; in the mass, they rest in
the symbols of culture which exist explicitly to give enduring meaning to the unconscious wishes of society.

Such is the psychohistorical schema. It is a system in
continuous disequilibrium and continuous evolution. Within each historical event, the entire panoply of symbols is
arrayed and regenerated: each event creates the world
anew; and from this event emerge the old forms reworked.

The most meaningful way to enter this system in the
West is through racism, for here the irrational underside
of our proud civilization is revealed most vividly. We can
now ask where in history the meanings of the symbols
black and white have arisen, and how they have changed.

The answer will take us surprisingly far. All we have to do is look at the record of our history, and discern within it the most general type of transformation which is in equilibrium with racism, and grounded in the same primitive fantasies.

CHAPTER 6
RADIX
MALORUM

Pleasure in the intestinal contents becomes enjoyment of money, which, however . . . is seen to be nothing other than odourless, dehydrated filth that has been made to shine.

Sandor Ferenczi, "The Ontogenesis of the Interest in Money"

THE WEST IS A WHITE CIVILIZATION; no other civilization has made that claim. White emblemizes purity, but purity implies a purification, a removing of impurities. This is indeed part of the meaning of white; for, though scientifically the sum of all colors, to the symbolizing mind it becomes the absence of color, that which remains when color has been removed. And it is upon this symbol of whiteness that the psychohistory of our racism rests.

Why be proud of such a negation? The answer is simple: the negation yields power, an energy so titanic as to shake the globe and perhaps destroy it. This power has been manifest in the West's economic amassment of sheer wealth; in its technological skill; and in the orderly organization of society. And all these achievements depend upon the application of a pure form of thought—rational, scientific, "whitened"—to the diverse problems of civilization. But pure thought has not been sufficient: the power has derived from a combining of science with a purified will, an élan, a zeal, even a fanaticism. These two factors —pure thought and restless zeal—have together been the guarantors of Western power; and it is the Western genius, that which above all else has yielded the pride in whiteness, to yoke the two aspects, so divergent in form and style, within one cultural entity. This also implies, however, that a splitting force is at the heart of Western culture. The ability to separate the polar dualities of reason and energy, and to keep them going together, is the distinct gift of the West. And it is this that we must understand, for it underlies the other splits and seams in our civilization, including that of race.

To this end, Western culture must be seen as an organism that permits the differentiation between reason and energy to occur in widespread and potent form. What kinds of conceptions of the world are needed for this, and what styles of action must be engendered in the inhabitants of the West to make them both so driven and so controlled? Let us look at certain crucial aspects of our culture for an answer.

Science

The scientific achievements of the West may well be its most important contribution to civilization. Certainly science has been a principal means to power. The work of the scientific mentality passes far beyond the laboratory or mathematical symbol—beyond even the technological apparatus which has realized their most infantile dreams of omnipotence. The scientific mentality has come to invest the whole universe with its own perspective.

Some aspects of the scientific viewpoint have been particularly useful in the objective description of nature. Most notable are the stubborn insistence upon empirical fact as opposed to wish or belief; the construction of the experimental method to ascertain and validify fact; and the development of abstract quantification, from the all-important concept of number itself to the most beautiful and elegant constructions of mathematics.

Abstract quantification is a very general example of the typical modern attitude. In itself, of course, it is indifferent to the objects of quantification: as such it is the province of pure mathematics. But pure mathematics is only a rarefied element of the Western scientific attitude. Central to this attitude as a whole is the belief that quantification can be applied to anything; or, to be more exact, to anything *worthwhile*: what is worthwhile is quantifiable. In this case, worthwhile means not only something that is valued, but something that is acted upon. And what is to be acted upon? Why, the whole material universe. And what is this material universe? Why, anything that can be quantified. The West has seen to it that this does not become a circular argument by constructing a symbolic belief about the nature of things which includes their quantifiability. All one has to do, then, is to apply the canons of scientific and mathematical thought to these things, to transform them into quantities, and to act upon them, aggressively if necessary, to change them into models of man's will. Being so tractable, they become worthwhile, appreciated, even loved.

A very profound and axiomatic belief is involved here, one of those general ideas that is never questioned in itself but only as to how it can be approached. The nature of this belief, or fantasy, has been best described by Whitehead, in his *Science and the Modern World*.

According to Whitehead, the fantasy imposed on nature by Western scientific man, and confirmed for him by his success in history, is the belief that the material world is composed of lifeless material bodies acted upon by immaterial forces. We see here the nuclear mental operation of Western man in its purest form: nature, which had been experienced in previous eras as an organismic and direct unity, is abstracted and made remote from men. Looking at it from a distance, Western scientific man reduces it to substances, "things"—dead things upon which a force can operate. The nature of the force is unimportant: it may be the Newtonian force of gravity (which was the most brilliant insight permitted by the abstraction) or the conquering force of men. In the primitive, axiomatic, nuclear form of this fantasy, both are equivalent. The result is the death of nature, which becomes "a dull affair, soundless, scentless, colourless; merely the hurrying of material, endlessly, meaninglessly."[33]

In spite of the protest which has been raised from time to time against this notion, the notion itself has become so engrained in us, so diffused throughout our culture, and so phenomenally successful as to resist the slightest dislodgment. This, then, has become the elementary belief of Western man: that the universe consists of dead matter distinct from us, and that the *us* who knows and works upon this matter is a dematerialized mind, a mind split from its own body just as it is split from the rest of the material world. There is nothing intrinsically wrong with the abstractions; the error (that is to say, the *fantasy* which has elaborated the scientific insights) has been what Whitehead termed the fallacy of misplaced concreteness, the application of the abstractions to the material, bodily earth. That is to say, the *fact* upon which we stubbornly and proudly perform our scientific operations may at times itself be created by fantasy. Whitehead continues to describe the mathematical-scientific approach as "entirely satisfactory so long as it is those abstractions which you want to think about. The enormous success of the scientific abstractions, yielding on the one hand *matter* with its *simple location* in space and time, on the other hand *mind*, perceiving, suffering, reasoning, but not interfering,

[33] Alfred North Whitehead, *Science and the Modern World* (New York, The Free Press, 1967), p. 54.

has foisted onto philosophy the task of accepting them as the most concrete rendering of fact."[34]

And so the West's material success, generated by applying this schema to reality, has transformed an intermediate stage of scientific understanding into a philosophical truth, and beyond that, into the substance of Western man's belief about the basic structure of the world.

Note that an intermediate stage of science yielded these principles. Twentieth-century science has demolished their right to be axioms of reality, to be anything more than the practical basis for technological progress. This demolition occurred on two fronts. First, on the physical, by quantum mechanics and relativity theory which demonstrated that the world consists, both in the fine structure of matter and in its gross relationships, not of distinct substance and separate energy, but of substance and energy immanent in each other and fused in time-space. The second front was psychological, when Freud demonstrated that the thinking of man grows out of his bodily desires and remains forever ingredient with them, even across the wall of repression. From a different approach, the Swiss psychologist Piaget showed experimentally that forms of knowledge are not independent, *a priori* givens, but spring organically from the child's concrete bodily operations. From every field, the truth (at least that level of truth permitted by our current stage of cultural evolution) has dawned: we are all one. There is an efficient differentiation of energy from matter, but the mind operates within a basic unity; and the bodily matter from which our mind is differentiated is but a part of the rest of matter, of the whole universe, including the bodies of other people.

[34] *Ibid.*, p. 55. Italics Whitehead's.

No matter: we will not believe it. It does not correspond to the culture with which we are saddled. We can only live in *this* culture, which is in turn the product of centuries of action upon the world which has made what is but a differentiation within a wholeness into radically separate entities; into mind-body and body-world, schisms which have devolved into whatever separates men, including the cleavage between races.

This most basic attitude is diffused throughout culture, and has found realization in many forms quite remote from the science that is its purest realization. Its practical effect upon history—including the history of racism—derives from its potent investment in other cultural patterns. We will now briefly consider these.

Economics

Here is indeed the central passion of the West, the first civilization to have created a type of man, the bourgeois, for whom economic activity is itself the end of life. This development in itself imposed a new differentiation upon humanity. Henceforth a distinct style of human being, and a distinct class based upon that style, would enter the configuration of society. The bourgeois also brought with him a deeper change in cultural attitude, not only toward the pursuit of economic activity, but toward the objects of that pursuit. He introduced a radical cleavage into the world that was congruent with the scientific attitude toward matter, but added to it a specific and highly meaningful activity: He made the world a market.

In its rudimentary form, this was nothing new. Forms of exchange existed from the first point of human social differentiation, even before the high-order differentiations of civilization were attained. One man had, by virtue of his distinct activity, something that another wanted, and the other, something that the first needed: the two were exchanged and the differentiation thereby became viable. The further differentiation went, the more elaborate the market became, involving material goods, services, implements, land and, eventually, an abstractification of these, money. As matters grew more complex a particular type of person arose to devote himself more or less exclusively to these transactions: the merchant. Thus the market was created. Whatever its complexities in prior epochs and in other cultures, one fact remained consistent: it was the servant of society, whose economic activity it regulated, and not its master.

In the West, however, as Karl Polanyi pointed out in *The Great Transformation*, the market came to rule the economy, and gain and profit became rulers of the culture. In the course of this process, the entire perceptible world was drawn into the market, and in this way, the West came to dominate the world. Economics, which had been the province of the community as a whole, became the almost exclusive province of a class of men who lived by the mystique of gain. What they gained, others lost; and in this process the community itself was broken up, differentiated radically, and splintered into those billions of fragments that have become the selves of modern men. The economic transformation of the West became, then, the principal agency of that excessive splitting which is distinctive in our civilization. The market divided the world; the bourgeois West conquered it.

Under the conditions of so-called primitive life, and throughout feudal times in the West, gain and profit were not paramount motives of men. This is not to imply that men were not greedy. Rapacity and greed seem to be virtual givens in humans, the result not of scarcity (which in itself impels men simply to take what they need), but of the life-long persistence of the limitless infantile strivings that are bound to be frustrated in the process of growth and separation. But greed and the desire for profit are not the same. The former is a relatively simple wish expressed in the act of taking—and what is taken is usually displayed narcissistically. The desire for profit, on the other hand, is an extended form of greed, a rationalized abstract pursuit which aims at the progressive accumulation of the media of exchange. Such an elaboration of greed was largely absent from human activity prior to the rise of the modern West. Without this systematic drive, men were by and large content to share within the provisions of the community. In more advanced civilizations, this sharing had been continually breaking down, as individuals arose who arrogated to themselves greater portions of the common good. But this was in fact the paradoxical sign of their advancement. In more primitive and simpler cultures, men saw themselves as less differentiated from each other and from the larger community. They identified readily with the community and often expressed their feeling about its bounty through the practice of gift-giving. Material objects hung lightly from them; they saw their bodies both as complete in themselves and as fused within the larger body of the community. Wholeness was expressed as exuberance: the more a man gave, the less he needed, and therefore the more complete he saw himself to be.

This attitude became completely reversed in the West. Giving was no longer proof of virtue; taking became its replacement. Even today, when philanthropy is considered an undeniable virtue, it is the virtue of a man who has taken so much that he can afford to give back in return. Furthermore, and this became crucial, the value of things taken within the market began to achieve, and has

progressively continued to achieve, a magical significance.
Wealth, the goal of the bourgeois West, was not just an
acquisition to be enjoyed, nor was its value even encom-
passed in narcissistic gain. Wealth became instead that
perfectly magical substance through which all of life's
meanings were focused.

The new world view of the West was fully realized in
the passionate pursuit of material gain. Now the external
world, that had previously been experienced in its intensely direct form, was abstracted and made into an idea
remote from the human participant in the world. And
from this distance, the idea could readily be seen as a material substance that was both *lifeless,* and so capable of
being worked on aggressively, and intensely *desirable* in
itself, so much so that when it was obtained by the person,
it became his and his alone, his very own *property.* Here
is a paradox of great importance: the subject of such
intense desire was also without life, and though it could
be sought with ferocious intensity, it could scarcely be
enjoyed once obtained. This deficiency forced a further
search for gain; and gradually the emphasis switched from
the goal to the means. The very process of seeking became the most highly valued part of the activity; what was
sought, and even worshipped, became, through the very
abstractification that made it attainable, more and more
remote, cold, and dead, and more purely quantitative.
The world was remade into dead things to be acquired;
and what was acquired was the coldest aspect of these
things: their money value.

Meanwhile, however, the joyless procedure grew mightily in power. By abstracting and quantifying everything
within reach, the ambit of the market could be widened
to include the whole world. Things abstracted can be
given a number, and numbers can be equated with each
other; hence the magical value of material things could be

widely spread to elements of the world that had never previously been held in much regard. The whole world became materialized in consequence of this abstraction. The basic mental process of the West had borne its strange fruit. And it was a potent operation, for now all the energy that had been directed by human greed toward the simple *acquisition* of wealth could be directed toward the *generation* of wealth. With this new mystique, the process of gaining could be continuous. Production entered the world through this reduction of everything to its abstract quality, and through the union of these abstractions into rationalized relationships. What was rationalized, however, was the pure desire to gain lifeless, pleasureless, and abstracted matter.

And so the whole world became things out of which more things could be made. As the process became generalized, these things, in order to be equivalent and related to each other, became even more abstract. In this way, they could be expressed in terms of their universal solvent—money, which, to use Karl Polanyi's definition, "is only another name for a commodity used in exchange more often than another." Money itself has become progressively more abstract as the logos of the West has worked itself out in the modern era. The concept of money began as a gift of something valued in itself, and passed through a stage in which valued objects were bartered for each other. Soon it was focused onto objects useless in themselves, though still concrete; then it became more abstract, until shells, stones, gold, coin and paper have led to cheques and credit cards. Soon, as the rationalization reaches its end state, it will become pure number. Money, which has been sought as the representation of all that is materially worthwhile, has become progressively more worthless in itself. And the economic system based upon this mental process, as it has perfected itself, has also become the representation of pure production as an end in itself, disgorging an endless supply of material things which, though more valued, are progressively less enjoyed.

Clearly, there is nothing intrinsically wrong either with a rational system of exchange or with material objects—just as there is nothing wrong with scientific or mathematical activity in itself. What *is* wrong, that is, demonstrably destructive to the living things on the earth, is the radical extension of the market principle to the entire universe, and the icy grip it has come to hold over man and nature. The mystique of property and productivity are only the most glaring signs of this grip, the vehicle for applying this principle to the world of living things, and making them fodder for acquisition.

True scientific activity is a paean to the beauty of nature, but the technology sired by science and the mystique of productivity makes nature into an inert mass whose inner forms are to be pulverized into property. Land is not really a commodity, since it was not made by men, but made them instead. Yet in making the land into a commodity from which endless wealth can be extracted, men have vented such aggressive energy upon it as to bring nature into abject submission. The submission is deceptive, since, as we are beginning to learn, nature so traduced by technology has its ways of recoiling. But the deception is all that is needed to provide men with what they want: an adequate symbol to realize their inner wishes. And these wishes include, as we can see by simply looking dispassionately and objectively at what has been done to the earth in the name of productivity, an immense hatred of nature, a desire to wreak upon it what can only be considered some sort of revenge. This hatred is not what our culture professes—all we want, we say, is to produce rationally as much wealth from nature as possible—but it is what our culture has done, and what we have done must correspond somehow to what we want to do.

Along with this rapine has come the peculiar transformation of man in the modern West, the most decisive of rationalized fissions and abstractions which characterize this civilization: the separation of work from the worker, and the removal of this labor to the pool of the market, where it is dissolved in its appropriate quantum of money. Again, there is obviously nothing inherently wrong with remunerating a man for what he does; any social system based upon differentiation—that is, one within which a high-level mentality can occur—must include such a principle. And again, what has been wrong with this system is its phenomenal accentuation; the intense abstraction of work away from the worker so that another person can *own* that work as though it were his property, can leave the worker with nothing but a lump of cash for his efforts, can, in short, dehumanize work and alienate the worker. This abstraction, as do the others, enables aggression to be applied more widely and efficiently to the world, and generates the considerable power of productivity. It has, in fact, been done in the interests of power; it rests solely upon the inner assumptions that underlie the generation of power.

That the alienation of labor is at the core of the dilemmas of our history follows from the fact that work is man's essential activity, and that his activity is the cardinal feature of his life. This is not, of course, a new observation; Karl Marx arrived at it in its most telling form in his youthful essay "Alienated Labor," written in 1844. There he stated the essential truth that the very intensity of the mystique of property derived directly from the alienated nature of work: "As the world of things increases in value, the human world becames devalued. For labor not only produces commodities; it makes a commodity of the work process itself, as well as of the worker—and indeed at the same rate as it produces goods.

"This means simply that the object produced by man's labor—its product—now confronts him in the shape of an alien thing, a power independent of the producer..." "...the [worker] falls under the domination of the wealth he produces and cannot enjoy—... capital ... from this premise, it is clear that the more the worker exerts himself, the more powerful becomes the world of things which he creates and which confront him as alien objects; hence the poorer he becomes in his inner life, and the less belongs to him as his own.... The life which he has conferred on the object confronts him in the end as a hostile and alien force."

This insight strikes the root of the multiplication of power into endless productivity that has propelled the West to the top of all civilizations. All the rationalizations of modern capitalism, far from erasing it, have only served to safeguard the core process: the abstraction of work and the extraction from it of an alien and powerful force which can be rationally multiplied to suit the dominative and acquisitive needs of culture. The effect it has had on people can be seen in the debasement of culture, in the creation of masses of poor, in the uprooting of millions of people to be shifted about by ever more impersonal forces, and in those extreme forms of dehumanization that crystallized into racism.

We will return later to this trend, to study some of the underlying fantasies that were derived from it and converged with it into the psychohistorical structures of racism. Before leaving this brief discussion, however, one more factor needs mention.

The power that became abstracted away from nature

and mankind and which was then recondensed into our powerful culture found both its actuality and symbol represented in one entity—the machine. The development of machine technology had of course begun with the beginning of humanity itself, when the first hominid picked up a tool. Its growth proceeded fairly steadily throughout history, being more marked before the advent of the machine age in some civilizations—such as China—than in others. Europeans were in fact rather inhibited in their development of the machine before the modern age. They had been detained by certain peculiar emotional attitudes toward the world, which we shall study shortly. However, once the nuclear solution of modern times had been achieved, machine technology began its unparalleled growth in the West. It was jointly spurred by scientific discoveries and by the new-found rationalized approaches to economic activity which we have discussed above.

At about the turn of the nineteenth century, the numerous advances in the development of machinery converged into something like a critical mass and set off what we know as the Industrial Revolution. This change was indeed of massive proportions, but it was less a revolution, that is, something that overturned a pre-existent culture, than it was an immense accelerator to the basic trends that had been germinating in the West since the sixteenth century.

From the Industrial Revolution on, the West came into its own. The imperial age had dawned. The rise of industrialism was the material certification the new kind of mentality had been awaiting. Machines became the best possible symbol of the inner strivings of Western culture —for the best possible symbol is potent actuality. Accordingly, the inner changes of Western culture leaped forward. In particular, the reliance upon men for the generation of power was replaced by the reliance upon the machine. A critical choice was posed to mankind, and its implications are still before us. The existence of machines radically multiplies all the potentialities in human nature. By freeing men from their abject dependence upon brutalizing labor, they release and magnify the self; and such freedom implies the possible realization of the undying dream of human liberation. But what is done with machines depends upon the nature of the self that is so magnified by their use. If it is a self devoted to the service of the life forces, then the machine can become the tool of Eros; if it is a self in thrall to domination and the endless production of lifeless substance, then the machine will become the tool of destruction.

These polar aspects are mixed in culture; history shows us which one has had the upper hand. Thus the machines so brilliantly devised by the Western mind have actually been used to accelerate the mystique of capitalism: the interminable abstraction of nature in the interests of the production of joyless wealth for the power of the few in control, and the degradation of those masses dominated by the powerful few. The machine thereby became the catalyst of what had evolved before it.

And with this development, the full force of the market took hold, for machines are expensive, they require capital investment, and they must produce an excess of goods to repay their owners. In the drive to justify this investment and to maximize the immense material potential of the machine, everything—land, labor, human values—had to be subordinated to the mechanical organs of production. In part, this meant that man himself was evermore diminished: the rise of the impoverished, rootless masses, and the dehumanization of labor attested to this.

At the same time, the new form of power energized a

revolutionary striving. Men questioned the old order; some, observing the ruin wrought by the unchecked force of Western productivity, dared hope for a better order. New governments arose, drawing upon some of the potentialities for freedom that were released by the rise of the West. And this abstract ideal of freedom was itself made possible by the creation of the idea of an individual, self-determining personality which followed from the new differentiations within Western culture. A belief in the power of rational activity and the strength of natural law was also a consequence of man's intellectual advance, and was used as the philosophical ground for these ideals of freedom and humanity. And this surge, dialectical to the dehumanization of the mystique of productivity, was also generated by the expansive energies infused into the West by the power of the machine and the scientific mind.

And so the historical process was generating many distinct trends, some clearly destructive, some clearly hopeful, some ambiguous. All shared in the common underlying differentiation of Western culture; all were invested with the intensity that such a rapid change involved; all would vie with each other in the historical developments to come.

Other Cultural Changes

Western culture progressively adapted itself to the new forces released by its scientific and economic expansion. Traced upon those changes were the cardinal trends of differentiation and abstraction; written into them were the dialectical divergences revealed in the coexistence of the ideals of freedom and humanity on the one hand, and of power and domination on the other.

The Church, which had once bound the West into one Christian community through its provision of one universal belief, also became fragmented; and from the fragments, forms of belief arose that brought into existence symbolic conceptions of God and man appropriate to the new stage of cultural organization. The process was bound to be violent since religious beliefs seemed to Western men the most vital symbolic expression of their whole relationship to the universe. The religious persecutions and wars of the sixteenth and seventeenth centuries bore adequate witness to this. Nowadays, preoccupied with a different set of secondary symbols, we find such intensities and hatreds bizarre in the extreme, and contrary to the "true" nature of religion. But men then took their religion much more seriously than we; and whatever changed in their culture had to be expressed in religious form. Out of these religious changes emerged new forms of belief compatible with the new stage in Western culture.

These new beliefs were summed up in the Reformation, which arose to *reform* the abuses of the established Church, and, more basically, to re-*form* the image of man and God. The etymological point is more than superficial. The new formation was expressed in terms of moral reform, and became itself the source of a radically different morality. Previously, morality had devolved from God through the mediation of an intervening institution, the Church. The source of the great influence the Church wielded in all spheres of life lay precisely in its institutional hold over moral judgment. Through its definition of good and evil in all spheres of activity, it held the cords which bound the West into a Christian community. Martin Luther would not have arisen as a great man had not that community been failing in its synthetic function, and this failure was nowhere more explicit than in the inconsistency between the professed values of the Church and its actual corruption. The corruption was primarily venality, an excessive and unbridled greed, itself the signal of a failure in sublimation, and a return to the original drive-centered form of materialistic impulses that were supposed to be held in check by the moral force of the Church. The massive anxiety and despair of the late Middle Ages bore vivid witness to the deterioration of traditional Christian values in the face of new historical phenomena. Clearly, the traditional culture of the West was failing, and a new form of moral restraint was needed.

Luther, a defiant, stubborn and creative man, found that restraint. He did so essentially by scrapping the moral mediation of the Church: henceforth, men would relate *directly* to God. It took all of Luther's strength and genius to abandon the hallowed nuclear ideas that, no matter how flawed, still served as the organizing principles of Western civilization. His central insight was that a principle of God was within man himself. Given this, men could relate directly to God and could express this relationship in faith alone, devoid of all institutional and worldly trappings.

Psychologically, this meant an internalization. What had been fulfilled previously by an external factor, the Church, could now be accomplished within the self. The way was cleared for the development of an individual sense of morality. Freed from its concrete bind to the Church, the mind was further free to doubt old values, and to explore and create new ones. It was a painful freedom, but it introduced a creative element into Western culture that seized upon other elements, including the Renaissance, and eventually led, through the great philosophical and scientific discoveries which followed in the wake of the Reformation, to the powerful, rationalized culture of the modern West. This internalization was a basic change—and it was basically a new plane of human differentiation. It also involved an *abstraction*, a reliance upon the abstract symbol of faith alone—on the principle,

or idea, of God—rather than upon His concrete images on
the earth. The vision of God that emerged from this
change contained the paradox common to all of our culture: He was a principle, to be related to *directly,* but
He was also more abstract and *remote.* Men could not
know Him; they could only have faith in Him. The power
of faith—and it was a driving force—overcame the paradox. The practical genius of Protestantism, which was no
less than the genius of the West as a whole, was to discover that the more remote a desired goal, the more
passionately a man would seek it. The new image of man
which emerged with the arrival of Protestantism was
equally paradoxical. Now he was freed to be an individual. Having God within him, he could be more of a unique
self, less of a cipher within a larger Church-centered community. The self grew greatly through this transformation;
split off from the body of the Church, it was freed to
undertake its astounding differentiation in the further history of the West. And, consistent with the God to whom
it related directly, this self was also more abstract, more
the creature of pure spirit, less embedded within its own
body. The self became greater, but also more remote from
the world in which it was grounded, including that intermediate part of the world, the body. The disjunction between mind and body, spirit and flesh, which Christianity
had dynamically infused into world culture, was radically
accentuated. God had become more abstract and could
no longer be suitably represented in concrete and plastic
images. By the same logic, the human body which, despite
all negation, remained concrete, ceased to be of value to
Him. Spirit was what He was; Spirit was what He wanted;
Spirit was goodness itself. The body, badness itself, was
of concern not to God but to his black antagonist, the
Devil.

Thus Luther abhorred material pursuits, especially the

pursuit of gain, thinking them to be the work of the Devil. He thereby intensified the primal Christian abhorrence of the sinfulness of bodily—ergo material—desires. From this point of fission within the development of Christianity, there appeared many divergent patterns of belief. Some were to proclaim a total ascetic denial of the body and a correspondingly absolute dedication to the spirit. In extreme form, this strand of Christian denial led to those sects who practiced mass castration lest they fall victim to bodily desires.

Another pattern accepted the body as the instrument of pleasure and life, as our given reality, and restricted their opprobrium to the materialistic pursuit of gain, the creation and acquisition of lifeless objects described above, which they discerned as the specific root of evil. This affirmative stream of Christian belief never took hold in the main body of Western culture, but it never died, either. It found instead a series of prophets, the greatest of whom was perhaps William Blake; remained fused to other, less specifically Christian elements of culture; and still exists in numerous forms—many not religious at all— in the modern age, where it is given dialectical existence by the current spasms of advanced industrial civilization. Its nature is perhaps best described and affirmed in the work of Norman O. Brown, and of others who have chosen to rebel against the icelike materialism of modern culture.

Nonetheless, Western culture has developed primarily along materialistic and rational lines. Blake, after all, never promised men power. And, though the outcome would have been abhorred by the men of faith who created the basis of modern Christian belief, the dominant culture also derives from the Lutheran revolution. What counted in this respect was not the dynamic belief in the destructiveness of material craving, but the form, style and structure of social action made possible by internalization. The Reformation resulted in an abstracted, inner-directed self remote from the God it believed in and the body-world it lived in. This abstraction and remoteness supplied room for maneuvering; there was enough distance now between the self and the outside world to allow for further inner change. And this inner change, involving the dynamic urges of mankind which had led to the concupiscent despair of the late Middle Ages, could be restructured into the efficient, scientific, practical, potent, rational, moral, productive and destructive styles of bourgeois activity. For this to happen, however, a further elaboration of the Reformation doctrine of religious activity was necessary; and history will always supply the means for what is necessary. In this case, it was the doctrine of Calvinism.

In Calvinism, abstraction and remoteness were carried one step further. God, no longer simply abstracted from the world, hated the world. For the Calvinists, men were damned in God's eyes, irretrievably foul in their bodily aspects, and clung to God only through their abstract spirit. This spirit had to *prove* itself to God, had to negate its corporeal handicap. It could not enjoy the filthy world, but could attempt to bring order to it, to clean it up as much as could be humanly possible. The logical outcome was clear: make, produce, work over the given world, control both it and the body, and you will have virtue, you will be revealed as part of the elect and will receive heavenly reward. Here on earth, however, virtue—moral perfection—was the sole reward. The sensuous enjoyment of reality was confined to pure activity—the cold efficiency of work for itself, gain for itself. What is gained cannot be enjoyed; it should not even be seen, but must instead be progressively abstracted until the only things that "matter" are money and moral purity—the former being the abstraction of a deadened filthy world, and the latter, the abstracted quality of a deadened, clean self. To be sure, there was no satisfaction intended by this system. All that "counted" was movement, striving for an endless goal that became ever more remote precisely through the process of striving.

This impossible situation generated fantastic energy for the benefit of its adherents. The more one strove, the less it was possible for one to enjoy. The less one enjoyed, the more one strove. Gradually, the material objects of the striving began to assume a fantastical aspect. Ever more desired, ever less desirable in themselves, they became ever more valued, and ever more hated. The only solace was moral perfection, the freedom from a guilt that was increasingly generated in the impulses toward freedom. The only recourse was further abstraction—splitting up the self and the world into separate, abstracted quantities by which the insensate dilemma could be, if not resolved, at least kept out of sight. By and large, the more abstractable an element of the world, the more pure, hence desirable it is; the more irreducible and concrete, the more impure, and the more hated. Unhappily, the world consists of concrete objects which exert a fascination all the more intense for their being hated.

We have isolated from the general stream of cultural history a process which can endlessly destroy any element of the world that happens to come within its domain. Furthermore, we have seen that this process is neither a discrete activity nor an aberration. Rather, it is an ingredient of the very aspects of our culture of which we are most proud—our science, our rationalized economics, our insistence upon personal autonomy. American history supplies endless examples of the dilemma. In the process of tearing Indians off their land, of enslaving and dehumanizing blacks, of exploiting great numbers of human beings besides Negroes and Indians, of raping the land itself—through this whole destructive process, a proud civilization has been built, replete with the highest ideals and cultural achievements. The tendency in dealing with this absurd paradox is to fall into the mental tendency basically responsible for it in the first place, and to see only one side: to either excoriate culture out of hand for its destructivity, or to praise it in the feeble hope that "basically things are all right," and that just a little tinkering with the system should right the wrongs. But it is in that root polarization, in that fleeing to ends of good and bad, of white and black, in the face of an inextricably fused reality, that our historical agony resides.

Let us say that the abstractions with which our culture is saddled arise from the human need to sort out what is real but mixed, into what is symbolic but separated. We have observed this kind of activity at two levels: in the human mind as it develops into a synthetic whole; and in human culture as it adapts itself historically. We are now at a stage of our study where it should be possible to make a fruitful comparison between the two levels, and to derive, from the pattern of history, a fuller realization of the nuclear ideas that lie within.

Recall that culture is organized into sets of symbols which are congruent with the structure of the personalities within it. Recall further that patterns of activity have a symbolic value of their own, and that these are of the greatest importance because of their decisive role in historical change. What kind of elementary symbolic value can be derived from the historical process outlined in this chapter? In terms of the symbolic matrix presented in the preceding chapter, what is the symbolic value revealed in Western culture's central activity—the creation, production, abstractification and rational acquisition of property, and the joyless passion which seeks ever more avidly that which recedes into remoteness through the process of seeking? There is a mythic quality to this unfolding process, and we must discover its content.

The first aspect to be considered is the emergence in the West of a style of activity that was both intensely driving and tightly controlled. We have noted that power has accrued to the West through the yoking of energy and reason within one cultural ego. Other cultures had the energy, still others had the control, and some even combined the two; but no culture carried the combination to such extremes. The very passion expressed by the Western drive to power is representative, on a cultural level, of the tapping of deep infantile desires. This culture, at once the most advanced, is also the most infantile—if by infantile we mean the presence of a cosmic yearning, an endless striving, a bottomless longing for the objects of desire. But then, so is man himself the most advanced and the most infantile of animals. The deeper one returns into infancy, the more profound and limitless becomes desire. However, before a certain point is reached, desire cannot be yoked with control or purposeful activity. This is the oral stage. Consequently, oral fantasies will not suffice to account for the Western innovation.

In the anal stage, however, passion persists and is critically linked with efforts to control the body, and to differentiate the self in a realistic way from the rest of the world. Anal fantasies can encompass both reason and energy, control and desire. The personality type which, when exaggerated into maladaptive pathology, is called the obsessive-compulsive, or anal personality, is also the normal variant of Western man: punctual, orderly, clean, emotionally controlled, reliant upon rational, discrete thought rather than upon emotional effusion, perceiving emotionality itself as a form of disorder. This personality type derives its structure from the negation of anal fantasies, which allows the fantasies to persist energetically in the unconscious while the conscious self pursues a life style dominated by symbolic extensions of efforts to control the excretion of bodily products. If these attempts break down under the pressure of overly intense unconscious fantasies, pathological states ensue. Western culture, however, provides an ample set of symbolic operations to encompass the numerous aspects of anal personality traits.

We know from studies of Luther himself[35] that his personality was to a considerable extent elaborated upon anal fantasies. Two of his personality traits, stubbornness and defiance, were of decisive aid to him in his rebellion against papal authority—as have similar character configurations aided countless other Westerners in their stubborn and defiant efforts to impose a new world culture upon other civilizations. Nor must we forget—though somehow almost everyone manages to—that the turning point in modern Western history, Luther's idea of the power of individual faith, struck him in a flash of inspiration while he sat upon the privy; and that this genius was not loath to stress the importance of this in applying fecal symbolism to all evil parts of the universe, and especially to the Devil, God's black antagonist.

In sum, then, control, stubbornness, defiance, orderliness, cleanliness, punctuality and thrift—all these complicated traits which have characterized the West more than any other civilization—devolve onto anal fantasies and the resolution of their logical incompatibility is achieved through an unconscious symbolic root in infantile fantasies about excretion.

[35] Most notably Erikson's psychobiography, *Young Man Luther* (New York, W. W. Norton & Company, 1958); and Norman O. Brown's section on Luther and Protestantism in *Life Against Death* (New York, Vintage Books, 1960).

A culture, however, must do more than define an ideal character type. It must also provide a view of the universe which enables this type to function. And so in the modern West, reality has been restructured according to the symbolism of the excremental vision of infancy. In both the historical and infantile systems, a universe is radically split along lines of goodness and badness; in both, what is good is pure, clean and white, and what is bad is impure, dirty, smelly and black. Both systems are dominated by the fantasy of dirt: the body is dirty; what comes out of the body is especially dirty; the material world corresponds to what comes out of the body, and hence it is also especially dirty. Not the whole world is dirty, but only those more concrete, sensuous aspects that are symbolically close to the concrete, sensing body. If something in the world can be made clean and pure, and if it can be made cold and non-sensuous as well, then it will meet the criterion of goodness. What is good in the world is identified with what is good in the person—not his body, but his mind. Thus, within anal symbolism, mental contents come to be considered especially pure and perfect differentiations. Words themselves achieve a magic power, which stem from the infant's magical preoccupation with feces; when the feces are repudiated as filthy, their power to represent the whole universe becomes displaced onto the mental productions which represent the universe. The mind, good, makes words and thoughts; the body, bad, makes shit and filth. And words are placed in the service of aggression toward the natural world, just as feces had been instruments of aggression toward the mother. The connection is negated (and so affirmed) in the childhood ditty: "sticks and stones will break my bones, but words will never harm me." And these words and thoughts are the instruments of Western scientific world domination, surely the most culturally potent form of aggression yet devised by humanity.

One overriding quality determines what is good and bad within the analized world: purity. And within the entire spectrum of reality, one aspect of knowledge fulfills this quality: *abstraction*. An abstract idea is a purified idea, freed from annoyingly concrete and sensuous particulars. Words themselves are abstractions. The non-sensuous senses, sight and hearing, are the mediators of abstract activity. Smell, taste and touch are concrete, syncretic, incapable of making the fine distinctions necessary to sort out what is abstract from what is sensuous. Abstraction means distance from immediate experience, the substitution of a relatively remote symbol for a given sensuous reality. Sight and hearing are thus those senses which best fulfill the possibility of a remote relationship to the world. Western civilization began its expansion with the discovery of perspective, and the perfection of remote, visually organized, abstracted activities—whether in navigation or in the development of firearms that could kill from a distance. The West became intoxicated with the idea of distant space, which was represented in the dream of a New World (and today, a new universe) to be conquered.

Abstraction in the service of power—whether in capitalism, science, political organization, or religious organization—is the cultural means of translating the infantile fantasies about dirt and the body into realistic action. It is thus a primary symbol, and forms of reality become secondary symbols of goodness or badness, according to whether they are abstractable or not. And of all substances, feces are the least abstractable, the most irreducible and undifferentiated to the mind, hence the most to be avoided. When we see through the arguments of another person, sense a falseness of conception, or a flaw in abstraction, we signal this by saying "that's a lot of crap"; or, if the person himself is to be reduced to worthlessness, then one adds "you're full of shit": no other word could be falser to our idealized image of non-bodily perfection.

But feces were once valued too, as parts of the narcissistic body grudgingly surrendered. Within the unconscious mind, the original valuation is never relinquished; it endures in all its infantile ambivalence. But the world can be segregated into good and bad representations of excrement. The good representations are those that can be abstracted: in their final form, we call them money. Money is to the Western world-image what words and thoughts are to the self-image: the most perfectible, desirable, abstracted form of symbolic realization. The symbolic equation of feces with money was an early discovery of psychoanalysis,[36] and its connection with abstraction was shown by Ferenczi, in his paper of 1914, "The Ontogenesis of the Interest in Money." Ferenczi traced how this most valued possession of man derives from the interest in feces; and how, in consequence, feces became the least valued of human possessions. Spurred by the repression of the sense of smell, the child shifts his attention first to street mud; thence, as mud becomes objectionable, to sand[37] (dried, deodorized and whitened); then to stones (hard as well); to artificial products like beads, marbles, buttons (no longer attached to the earth—indeed, the first objects of exchange, and the first desirable possessions); and then to shining pieces of money, gold being the most desirable because it is the least concretely useful, the most abstractly

---

[36] Cf. Freud's paper *Character and Anal-Eroticism* (1908), in *Standard Edition*, Vol. IX.

[37] The sense of sensuous enjoyment meanwhile, according to Ferenczi, has become split off, sublimated and displaced to other subjects, and finally to aesthetic pleasure.

mysterious of metals. Here the infantile stage is complete.
Further transformation into paper, checks, etc. and eventually into pure quantity, depends upon the development
of the full symbolic power of the adult mind and its ability, under our cultural conditions, to transform all of
reality into media of exchange. Thus money is the most
acceptable of all possessions, since it is the most abstract
—but all men share in the infantile magic ascribed to
excreta.[38]

As Norman O. Brown demonstrated, the spur to this
process, which, though universal, has reached utterly new
proportions in the West, is guilt. "Money is symbolical
because it is derived from unconscious guilt and because
there is nothing in reality that corresponds to it."[39] It derives its life in culture "by inheriting the magic power
which infantile narcissism attributes to the excremental
product." It is through this magic power that the infant
seeks to master the agony of his individuation by displac-
ing the rage of separation, first onto his parents, then to
the self, then to the bodily-self, and finally to his (expelled,
hence separated) excrements. And it is because of the
basic human intolerance of separation—that is, through
man's eternal desire for reunion with the source of his
being—that we cannot even give up that which we hate
and are disgusted by, but seek to return abstracted portions of it into the self. Insofar as this is done, then self-
hate and self-disgust—that is to say, guilt—becomes
permanently established within the personality and spurs
it onward to further abstract differentiations. And it is this
primitive and universal fantasy that the West has mobilized in its culture, and turned to the generation of material power—an endlessly transformed guilt. The guilt may

[38] The German word for possessing is *besitzen*—to sit upon.
[39] Brown, *Life Against Death*, p. 271.

be denied; but it is most commonly projected outward onto scapegoats of one sort or another where it persists as a goad within culture, held fixed by the synthetic needs of the human organism.

Indeed, the problem of guilt looms even larger in culture than in the individual, as it becomes progressively abstracted out of the individual and onto culture with the passage of historical time. This happens because, in individual development, men seek happiness. The need for happiness is balanced against the need for restrictions, expressed by the internal, guilt-producing mechanism of the superego. Within this balance the scales may frequently tip themselves toward the production of guilt and pain; but there is, except in severe psychopathology, an equilibrium of forces.

Yet culture has no intrinsic desire for happiness. "Here," as Freud wrote in *Civilization and Its Discontents*, "by far the most important thing is the aim of creating a unity out of the individual human beings. It is true that the aim of happiness is still there, but it is pushed into the background. It almost seems as if the creation of a great human community would be most successful if no attention had to be paid to the happiness of the individual." And, as the community widens, the conflict of the individual "is continued in forms which are dependent on the past; and it is strengthened and results in a further intensification of the sense of guilt. . . . If civilization is a necessary course of development from the family to humanity as a whole, then as a result of the inborn conflict arising from ambivalence, of the eternal struggle between the trends of love and death—there is inextricably bound up with it an increase of the sense of guilt, which will perhaps reach heights that the individual finds hard to tolerate."

Freud emphasized the oedipal, and especially the parricidal, source of this guilt. There can be no doubt from the record of history and myth that this has been the enduring system which generates guilt and incorporates it into an endless cycle of historical domination. We would add to this the insight developed so powerfully by Brown: that in modern Western civilization, this primal source of guilt has been at once defended against and furthered through the cultural marshaling of pre-oedipal fantasies, principally centering upon the anal zone and its excremental product. How this has progressed will be the subject of our next chapter. For now, let us summarize the mixed blessing brought to mankind by the inventive genius of our civilization.

The West succeeded in institutionalizing its guilt into efficient systems of production. Through the expedient of abstraction, most forcefully expressed in Calvinist theology, a God-symbol arose to justify individual suffering by turning it to economic use in the compulsions of work without pleasure and gain without joy. Much has thereby been acquired besides that most valued commodity which is, to quote Ferenczi, "nothing other than odourless dehydrated filth that has been made to shine." A world has been gained—but at the price of its death. This ambivalent attitude toward the world is coordinate with the sense of guilt so active in the modern history of the West. The guilt is, then, in its deeper sense, guilt over the persistence of an impossible infantile fantasy—the wish to both take in what is fancied to have been lost from the bodyself, and to destroy it. In order to save the self from being destroyed as well, it, and everything it values, becomes abstract—cold and white. Everything it takes in but destroys is concrete, sensuous, and black. The self of modern man is thus gained, along with the idea of its freedom. But the freedom must include the freedom to hold onto those deadened parts of the world called property. Thus property rights in the West far surpass what libertarians call "human" rights. And by implication, what is human and which kinds of people are to be more human than others, is culture's province to define.

CHAPTER 7
THE PSYCHO-HISTORICAL MATRIX

No one knows who will live in this cage in the future, or whether at the end of this tremendous development entirely new prophets will arise, or there will be a great rebirth of old ideas and ideals, or, if neither, mechanized petrification, embellished with a sort of convulsive self-importance. For of the last stage of this cultural development, it might well be truly said: "Specialists without spirit, sensualists without heart; this nullity imagines that it has attained a level of civilization never before achieved."

Max Weber, *The Protestant Ethic and the Spirit of Capitalism*

IF BOTH CULTURE and personality are congruent systems mediated by a set of symbols, it should be possible to array those symbols into a coherent form which expresses certain critical historical relationships. This form cannot be linear, that is, one-to-one between personality and cultural structures. Neither system is linear in itself; both are organic—unified synthetic entities within which interlocked elements play out a myriad of connected relationships.

Thus our array of symbols must be multidimensional. We have already used the term *matrix* to express the organization of symbols; now let us develop this concept further. The word is itself a symbol, and like all important symbols, has numerous related referents. In its most elementary form, it refers to the womb; more abstractly, it refers to what the dictionary describes as "a place or enveloping element within which something originates, takes form or develops . . . that which gives form, origin, or foundation to something enclosed or embedded in it." The matrix is the natural material in which something is embedded—and it gives form and development to that which is embedded within it. In biology, it is the substance between cellular elements; in history it is the array of symbolic elements out of which *both* cultural and personality structures take form and develop. Matrices are often expressed mathematically, and we shall express our psychohistorical matrix in a similarly formal way, in order to express the differing functional relationships which symbols serve.

According to the definitions of Chapter 5, symbols which are free of external referents are the primary symbols; those realized by application to cultural objects are the secondary symbols. These symbols can be further differentiated according to whether they are involved in the functions of the id—the collection of repressed, biologically rooted infantile fantasies; the ego—the collection of functional operations adapted to reality and the needs of defense; or the superego—the collection of controlling and directing operations within the ego. Each of these systems must naturally influence all the others if the personality is to remain a coherent whole; and each system must have its representation in culture, if culture is to meet the needs of man and maintain its own wholeness. The mutual influences between the four main dimensions of id, ego, superego and culture are what give the matrix its formal symmetry.

The matrix presented here can be no more than a limited beginning to the comprehension of this underlying order. One of its ironies is that it is composed of words, which are but the symbols of the symbols of the matrix. More serious than this is the tendency to simplify the staggering complexity of human reality in the interests of deriving lawful relations. Whether this simplification has been to a *reductio ad absurdum,* I must leave to the reader to decide. My hope is that it provides a way to grasp the progression of what has actually happened to make the modern Western world unique among civilizations. Every human and, by extension, every human group, has had to deal with the same set of nuclear problems. Each has elaborated it specifically, and the evidence presented in the previous chapter suggests that what is *specifically* important about the psychohistory of the West has been the elaboration of certain primitive bodily fantasies into a comprehensive world view. The matrix hopefully sheds at least a dim light upon some cardinal aspects of that world view; it also hopefully takes into account the coordinated development of a high degree of rational activity with bloodshed, domination, confusion and torment. The "higher" mental functions do not arise independently of the "lower"; reason emerges as a plant does from the soil, but, like the plant, it needs the soil and needs to have its roots within it.

In the diagram of the psychohistorical matrix (see Fig. 2) the four dimensions—id, ego, superego and culture—are arrayed both horizontally and vertically, so that mutual influences can be shown. Where horizontal and vertical aspects of a dimension intersect, a box is drawn around the symbols. These boxed symbols are to be considered the specific character of that dimension under the conditions of modern Western expansion. The influences

Figure 2.

PSYCHOHISTORICAL MATRIX—STRESSING ANALLY ROOTED SYMBOLISM

	ID	EGO	SUPEREGO	CULTURE
ID	world as feces: good: to be included, saved (property) bad: to be extruded destroyed (dirt)	conative striving defiance	unneutralized harsh, full of self-hatred	matter an object of disgust the indifferent recipient of aggression
EGO	defend against anality reaction formation increasingly differentiated	self-pure & discrete rational abstracted controlled clean punctual industrious, etc.	intensely moralistic purifying	—rise of modern, bourgeois-democratic state —Industrial Revolution —Technology all articulated, abstracted, rationalized labor alienated
SUPEREGO	actively repudiate: world is of the devil	striving for mastery —self-perfection: to reclaim loss —guilt-ridden to destroy —closely watching	intense idealistic self-righteous	object to be reclaimed-reformed destroyed-re-formed
CULTURE	—scapegoats —despised races —technological destruction —warfare —pollution	distant, abstracted transactions, e.g., —impersonality —bureaucracies —money	—helpless, oppressed people to be saved —church —state —remote, judging god	The Market—the world as abstracted property self-contained social systems ever asserting their autonomy

a dimension has received from the others may be read in the vertical column under its name. Thus the boxed symbols are the psychohistorical integral of the vertical column of symbols. Similarly, the horizontal line proceeding from each dimension expresses its activity upon the other dimensions.

Thus, for example, the Western ego receives its conative striving, etc. from the id, its striving for purity from the superego, and its distant, abstracted operation from appropriate cultural forms such as bureaucracies. Out of these influences (and by its own activity), it emerges as a driven, pure, rational, clean self.

Similarly, the ego defends against the anal sadism of the id, creates in itself an intensely moralistic superego, and has created in culture such forms as the modern State, the Industrial Revolution, and technology. That these forms are also influences upon the ego is but one of the word-limitations of the matrix. The same construction may be applied to the other dimensions. In sum, then, the psychohistorical matrix is a way of representing mutual influences of different functional entities within a culture. It does not itself propound any immanent, Hegelian law of history; the only principle to which it is faithful is that of the parallel organicity of culture and the psyche.

Both culture and the psyche are in the process of continuous historical change, but the temporal element within these symbolic relationships cannot be charted; we must trace out its broad workings. This temporal dimension begins at the point in history when the particular fantasies represented in the matrix diffused meaningfully over the entire cultural world.

Each civilized group will show significant precursors of what is to become its mature form, and the West is no exception to this general rule.

The precursors extend far back into the history of our civilization. Perhaps the most important element was the tendency to internalize aggression in the interests of group cohesion and intellectual activity. The West owed this boon to the Jewish people, and the guilty pains associated with the change became forever after the justification for the scapegoating and persecution of the Jews. Pain aside, what this creative development ensured was the appearance of coherent superego systems, both in culture and in the individual. Internalization has occurred before, of course, and occurs in all forms of culture; it must exist wherever mentality does. The Western style had a coherence and extension, however, which the others lacked. Here was the nuclear synthesis of man and his world that could become extended into infinity. A price had to be paid, however. The unique father–God—who had overthrown the pre-existing mélange of polytheistic and matriarchal deities and who had by his uniqueness thereby certified to the Jews their chosenness—this one God had to receive all the mixed feelings hitherto deployed throughout a pantheon. But hatred and love could not be at the same time directed toward a deity without destroying his synthetic unity. Hatred—the inevitable consequence of the eternal ambivalence of the human situation—had to be kept out of awareness; and, since aggression could not be kept out of human life, hate had to be turned inward. "There was no place in the framework of the religion of Moses for a direct expression of the murderous hatred of the father," wrote Freud in *Moses and Monotheism*.[40] "All that could come to light was a mighty reaction against it— a sense of guilt on account of that hostility, a bad conscience for having sinned against God and for not ceasing to sin."

[40] *Standard Edition*, Vol. XXIII, p. 134.

This bad conscience was never to leave the history of the West. Indeed, what is specific about Western history has been the progressive enlargement of an aggressive conscience and its steady accumulation, through historical events, of deeper and wider senses of meaning.

Christianity widened the process by adding to the patriarchal religion elements of an older, matriarchal one. Out of the union emerged a son-religion to replace the father-religion: a desexualized Son of God appeared who widened the range of inclusion by his assumption of generalized guilt. Guilt had been growing within classical culture, where it had appeared in harsh, unneutral forms, as in the orgiastic and self-castrative religious rites which abounded in the Mediterranean world at the beginning of the Christian era. The Christ legend offered a subliminatory way out of the self-mutilating trap by providing a purified and highly ethical cultural superego to replace the nakedly self-destructive forms of guilt that were uselessly torturing mankind. The new superego would turn men away from their bodies—would, as has been the case throughout our history, abstract them further—and relate them to an abstracted version of the Judaic God. Any study of the early Church, and especially of its asceticism and martyrdom, reveals that this process of sublimation was faltering at best. Nonetheless, the nucleus of change was presented, and, as the regulatory systems of classical civilization were plainly inadequate to men's needs, it would only be a matter of time before the West would grow into the new development.

Throughout this intermediate stage—and we will continue to gloss over eras and vast changes to present but one elementary aspect—Christianity spread over the West and created a community out of what had been barbarian splinters. It did this through the power of a concrete institution, the Catholic Church. It was the Church's imme-

diate influence that held aloft the subliminatory ideal of
Christ and, through that ideal, gave Europeans a scaffold
of identification with which to bind themselves into a
unified civilization.

Men, however, remained men, torn and driven by their
obscure passions into strivings for greed and domination
which culture could scarce regulate. Intense aggression
resisted the Church's unification, continued to plague
European culture, and delayed its growth. Within the
original Christian world-view, there was no way to rationalize or include the strivings for greed and domination
that persisted within civilization. After all, the Christian
revolution was superimposed upon a basically dominative
way of life. It could only account for the guilt that arose
from the dominative style of society by turning away from
the given world. This introduced a split into the cultural
universe—one which left unchanged the very real and
persistent dominative urges in humanity. Christian culture
could only curse from a distance; and with time, the distance became greater, the urges of domination and greed
went undiminished, and the West became faced with an
increasing gap between its superego ideal and its ego
practice. As long as ideals remained without—in the institution of the Church—they could not penetrate sufficiently
into personal styles of action. This failure corrupted the
Churchmen themselves, who, as their institution exerted a
greater moral force in the life of culture, saw fit to avail
themselves of the opportunities for temporal gain granted
by spiritual power. The further they indulged themselves,
however, the weaker they became as objects of identification, and the weaker became the normative power of the
Church to bind up the guilt of its culture. And as this
moral power declined, anxiety mounted and led to a further desperate leaning upon the Church for guidance, a

further increase in the temporal power of the Church, a further corruption of Churchmen and, in short, a furtherance of what was clearly a vicious cycle that could be broken only by radical intervention.

People were capable of experiencing much more intense feeling then, and everything in the world held a vivid value for them. Value inhered in each concrete thing; the universe was seen to be alive; abstract concepts were themselves alive. To live in this world was both intense delight and torture, for even that which was hated had value. It was this intensity of experience which gave such an agonized quality to life in the late Middle Ages. "To their epoch," Huizinga writes,[41] "cupidity becomes the predominant sin. Riches have not acquired the spectral impalpability which capitalism, founded on credit, will give them later; what haunts the imagination is still the tangible yellow gold. The enjoyment of riches is direct and primitive: it is not yet weakened by the mechanism of an automatic and invisible accumulation by investment; the satisfaction of being rich is found either in luxury and dissipation, or in gross avarice. . . . [The] primitive pride [which also preoccupied the medieval mind] has now united itself with the growing sin of cupidity, and it is this mixture of the two which gives the expiring Middle Ages a tone of extravagant passion that never appears again."

The disappearance of this extravagant passion was a necessity: it had become intolerable. The more men cursed gain and cupidity, the more, obviously, did they desire it: the strength of a moral imperative is generally in direct proportion to the intensity of the wish it opposes. The medieval mind cursed cupidity and hated material pos-

[41] Johan Huizinga, *The Waning of the Middle Ages* (New York, Anchor Books, 1954), p. 28.

sessions. On the other hand, medieval man intensely desired the pleasure so forbidden. The logical incompatibility of their conflict is easily understood if we recall the symbolic root to bodily products, and the primitive infantile ambivalence toward the body and the separated world which is thereby revealed. Lucre was filthy; everybody knew it, and everybody wanted it anyhow, at least in its partially abstracted form, gold. What was needed, of course, was to abstract things further, to deaden their intensity, and thereby to rationalize gain.

As Lewis Mumford notes in *The Myth of the Machine*, models of rationalized work in the medieval world were provided by monasteries, especially by the Benedictines. Significantly enough, this rationalized activity occurred only in a desexualized atmosphere. Here, free from disturbing passions, Western productivity took hold. It was a nucleus that could later be drawn into more far-reaching systems.

The new systems would, of course, have to encompass the full range of human passions, including sexuality— such is the synthetic task of culture. And this was the gift of Luther, Calvin and those other Protestant radicals who at last resolved the dilemmas of medieval Christendom by further abstracting men away from their world and by deadening the world that had been such a source of pain. But to anesthetize reality in this way required an immense inner fortification as well as an external devaluation. It required defiance, obstinacy and controlled passion; and it required a fantasy elaboration that could at last render the world sufficiently disgusting to make the turning away from it seem a relief, and to make the aggressive workings of men thereupon a moral imperative: it required, in brief, the analization of culture and the inception of the anal psychohistorical matrix.

Excrement had held an ambivalent fascination for men throughout their history. In agricultural societies, Mumford notes, feces used in manuring had a religious, life-giving quality. Their very sacredness was the token of ambivalence: what is sacred has magical power, but is also to be avoided, shunned, even considered disgusting. This intense ambivalence toward excrement is apparent in numerous myths and practices, and coalesced in medieval Europe, as Brown observed, into the myth of the Devil. It was the excremental Devil whom Luther invested with all the corporeal evil of the world; and it was from this symbolic turning point that anality spread, by repression, sublimation and abstraction, onto the entire cultural world. "A new stage in the history of the money complex begins in modern times, with the Reformation and the rise of capitalism. On the one hand definitive sublimation is attained at last by a final repression of the awareness of the anal-erotic sources of the complex: up till then the pursuit of money appears to have been inhibited by the knowledge that Lucre is filthy. And on the other hand there is a turn against the sublimation, . . . a desexualization of the sublimation itself."[42]

From this point on in culture, only the id retains its fantasy interest in excrement. The superego becomes pure—Puritan—and holds, through its repression of anality, the reins of culture in its hands. The ego, forced into its pure mold, makes reality into bits of isolated, undifferentiated, empty, dead, non-living matter—shit to the id, but workable substance all the same. "Accordingly," writes Whitehead, "the Cartesian scientific doctrine of bits of matter, bare of intrinsic value, was merely a formulation, in explicit terms, of a doctrine which was current before its

---

[42] Brown, *Life Against Death*, pp. 302f.

entrance into scientific thought or Cartesian philosophy. Probably this doctrine was latent in the scholastic philosophy, but it did not lead to its consequences till it met with the mentality of Northern Europe in the sixteenth century."[43] This "gave stability and intellectual status to a point of view which has had very mixed effects upon the moral presuppositions of modern communities. Its good effects arose from its efficiency as a method for scientific researches within those limited regions which were then best suited for exploration. The result was a general clearing of the European mind away from the stains left upon it by the hysteria of remote barbaric ages."

The beneficial effects of the modern transformation culminated in the Enlightenment, and in those humanitarian ideals of freedom which still stir us. But the ideals are tragically yoked in the cultural unconscious to the destructive effects of our matrix, which in turn live on through their generation of material power.

Indeed, each sublimation of Eros, each binding of the modern community with high ideals, has brought what Freud described in *The Ego and the Id* as a coordinated freeing up of aggression. This aggression is turned inward, filtered by the abstracting qualities of the ego and superego, and turned outward onto the fecalized world to further deaden it. A materialized world without intrinsic value is acted upon by a self freed from that world by an inward turning. Superego at last moves inward to rationalize gain and production decisively, and so becomes the lord of history.

The new class whose rationalized activity so transformed the globe was given its definitive description by Max Weber in his *Protestant Ethic and the Spirit of Capi-*

---

[43] Whitehead, *Science and the Modern World*, p. 195.

talism. This work has been widely misinterpreted by those who have assumed, as Weber carefully denied, that he was proposing a one-to-one causal relationship between these two broad cultural movements. He was actually looking for an example of the organicity of culture—how, in this case, the "spirit," that is, the psychology, of capitalist activity, was decisively influenced by the new style of religious activity devised by Calvin, and by Luther before him. Religion has been, up to recent times, the source of our cultural world-view. A world-view must be presented as a set of normative controls, which must in turn be equilibrated with the superego structures of the individuals within culture. Thus the decisive change in the development of the capitalist spirit was the granting by Protestantism of a stern inner conscience to direct productive activity rationally.

The early capitalist conscience was a harsh structure. As Weber points out, the system of justification through works that the Calvinist brought back from Luther's insistence upon pure faith, and which he made into the knife-edge of his whole approach to the world, was undertaken not so much to purchase salvation as to escape damnation. The remoteness of the condemning God reflects the distance driven by superego between ego, id and world. God is still the angry patriarch who had dominated Judeo-Christian culture since antiquity, the mass-projection of the oedipal father, but He is distant now, and history makes Him more so. Modern bourgeois man, who began his development propped up by Protestant faith, succeeds in pushing God aside even as he worships Him. Pushing the father symbol to the periphery of culture continued the original Christian solution by granting to the sons both the anxiety and the freedom to construct the modern order. And the modern order in turn fills the void left by its own creation with material precipitates of deadened yet potent body symbols: machines and possessions. Capitalism thereby frees itself from religion and becomes autonomous. And material goods, Weber states, first gained according to a religious asceticism which sacrificed enjoyment of wealth to its accumulation, now have "an inexorable power over the lives of men as at no previous period in history." The care for material goods has become, in Weber's words, an "iron cage." The decades that have passed since he penned these words have done nothing to diminish their truth.

The remote, internalized and abstract style of life within the new order favors sublimation of the basic process of domination. Efficiency makes this possible. What had been direct, and accomplished by at least the vivid threat of physical force, becomes indirect, and capable of mediation by reward rather than threat. This is accomplished through each man's internalization of the norms of his culture, i.e., by the rise of the individual superego as the coherent directing agent of the self within culture. Accordingly, the living realities of domination can be repressed and substituted for by the abstract commodities generated by the productive power of bourgeois civilization. To quote Herbert Marcuse,

We have seen that Freud's theory is focused on the recurrent cycle "domination-rebellion-domination." But the second domination is not simply a repetition of the first one; the cyclical movement is *progress* in domination. From the primal father via the brother clan to the system of institutional authority characteristic of mature civilization, domination becomes increasingly impersonal, objective, universal, and also increasingly rational, effective, productive. At the end, under the rules of the fully developed performance principle, [Marcuse's term for the specific form of Freud's reality principle in our civilization] subordination appears as implemented through the social division of labor itself (although physical and personal force remains an indispensable instrumentality). Society emerges as a lasting and expanding system of useful performances; the hierarchy of functions and relations assumes the form of objective reason: law and order are identical with the life of society itself. In the same process, repression too is depersonalized: constraint and regimentation of pleasure now become a function (and "natural" result) of the social division of labor.[44]

Superficially, nothing seems "wrong" with this progression. People are treated more fairly and less brutally, material rewards are greater, and overall productivity is vastly increased. But that there is something wrong with such "progress" can be inferred directly from the chaos and destruction left in its wake; and the something that is wrong will emerge from deeper examination, if we bear in mind that the schema of indirect control so brilliantly perfected by modern civilization is organically continuous with its historical roots, which are symbolically portrayed in our matrix. Indeed, the entire process of rationalization and abstraction can be seen, if a broad enough vantage is found, as only a partial stability within a larger, uncontrolled system. The surface has been frozen to hide what goes on underneath; and the surface has served as a lid, increasing the pressure of what it hides, and thereby furthering the need to keep what is hidden out of sight. Despite all defense, the splits introduced into the matrix of culture and ego, like the often invisible flaws in mountain snows, have loosed an avalanche.

The same symbolic matrix informs both the most sublime and the most base aspects of our civilization, and ties them together even as their inner contradictions drive them apart. Justice, freedom, rationality, the repertoire of morality itself, have been in part historically grounded in the symbolic flight away from the anal-sadistic view of

[44] Herbert Marcuse, *Eros and Civilization* (New York, Vintage Books, 1962), p. 81.

reality. No reductionism is intended here, nor any facile relativism. The ideals of civilized life can be derived independently of sexual and aggressive influence; their content depends upon the perception of an order in the universe beyond any simple attempt at delimitation. But no aspect of human life exists independently of any other; and the ideals of freedom, justice and ethics, whatever their independent substantive origin, become, in the course of human development, modified by the ego according to its synthetic need to mutually regulate all the strivings of the organism. When these strivings are grossly incompatible, the ego may be forced to intensify some of its ideals, falsify others, and to react so that what is denied to the body becomes subtly affirmed through its spiritual negation. Distortion of this kind may be observed in the individual by psychoanalysis, and in the cultural accumulation of individual egos by psychohistorical study. In the modern West, such study reveals the symbolic roots which the ego has found between our lofty notions and certain derivatives of anal sadism, to be presented in the fantasy which seeks both to include and save the world and to extrude and destroy it. This impossible wish is realized in the mystique of production, by which the world is reduced to abstract form and then worked over aggressively. What we allow ourselves to see of the product is considered "saved," created by order out of chaos, manufactured, and worthy of inclusion. But our products are also things that have been killed. The contradiction appears everywhere in our modern life, and is diffused endlessly through culture.

Bemused by Muzak, we shop in the supermarket for the hygienically wrapped and carefully labeled piece of meat. The circumstances of this act ensure that we can avoid seeing that the meat came from a scientifically raised animal whose slaughter, despite its rationality, is still a slaughter. Nor will we allow ourselves to make the mental connection between the clear plastic wrapping of the meat (that reinforces the defense against realizing the killing, for something so cleanly wrapped cannot have been bloodily slaughtered) and the processes necessary for the manufacture of this plastic: the oil wells, say, in the midst of the human city of Long Beach, California; the petrochemical plant outside the city, whose orange smoke creeps over the skies and into human eyes and lungs; the trucks carrying the produce, whose diesel exhaust and horrid roar equally assault the human body; and the roads over which the produce is efficiently carried, knifing through the human city and perpetually turning it into a stone monster whose awesome power cleaves the human selves within. We do not see that all this—and the infinitude of linked processes within advanced industrial civilization—form an organic, symbolic whole, within which all our impossible wishes are expressed alongside of, or rather, as a part of, our rational needs. Isolation, abstraction, splitting—"segregation"—makes possible the representation of what would be intolerable as a whole. We live in isolated fragments of this whole: cooling off in the air-conditioned supermarket, free from awareness of what goes into the preparation of its foodstuffs; perhaps reveling spiritually in apparently isolated aspects, such as the efficient order of it all; perhaps identifying with and reveling materially in the profits of the giant corporations which make and move the foodstuffs; basking in the afterglow of the canned television show sponsored by some of the same corporations; perhaps doubly relieved to enter the rationalized supermarket because we had to drive to it through the smog, along the superhighways, and between the trucks that contribute organically to the foodstuffs so enjoyed.

We live in isolated fragments of this monstrosity because we experience ourselves as fragmented, isolated both within ourselves and from one another. The splits are kept in motion by a twofold gain: power and defense. The more we fragment ourselves and the world, ignore the whole situation, and deal instead with deadened, abstracted individual aspects, the more we will be able to buy in the supermarkets, the more of that mysterious stuff, money, we will be able to derive from the supermarket that is our whole culture; and the more split up we become, the less we will have to see what is done in the name of our productive acquisition, the destruction which is presented to the modern self, in morally neutral, avoidable form, as "objective necessity." Rationalized destruction has no end; for each resultant gain in power presents itself as a threat to our values of justice and love, and each such threat is handled by further abstract splitting, by further removing ourselves into the supermarkets and away from the pulverized world of production, and, by that very removal, further pulverizing that world—i.e., generating more material power upon its lifeless body, and so renewing the cycle. Nor is the cycle of a single intensity; it is always accelerating. It is as if the splitting releases a kind of energy of fission; or, rather, as though the same degree of energy becomes multiplied through its efficient deployment onto more abstract, hence less resistant, forms of reality. Whatever the model, there has been a "fantastic" acceleration in the generation of material power, and an equally accelerated need for defense. The more moralized the culture, and the more refined the people within it, the less able they are to bear the burden of guilt that accrues from culture's aggression; the further, then, must they remove themselves from actuality, and the freer and more autonomous become the processes of production. With this delusion of objectivity, men can stimulate themselves into infinite reaches of narcissism.

Yet each man retains his id, grounded in biology and with its own cultural forms of realization. The abstraction and splitting of the world is an attempt to attenuate the connection of ego with id. But they fail to break the synthetic web of symbols which extends across the barrier of repression: the id lives on, timeless, unconscious, an indestructible piece of biology. At the same time, each progressively remote and refined process proves its validity in the struggle for existence by the power it affords over nature and man. And so the dialectical struggle is replayed according to the same terms: more potent cultural abstractions are invented to be marshalled against recurring anxiety, against the threat from within of id, trumpeting that this whole panoply of nature and society is but inert matter to be worked over destructively, foulness to be refined: shit. And this shit that we so abhor is but the concretized part of our body-ego, bearing in its harmless, dark, odorous, undifferentiated substance the accumulated rage at separation from our maternal matrix. Maternal, matrix, matter—the same etymological root, the same symbolic root: a dimly receding, ambivalently held ground of being, pushed away by historical progress.

This is not a tirade against rational science or rational ethics. On the contrary: it is a specific attempt to see how our highest achievements have been usurped by dominative and acquisitive needs, and falsified to these ends, so that one watches in horrified frustration as the ideals of the West are progressively swallowed by its machines and used by them to blind men to the operations of history. The contentions that the material world is horrible, or that it is not to be enjoyed, or that possessions are *per se* tainted, are not true; but our history has been propelled destructively by the operations of fantasies that proclaim them to be so. If people would in fact enjoy and be contented with the bounty they have been able to create by the application of reason and science to nature, the matrix would be negated, and history quite literally brought to a standstill.

This is really not conceivable, considering the present terms of our culture, a present that automatically extends itself into the future. Rather, we see an ever-accelerating system of striving and craving, which fills itself up with material pleasures that evaporate inside the abstracted self. Instead of enjoyment, we get the illusion of enjoyment, served up by an incredibly remote system of manipulations in the coherent interests of both rationalizing production and stimulating demand. No, the reason and science which have been generated by the positive side of our history—and, despite their ambiguities, we need them badly to master our situation—are in continual process of being swallowed up into the endless mystique of destructive production.

Other important aspects of the situation of advanced industrial civilization follow directly from the operations of the symbolic matrix. Abstraction and splitting gain power without awareness, and so serve the needs of repression. But they also diminish the self, and progressively cut it off externally from what is done to the world. The result is an inner void, which is filled synthetically, just as the machines fill in the gaps in the natural landscape torn up in the name of production. And what is added synthetically may be pleasurable and enjoyed free from guilt. But, just as the machine grows in cultural status through its power to fill nature with dead things, so is the self diminished by being filled with abstractions. The qualities of such a self are drabness, puppet-like acquiescence, a bland friendliness that barely conceals an inner coldness, an inability to spontaneously affirm or feel a genuine community with others—all representing the strangulated voice of inner hopelessness, clinging to what it is told out of fear of its own emptiness, and filling itself compulsively with the manipulated tokens of dead, manufactured things. The synthetic pleasure so attained is little more than comfort embellished with titillations and an occasional thrill. It is not that sensations are no longer strong, but that the modern self can no longer vividly experience what is sensed. As a consequence, sensations—manipulated along with everything else—have to be made increasingly violent to arouse the dulled perceptions of the abstracted self. And this too leads only to further craving. Even as the material "goods" with which we so sate ourselves grow in incredible profusion, the elementary striving that is mobilized to seek them becomes less differentiated. It is as if the further culture proceeds, the more primitive become the fantasies with which it must tie together the selves of the men who live within it. The modern age was ushered in with the analization of the world. This was necessary, though not sufficient, as we have seen, for the creation of bourgeois-capitalist culture. But capitalism becomes ever more autonomous with time. Just as it rejected the Protestant Church after having fed sufficiently upon it, so it is now, in a further stage of maturity, shaking itself free of some of its dependence upon anal fantasies and admixing them with oral ones. This is because of what Galbraith described, in his *New Industrial State*, as the paramount need to stimulate demand in the interests of rationalizing productivity. Accordingly, pleasure in intake must be emphasized and the more disgusting aspects of the world further repressed. The Calvinists, those capitalists of an early, harsh form, conceived the basic idea of gain without pleasure. While remaining the mainspring of capitalist culture, this fantasy does not suffice to match its inner needs for expansion. Stimulation of demand is also necessary; and so gaining without pleasure must be layered over with still another illusion: that of needing, craving and being obligated to take in what is wanted. This new illusion involves the energetic elaboration of a fantasy from an even earlier level of experience than the anal. Any logical incompatibilities between fantasies can be abstracted out and repressed by the techniques of modern manipulation. Once repressed, desire belongs to the unconscious mind, which knows nothing of logic. The result is an endless striving to take in material goods. A side-product is the appearance, in clinical psychiatric practice, of an increasing number of addictions, and, in culture at large, of the extraordinary craving for drugs in the interests of obliterating pain, achieving pleasure, and simply losing the sense of self.

The self has become especially burdensome under the modern conditions of our culture. On the other hand, machines, those external projections of our bodily desires, continue to grow in fascination for and power over the atomized men who gave them being. It is herein that the matrix retains its full force. Extracted away from men, it comes to rest more and more upon machines, which take on a life of their own in fulfilling the bodily desires that have become lost to us in direct form.

This phenomenon is of the largest significance. What we have thought to be an increase in our individual power and freedom granted by modern progress, is in reality a much more ambiguous and complex process. To a large extent, people have been freed by handing over to culture their autonomy, for which they are repaid with material bounty and the freedom from manual toil. These are substantial boons, but for the mass of men, they are obtained at enormous cost. For, along with the diminution of self-autonomy, occurs the complementary growth of culture and its magical machines. As the self becomes de-differentiated, society takes over the process of history, becoming both more articulated and more controlled. It may be that the decline of individual personality will usher in a new stage in human evolution, based upon the recurrence of the imperial forms of Egyptian and Chinese antiquity, but removed from them by another order of mechanization, in which society will become the dominant organism, and people so many cells within its body. We are talking, of course, of that unique modern phenomenon, totalitarianism, which we have already seen in this century in particularly horrid, and perhaps premature, forms, but which seems to be given existence simply by the natural unfolding of the logos of Western civilization.

The modern State, a new form of social organization much better adapted to mature industrial capitalism than the Protestant Church was to primitive Puritan capitalism, is the heir to the process of abstraction and splitting. And the genius of this State is to ensure its power, not through direct domination, for this risks rebellion and the kind of disorder incompatible with mature, rationalized productivity, but through indirect, lateral domination—through an intrusion into personality. "Total domination," writes Hannah Arendt in *The Origins of Totalitarianism*, "which strives to organize the infinite plurality and differentiation of human beings as if all of humanity were just one individual, is possible only if each and every person can be reduced to a never changing identity of reactions, so that each of these bundles of reactions can be exchanged at random for any other." The means of this domination are the rationalized, "objectively necessary" forms of bureaucratic administrative control, which we all accept because a), no one person seems to dominate us directly; b), the control seems fair and is apparently in everybody's interest; and c), the control ensures an increase of the material productivity we all value so intensely, for the reasons we have discussed. Nonetheless, the bureaucratic control ensures the overall workings of culture—and does so with exquisite success, by obliterating our awareness through its remote and abstract transactions. To paraphrase Herbert Marcuse, administration is the pure form of domination.

How can we conceptualize this intrusion, this reduction of humanity and augmentation of the State? The means are at hand in our psychohistorical notion of control, which, because of a very real connection with the individual superego, is termed the cultural superego. The idea was Freud's, who, in *Civilization and Its Discontents,* asserted "that the community too evolves a super-ego under whose influence cultural development proceeds . . . [it] has an origin similar to that of an individual." Indeed, the two systems are "always interlocked." The conscious precipitate of the individual superego is conscience, and of the cultural superego, morality; but both systems extend much further and deeper, to include all the mental representations of control and direction. And it is through the symbolic harmonization of the individual with the cultural superego that the individual becomes adapted into society and at the same time enacts culturally a measure of the impossible contradictions left by the oedipus complex. In the individual, the superego turns inward the aggression that had been directed at his parents, and which is freed up by the weakening of Eros that occurs with the renunciation and sublimation of incestuous desires. Then, through adaptation to culture, the harsh aggression which had threatened the ego from within is redirected outward to approved social pursuits, according to the dictates of the cultural superego. As society perfects itself, and further sublimates erotic interests to form its structure, the amount of exteriorized aggression grows.

With the plasticity of human drive, cultural aggression can assume numerous forms, some of which we shall discuss shortly as they appear specifically in racism. But one of these forms, perhaps the most decisive for the internal ordering of society, is to be found in the cultural superego. This particular kind of development is coordinated with the growth of indirect domination, and both have proceeded in parallel during the course of modern Western history. The formation of the intense Protestant conscience did not long remain unaffected by the forces of history. The guilt and joylessness of this conscience were too much to bear, and became ever more intolerable as society grew in material power, and, correspondingly, increased guilt. Abstractive splitting became the defense against the force of this conscience, just as it had contributed to its formation. By giving culture the control, individuals were freed from guilt. Equally decisive, because what transpires psychohistorically must at once generate power and provide psychic defense, the passage of control to culture at large allowed—through those transformations we have mentioned—the development of enormously increased material power.

Thus in modern times culture grows both in material power and superego control. The balance of forces gradually shifts to the cultural superego which, aided by technology, gradually obliterates individual personality in its effort to weld mankind into a gigantic machine. Its commands are as reasonable as the continued generation of material power allows; and, as the overall rationalization of culture and the identification of people with its aims proceeds, material power becomes increasingly secure. Hence the modern cultural superego operates free from that harsh self-punitive intensity seen at the height of the Christian era. Substituted for this sense of unbearable guilt is a pervasive, rigorous system of controls, whose perfection awaits only the final ascendance of computer technology—at which time we shall all have numbers, or, rather, *be* numbers, just as our money shall all soon be numbers. The spiritual body and the excremental body shall meet again on the pure plane of quantity. This poses certain crucial questions on moral behavior which, as we shall discuss, play very directly into the current struggle against racism. But it also poses an even larger question.

What of the aggression now at the disposal of the State, amplified by machines, controlled by well-socialized technocrats? And what of the further consequence of abstractive splitting: that symbols are progressively removed from their referent, retaining only one link, an all-important one in an unconscious mind that seems impossibly removed from the rationalized operations of society? The combination of these two factors is devastating. For the abstracting processes of modern industrial civilization have made the real consequences of our actions too remote to be conceivable, while its technological power has made them too destructive to be allowed the kind of free rein they now enjoy. With the dedifferentiation of matter and personality, symbol and referent have diffused so widely through our symbolic matrix that the possibility of a healing confrontation seems absurd. But nothing is more absurd than death; and is it not so that the increasing and seemingly mindless aggressiveness of our nation-state in recent years falls into just that pattern, that it reveals an extroversion of aggression abstracted from individual sources, removed from awareness, and turned outward to appropriate enemies? When the Marine officer described the American obliteration of a city in Vietnam by explaining that "we had to destroy the city in order to save it," was he not expressing in the succinct form given by such an extreme situation, the pure, nuclear fantasy underlying Western history—to save and destroy, include and extrude? And what of the prime means of our warfare: bombing? Is this not also the external, societally mobilized, endlessly rationalized enactment of an immemorial infantile, anal-sadistic fantasy: the efficient, rational, distant (no pilot sees his victim) operation of a machine—a machine as articulated as the principle of its usage is undifferentiated, and used to pulverize, really deaden, hostile matter? The relationships seem endless if one thinks a little symbolically. What do the bombs themselves represent? What do pollutants represent as well—that endless stream of garbage shat onto the earth by our rationalized yet uncontrolled civilization?

Indeed, splitting, fragmentation, isolation, remoteness —all the paradigms of modern society are furthered by the vicious cycle of their own aggressive potential. What we are witnessing now may be the pushing of this process past the synthetic capacity of the human ego, for people can only go so far in the loss of their autonomy before anxiety sets in. And the anxiety is with us, expressed, as would be expected, in external, remote, disguised forms, but ready to be recombined into new historical ventures. The symbols of our anxiety are the same as those of the underlying fantasies, now promulgated with a frenzy which reveals the panic latent in them. There is substantial feeling today that events are out of control, that the very abstractive and rationalized means of control we have historically chosen are no longer of use. The disquiet is revealed in various ways—for example, in the increasing preoccupation with "law and order," which may be the harbinger of a new fascism. Indeed, fascism is but a regressive return, within the conditions of modern civilization, to direct domination, a return forced by the anxiety produced by the failure of the psychohistorical matrix to contain the energy of humanity. The solution has an ominous appeal, in its return to the certitude of the acceptance of the authoritarian father whose simple force negates the ever-present potential for disorder. And from another potent corner of our culture, the media and advertising agencies who now hold the main force of the cultural superego, comes a redoubling of effort, a perhaps agonal attempt to muster forth all of the purification they sponsor. One sees this, in the clarity reserved only for myths and rituals of great symbolic importance, in the great outpouring of advertisements which seek to counter those anal fantasies which, it might be thought, people have at long last repressed. Yet our communications media are saturated with reminders of a new "washday miracle," a new deodorant that will at last ensure perfect acceptance, a new whitener, a new brightener—all proposed to a manifestly anxious housewife in the grip of some unseen filth. The cleaner she gets, the more she needs to clean. It is the societal counterpart of an obsessive-compulsive handwashing neurosis, and, like the endlessly repeated neurotic ritual of cleaning, it betokens the awareness of the breakthrough of a repressed aggressive wish, the wish to soil and destroy in an orgy of anal sadism. The combination of these factors reached perfection of form in the appearance recently of an ad in which the clean, anxious housewife was, with her fixed smile, assaulting an unknown bug with a new insecticide (an Aerosol, to be applied finely, at a distance) entitled "Clean and Kill."

Clean and Kill at home, search and destroy in Vietnam, the aggressive purification extends endlessly outward, the inner control attenuates, its fascist regression all too close —such is the grim picture of contemporary American life. Only a fool would predict with any certitude the outcome of the present shifting and confused balance of forces. One thing alone is certain: the current state of our culture is inadequate to meet the full human needs of its people. The younger generation has voiced this in a resounding vote of no confidence, but their own direction is uncertain.

Although we cannot predict the future, we can see what is pressing from the past: a coiling spring behind a veil of repression, a gathering cloud of unresolved debts, vapors in the rarefied air of Western abstraction, ready to condense themselves into storms, blowing culture ahead lest that condensation occur. We have seen such storms in this century, and uneasily fear a recurrence we would desperately wish to avoid. We have seen Germany, the most culturally advanced nation in the West, and the most inwardly split, resolve itself under the pressures of history into a regression that still blanches us in horror. We should know by now that Nazism was not a particular problem of the German people, but the general problem of men under the conditions of a civilization such as the modern West. Germany degenerated because of historical contingency, and, fundamentally, because she had gone furthest in progress and splitting, had pushed herself to that extremity beyond which is the abyss. Now other contingencies arise; and other peoples, further yet to the West, move themselves to an extreme.

It is as if a plague were afoot in Western culture. The metaphor derives from the title of Albert Camus' work, which presented the disorder vividly and concretely as the visitation of the plague bacillus, Pasteurella pestis, the immemorial bane of civilized life, upon the city of Oran. The most evident allegorical meaning of the plague is that it represents the invasion of Europe by Nazi Germany. So much was deadly clear, especially in the Bosch-like visions of the crematoria *cum* concentration camps. But the full point is revealed precisely in the allegoric transformation:

for the plague, Camus repeats over and over, is nothing less than a protean symbol for all the related afflictions of modern civilized life. Oran itself, "a dry place," is the paradigm of bourgeois banality, a city dominated by commerce, the regularization of pleasures, and the ugliness that ensues from such destructive sublimations. ". . . The real plague," Camus' Rieux concludes at one point was "a skilled organizer, doing his work thoroughly and well." These political structures are echoed psychologically by whatever it is that separates a person from his beloved, by whatever attenuates the forces of Eros, makes a man remote, unspontaneous, unaffirmative, helpless in his inner self—by the cold hand of abstraction upon the living soul. Tarrou, the personification of this attitude, *needs* the plague to keep him going, needs it as a projection of his inner death force, needs it so much that he dies when it wanes. All of the deaths in the book occur to people who experience this despair that is the very plague itself in attenuated form and that passes directly into its bacillary phase. The attenuation and abstraction of civilized life creates the grounds for this despair, and, from it, the need for the existential act, a form of grace to rival Luther's, a spontaneous, inner spark which arcs across the symbolic gap to fight plague through the affirmation of unity with others in the common struggle. As Rieux observes, "when abstraction sets to killing you, you've got to get busy with it."[45]

The spark is a form of light, and so of life. But light symbolizes more than life. The plague has a light too, a light akin to the smouldering of industrial fires or the smouldering of corpses in its crematoria: the baleful light of false knowledge, the light generated by men in the course of their separation from life and their coordinate

[45] Albert Camus, *The Plague* (New York, Random House, 1948), p. 81.

fear of death, as told in the plague-myth Camus draws from Lucretius: "the plague-fires . . . which the Athenians kindled on the seashore. The dead were brought there after nightfall, but there was not room enough, and the living fought one another with torches for a space where to lay those who had been dear to them; for they had rather engage in bloody conflicts than abandon their dead to the waves." This en-lightened fight amongst men is as much the plague as the bacillary disease; its torches, whether they be napalm bombs, the burning of libraries, the ignition of industrial pollutants, all represent the corrupted Promethean act of defiance, the destruction wrought by humanity as it separates from its being and brings upon itself the plague. Only Rieux prevails, and even he at the price of loss. Behind him stands his mother, patient representative of the source of being, who, "dim and silent though she was, . . . quailed before no light, even the garish light of the plague." Falling away from this radiant center, the men of the book, as the men of history, succumb to greater and greater variants of the plague.

As they do so they come upon darkness, the antithesis of light, and equally ambivalent. For, just as light can represent both the burning of matter and the soft maternal glow, so does darkness represent both the condition of death, or separation, and of sleep, or reunion. Light and dark are only gradations of energy in nature, neither good nor evil in themselves, except as they have become split apart and worked upon by the forces of the plague: then they can represent men's power, their illusions, their despair and their disgust. Here the specter of anality intrudes again upon the stage of history. People die, "in a stench of corruption." Plague dehumanizes both life and death and drives each to the equally false extremes of cold efficiency or fecal disgustingness. This latter aspect is symbolized by the rats, which are the concrete harbingers of the plague. Rats are, as Freud taught us, virtually universal symbols for feces. In Oran, as the plague announces its return to open form, the rats would be found "piled in little heaps" all over the city. . . . "People out at night would often feel underfoot the squelchy roundness of a still warm body. It was as if the earth on which our houses stood were being purged of its secreted humors; thrusting up to the surface the abscesses and pus-clots that had been forming in its entrails."[46]

Rats are in actuality but a form of life too, as worthy as any other. But they have been made, by their association with the sewers of the cities of men, into the representations of the products of the sewers of the bodies of men—their intestines and their fecal outpourings—and so into the symbolic carriers of our emotional plague, as well as the biological host of Pasteurella pestis. It is men who have made the sewers of their cities; and it is the presence of these city-bodies, and the guilt entailed in them, that gives symbolic, disgusting force to the fantasy of dirt and bodily filth. The historical nexus generates from itself dark fears of dark secondary symbols of filth: shit, rats, human "low-life," human "trash," "bums"—untouchables all, our running historical sores, the carriers of plague, or, rather, the projections of our own plague that we flee through abstraction or by the idolatry of washday miracles.

In America, in Oran, in Nazi Germany—the plague has long been with the West, since, in fact, medieval times, when both Pasteurella pestis and universal disgust took hold of our civilization. As sewage has been kept underground and sent out to sea to forestall the biological plague, so has the historical plague been put underground, forced out to sea and onto foreign shores. Most en-plagued

[46] *Ibid.*, p. 15.

of these has been Africa, the Dark Continent itself, cloaca of the West. The darkness of Africa is symbolic too, and historical as well, the symbol itself being generated by historical activity.

Joseph Conrad saw this in *Heart of Darkness*. Kurtz is the pivot of the book, and the voyage to him and back becomes the progressive unfolding of what he is, what Europe is—"All Europe contributed to the making of Kurtz," notes Marlowe—and what Africa is insofar as it has been acted upon by the Kurtzes of the West. It is an unfolding nightmare, culminating in Kurtz' own awareness at the moment of his death of what he had been about, and expressed by his last words: "The horror! The horror!" The voyage into Africa and into the spirit of Kurtz is the Dantean quest into the imperial version of hell, set physically in the dense and overwhelming jungles of Africa, but basically in the jungles of the Western mind. For, even at its most feral, it is the recurrent vision of the West projected onto the wilderness that strikes terror into the voyagers: "We could have fancied ourselves the first of men taking possession of an accursed inheritance, to be subdued at the cost of profound anguish and of excessive toil."

And subdued it had been—at least that illusion had been attained—by the ferocious activity of those restless offshoots the West sent outward to do its will. These offshoots expressed all the layers of the Western personality and our symbolic matrix. Some, representing, as it were, the id, were nothing but "sordid buccaneers: . . . reckless without hardihood, greedy without audacity, and cruel without courage; there was not an atom of foresight or of serious intention in the whole batch of them, and they did not seem aware these things are wanted for the work of the world. To tear treasure out of the bowels of the land was their desire, with no more moral purpose at the back

of it than there is in burglars breaking into a safe."[47]
There were others, representing the ego, to do the work
of the world, to organize wealth into systematic pursuits.
These, such as the accountant Marlowe meets at the out-
set of his journey, were greatly fortified by purification:
"in the great demoralization of the land he kept up his appearance. That's backbone. His starched collars and got-
up shirt-fronts were achievements of character.... this
man had verily accomplished something. And he was devoted to his books, which were in apple-pie order." Account books provide the energetic nucleus of rationalization, but also the ability to deny guilt, to retranslate it
into anger. The accountant, for example, looks at a sick
native (one of great numbers lying marasmically about
the station, in fact one of the millions dying in despair
in the Congo at this time) and says to Marlowe, " 'He does
not hear.' 'What! Dead?' I asked, startled. 'No, not yet,' he
answered, with great composure. Then, alluding with a
toss of the head to the tumult in the station-yard, 'When
one has got to make correct entries, one comes to hate
those savages—hate them to the death.' He remained
thoughtful for a moment. 'When you see Mr. Kurtz', he
went on, 'tell him from me that everything here ... is
very satisfactory.' "[48]

And Kurtz is the reference point, the man whose noble
words and infinite capacities will, it is held, get him very
far, the man who justifies all with the ideals of a culture. If rapacity is id, and efficiency ego, then Kurtz is
superego—all these tied together with the vaulting qualities of belief and guidance, the highest stage of the personality, the highest phase of the culture, godlike. Indeed,
Kurtz has become a deity to the benighted natives under

[47] Joseph Conrad, *Heart of Darkness* and *The Secret Sharer* (Signet
Classic ed.; New York, The New American Library, 1950), p. 98.
[48] *Ibid.*, p. 84.

his jurisdiction. And to the Europeans who rule the heart of darkness, he is nothing less: " 'The chief of the inner station. . . . He is a prodigy. . . . He is an emissary of pity and science and progress, and devil knows what else. We want . . . for the guidance of the cause intrusted to us by Europe, so to speak, higher intelligence, wide sympathies, a singleness of purpose . . . and so *he* comes here, a special being, as you ought to know. . . . You are of the new gang, the gang of virtue."[49]

But Kurtz overreaches himself; or, rather, the quest upon which he is sent forces him to extend himself beyond the bounds of ordinary controls, such as are given by the humble regularities of organized civilized life, forces him to extend himself into illimitable wildness. "The wilderness had found him out early, and had taken on him a terrible vengeance for the fantastic invasion. I think it had whispered to him things about himself which he did not know, things of which he had no conception till he took counsel with this great solitude—and the whisper had proved irresistibly fascinating. It echoed loudly within him because he was hollow at the core. . . ."[50] And being hollow, what does Western man desire but to fill himself up with abstract, dead negations of living substance? And so what does Kurtz, this avatar of the highest in the West, crave when he is thrown back upon himself in the darkness? What, indeed, but ivory: white, hard, smooth, odorless, dehydrated—in effect, white gold with the same fascination that the yellow, odorless, shining stuff has held for men. Perhaps even a greater fascination, because ivory is the dead part of living substance, a bodily excrescence, the extrusion of keratin, but completely and utterly denying by its purity its association with filth and darkness. "Evidently the appetite for more ivory had got the better

[49] *Ibid.*, p. 92.
[50] *Ibid.*, p. 133.

of the—what shall I say?—less material aspirations." Indeed the split proceeds in an endless, and continuously accelerating spiral, until Kurtz is seen with his mouth open, "as though he had wanted to swallow all the air, all the earth, all the men before him." There is no limit intrinsic to this passion. Thus an account of Kurtz, addressing a devotee who has a small cache of ivory: "Well, he wanted it, and wouldn't hear reason. He declared he would shoot me unless I gave him the ivory . . . because he could do so, and had a fancy for it, and there was nothing on earth to prevent him from killing whom he jolly well pleased." At the moment of his death, about to be freed from what had held him back from total fusion with the universe he sought to include, and at the point of uttering his final, horrific words, Kurtz is described as having an "ivory face." He has at length fulfilled the infantile dream of the denial of separation, and, rejoining with what he had wanted in its projected form, has become ivory itself.

But only to die . . . and to have killed in the wake of his return. Superego is built on id-negations and dissolves in the moment of regression. In the writing of a report for the "International Society for the Suppression of Savage Customs," Kurtz noted, in the high-flown style that had won him moral leadership, that the whites, by virtue of their virtue, had a spiritual burden, the white man's burden itself. " 'By the simple exercise of our will we can exert a power for good practically unbounded,' etc. etc. From that point he soared and took me with him. . . . This was the unbounded power of eloquence—of words—of burning noble words. There were no practical hints to interrupt the magic current of phrases, unless a kind of note at the foot of the last page, scrawled evidently much later, in an unsteady hand, may be regarded as the exposition of a method. It was very simple, and at the end of the moving appeal to every altruistic sentiment, it blazed at you, luminous and terrifying, like a flash of lightning in a serene sky: 'Exterminate all the brutes!' "[51]

And he and many others made a fair start, in the row of sacrificed native heads impaled in front of Kurtz' jungle temple, in the marasmic bodies lying dying about the ground of Western enterprise. Enterprise, moral fervor, efficiency, rapacity—all have been tied into one organic package, limited only by the inertness of the bodies, whether human or inanimate, upon which the West has laid its hand.

Millions of such black bodies lay strewn inertly about the floor of Africa; and other millions were consumed by the same process, and taken westward as Europe sought to project and perfect herself onto the dim expanses beyond.

New conceptions of blackness arose thereby, from which another chapter in psychohistory—the story of American racism—may be derived.

[51] *Ibid.*, p. 123.

CHAPTER 8
THE PSYCHO-HISTORY OF RACISM IN THE UNITED STATES

RACISM IS ULTIMATELY INDIVISIBLE from the rest of American life, a fact few of us wish to face. Most commentators who wish America to eliminate the blight of racism simply observe the discrepancy between what we espouse and how we act, and conclude: see, we are not living up to our ideals; let us do so, abjure racism, become true to ourselves, or else face the consequences, which have become painfully glaring by now. But they stop here, for to go on is even more painful than to continue participating in the presently disastrous state of race relations in America. To go on, in a manner truthful to ourselves and our history, would mean seeing and dealing with the full indivisibility of our situation. In short, it would mean confronting the fact that racism has not been a matter of ignorance or oversight, nor an inexplicable evil in human nature, opposed to our ideals and better feelings. We would have to confront the fact that both the racism and the ideals spring from a deep, common, unconscious unity; that, in fact, the height of our ideals has been historically nourished by the depths of our passions, including the passions of the fantasies of race, and that these live on in dialectical union with our ideals. In fact, the West would not have needed such high ideals if a part of it had not plunged so low in the pursuit of its desires. Of course a pseudoseparation is made, by repressing the connection between the various elements of the symbolic matrix that constitute our racial situation. Otherwise we could not go on.

Repression is what gives the quality of banality to great evils. Racism, as great an evil as has been wrought by men —perhaps the greatest, since it has been and is perpetrated by advanced men who claimed virtue and could have known better—is in itself the most ludicrous and absurd of beliefs: imagine making such a fuss over such an objectively meaningless datum as the color of a man's skin! Any extraterrestrial life endowed with the most elementary intelligence would stand appalled and baffled by the immense delusions woven by humans out of this gossamer thread. Yet we here on earth, conditioned by our relations on and with this earth, "know" differently—we *know* that this nonsensical dividing line between peoples, who, our ideals inform us, are all one beneath the skin, is of the utmost importance. We know that a great deal of the history of racism consists of the creation of pseudoscientific rationalizations to account for the inordinate importance ascribed to skin color. These can be dismissed with a wave of the hand; it is useful to know of them, to be sure, but only because they are indicators of what people required in the way of illusions at certain times in their history. But the real knowing that informs racial belief is of a different order than these fantastic tissues of rationalization: it is the knowing of what is unconscious across the barrier of repression, an uncanny, obscure knowledge that reveals a deeper, psychohistorical logic to the banalities of racism.

In essence racism has never been an internally coherent structure. Although it has a structure of its own, with a set of inner relationships, these hardly exist without reference to the broader stream of cultural activity. And so racism has lived as a kind of delusional parasite, an elaboration upon the mainstream of historical development. The set of racial fantasies, and the structure of their elaboration, have been created by the historical ego—not with the purpose of arriving at any real understanding of the racial situation itself, but only to tie together what had been presented to it by the onward rush of its historical activity. Certain elementary themes have persisted within racism, but only by virtue of the fact that basic historical activity has retained a coherent inner shape despite all the changes wrought by time, and, more immediately, that the oppressed peoples upon whom these fantasies were being discharged acquired complementary traits and kept reproducing themselves. Racism exists only because of the actual presence of oppressed races. And since racism has been, despite its necessity, burdensome to everyone who has tried to assimilate his conscience with his ideals, the prospect of actually ridding the nation of its objects has occurred at numerous points in our history. This has been the main impetus to the efforts actually to deport blacks that have occurred from time to time; it accounts in considerable measure as well for the psychology of segregation; and it provides the nucleus of truth, upon which paranoia always feeds, to the accusations by black extremists that the real goal of white America is black genocide. By the same token, racism ceases whenever a black has accumulated enough Caucasian genes to "pass" in the white world. America is full of people who pass for white, yet hide a trace of Negroid genealogy; and likewise, most black people in America had been obsessed, until the recent upsurge in their pride reversed the trend, with valuing the whiter aspects of themselves, hoping for lighter skin in their spouses or offspring and, in general, prizing that which they were not, and the lack of which oppressed them.

Anti-black racism has held a unique position in America. To be sure, racist thinking and belief has been applied in this country toward a whole host of non-Teutonic peoples. Even without blacks in our history we might still have been a significantly racist people. But it is to be greatly doubted whether we would have been *equally* racist. For the accidental blackness of black skin, and the special circumstances of black life in America, have combined here to bring about an extraordinary intensification of racism. It is likely, though not provable, that much else that is special in our national experience—for example our extreme materialism or our history of sexual prudery, even our peculiar idealism—has been intensified by anti-Negro racism. And, most likely, the other varieties of racism with which we have been afflicted have borrowed strength from the predispositions produced in white Americans by their relations with black Americans. Yet none of these other varieties cuts so deep into American experience as anti-Negro racism—none is so profound, so axiomatic, so destructive, or so deeply rooted in our history.

In the previous chapter we touched upon the one phenomenon which, when observed in American history, sheds the most light upon the way the matrix of our psychohistory became elaborated into its racist form. In our brief discussion of *Heart of Darkness*, we observed how the very limitlessness of Africa brought about a disintegration of Kurtz' moral ideals into the primitive impulses upon which they were built. Something of this sort happened in the history of America too, produced by the absence of institutional restraints. Institutions are the cultural analogues of the ego and the superego: when they exist, sublimated activity can take place; in their absence, a breakdown of sublimations may occur, with a freeing up of energy, both creative and destructive. To the West, Africa was the dark place, bereft of orderly institutions, a region in which the dark side of human nature could be played out. America too was a wilderness, and presented the same unbridled possibilities. But there was a distinction between America and Africa which gave the two great continents literally complementary roles: Africa was to be consumed, but America was to be settled and developed, and was destined to become the new home for Western civilization. Geography, historical newness, and many other factors all played a role in this crucial distinction, which led in time to the utter ruin of Africa and to the establishment in America of the most powerful nation the world has ever seen. Africa was to become the cesspool and cloaca of the West; America, its lofty vision and creation. Correspondingly, the deinstitutionalization of Africa allowed the West to discharge upon it whatever was forbidden and dark, while that of America led to the creation of a new, White, institutional order.

The stimulation of empty expanse accelerated the growth of whatever was latent in the logos of the Western symbolic matrix. A force, already under pressure, expanded into a moral vacuum and gained, as we know, great power. But the other terms of the matrix also had to be accentuated. Thus what is distinctly destructive about Western culture also achieved its most extreme realization here: a greater denial of the body, a greater reduction of matter to inert, dead substance, a greater reliance upon anal-negative character traits, a greater elaboration of the market economy—all these self-generating qualities received their most vigorous development on the new, vacuous land of America. Not only was the process of abstractive splitting most highly stimulated here, but the vastness of the land, the virtual limitlessness of the possibilities for

material growth, and America's isolation from European
power struggles all combined to keep abstractification unchecked. The immense landscape, stretching endlessly onward and drawing Americans to its receding horizons,
itself became symbolic nutrient. It became represented
inwardly as the idea of spaciousness, an expansiveness of
personal style; and an accompanying inner sense of blankness that was to fuse with the whiteness of the settler's
skin into the conception of a self both pure and unbounded, a self that had the right, the necessity and the
manifest destiny to dominate the continent and the darker
peoples upon it. A self grew in this symbolic soil that
could abstractively split apart its universe as readily as it
cleaved the unstructured land. The material success of the
matrix in America, and the coordinated facility Americans
showed in putting aside what they could not bear, both
contributed to the optimistic and easy-going image of our
national character. European nations, hemmed in by one
another, were forced to limit the audacity of their splitting up of the natural world, and were driven to make an
inner balance that was not required by the American experience. To be sure, even in its limited version, this splitting did not work very well for Europe either, and led to
desperate showdowns, first in imperial expansions, then in
global holocaust. Meanwhile, Americans lolled about in
idealistic self-congratulation. Our showdown, the sound-
ing of inner limitations, would have to await present times
—and with the showdown, our innocent optimism fades
into the anguish of those who, Kurtz-like, at long last
begin to become aware of what they have been doing.

One very real linchpin exists between the Western experience in Africa and in the New World: the black people who were taken from the former to work the latter.
We have observed that there was much in the history of
the West, and especially in the torments of its late medie-

val period, to make Western man regard blackness with awe, horror and loathing. The black death of the biological plague, the blackness of the devil that was the plague within the spirit, all had given Europeans ample advance reason to regard colored peoples, with irrational intensity, as appropriate subjects for less-than-human treatment. And a powerful material need for such inhuman treatment was not long forthcoming.

By the dawn of the modern era, as we have noted, Europeans already were characterized by an exceptional ambivalence toward material possessions, at once desiring wealth avidly and condemning its acquisition. Since they were still in a relatively concrete stage of mental organization, gold, the concrete shining negation of bodily filth, was desired above all. Along with it, however, Europeans also wanted the other concrete forms of wealth that could be taken from the land. The New World provided their opportunity for obtaining such riches, and the Pope smiled with distant benignity on their endeavor. It was easy to rationalize such a remote pursuit, when its living consequences upon the native peoples of Africa and the Americas could scarce be appreciated. Consequently, the Europeans set about their exploitation with a will; and, when it became apparent that the job was both too big and too forbidding, readily found the answer to their labor problems in the native peoples whose darkness and strangeness seemed the perfect correlate to all that the task required. So far, matters were cruel, crude and destructive; but they were not yet those which became specifically characteristic of the United States. The early European process was not racism, but a straightforward, if slightly rationalized, oppression. One might call it pre-racism, to imply that the elementary qualities of racism—aggression, greed, guilt, willingness to distinguish another on the basis of a simple quality like color, and so to oppress him—were present. What was needed in order for this early pattern to develop into the phase of dominative racism, was the unifying of all these separate elements into a comprehensive *Weltanschauung,* and their absorption into some kind of acknowledged productive system—in short, what was needed was the creation of an organic cultural structure out of these loose, pre-racist ends.

For racism is an *organization* of the world of racial relations, the creation of a new entity, and it required for its inception an organizing mind, more potent, better able to undertake the heroic task of civilization-building in the wilderness: a Northern European mind, Protestant, market-oriented, modern and abstract.

The Northern Europeans, especially the English, added the cultural advances of their bourgeois revolution to the special needs for dominated labor in the New World. From the fusion of these strands arose North American slavery, which henceforth supplied the entire nucleus for the further history of American racism. It is no exaggeration to claim that here—in one of those premonitory flights by which an early phase of development bolts forward into its logical fulfillment—was the most extreme version of the Western symbolic matrix ever devised. In the institution of slavery, the abstractification and splitting of the world extended not simply to nature, to manufactured commodities, nor even to labor, but to human beings—and from this extremity, to an entire civilization organized about slavery. Humans were made into things, into abstract equivalents of bodily filth to be regained by the white Western self. And with this one audacious stroke, sufficient energy and guilt were built into the system of slavery to make it that institution necessary for the formation of racism, and to keep racism in motion by its own further unfolding.

We oversimplify, to be sure, in the interests of emphasizing this central point. As our brief historical survey indicated, American slavery did not occur in one stroke; it was the tentative summation of numerous possibilities and contingencies. Slavery in America had many early variants, and took generations to harden into quintessential form. But an abstract dehumanization was the psychohistorical change inherent in the American form of chattel bondage, and was born by the burst of energy associated with the bourgeois cultural revolution, and, most critically, by the tremendous challenges, stimulations and difficulties which the New World presented to the pioneers. The wilderness that stimulated Americans into their expansion was also an ambivalent symbol of darkness[52]—a darkness which combined with the color of enslaved skin to stimulate the particular American response to blackness. And it was a response that swept the history of racism—indeed much else in American history—along with it. Here we have the nuclear creation: the radical dehumanization —the "thingification," with all the excremental implications it involves—of black people. By making property of men, Americans raised the mystique of property—and with it, the whole matrix of anality—to untold powers in their culture; from then on it was to become engrained indelibly and increasingly in American history.

We have seen that the black man entered the stream of Western history as an exotic, the bedeviled son of Ham, a symbol of instincts run wild, degenerate Oedipus himself. As the impulses which Africans represented to the West were but poorly repressed by Western culture of the time, the threat and stimulation posed by blackness to Europeans at the dawn of the Modern Age were not inconsiderable. Nor has the main strand of black symbolism changed essentially over the generations: after all, the

[52] Cf. Oscar Handlin, *Race and Nationality in American Life* (Garden City, N. Y., Anchor Books, 1957), p. 114.

bigot *knows* even today that blacks are wild, impulsive, hypersexual, violent, potential insurrectionaries. From the beginning, such a tempting creature could not be incorporated whole into an expanding civilization desperately in need of controls. Imagine the results if such individuals as white fantasies make of blacks were to be "let loose" in the midst of a white bourgeois community at any stage of our history; that is, were to be given freedom and power: the whole fabric of society would break down. And yet, the whites needed their black—needed him as long as repressions and undying desires were present within them, needed him especially when repressing institutions were weak. And besides—we must stress again the inner relationship between economic and instinctual activity—whites most needed labor for the illimitable assault on the darkness of a new continent when institutions were at their weakest.

The solution to this predicament was furnished within the Western psychohistorical matrix of anality: include the black—retain his instinctual appeal and the strength of his labor—but *control* him utterly. Subject him to a twofold control: first, reduction to a subhuman being; and, second, defense of one's white self against the ever-present temptation personified in the blacks. For both of these ends, abstractive splitting works eminently well—at least for a considerable time. Thus, raise the living human presence to an abstraction, then split the abstraction: retain in one part the simple, sexually and aggressively tempting body, and lower another part to a piece of filth—manageable, non-living, workable, beyond moral concern. Then proceed further: make of the filth a commodity, expose it to the further abstractions of the market, handle it rationally and, above all, possess it.

Possession above all, because only so could the necessary control be maintained: without the mystique of property, the entire system of splitting, the whole panoply of projected wishes, the entire freedom from moral restraints, would all break down. Property in the modern Western matrix is filthified matter to be controlled and enjoyed without conscious guilt. The further the black person was subjected to the force of the market, the further the white could proceed in his quest for the guilt-free realization of his illimitable desires. He could, in the ideal form which this situation attained eventually in the deep South, obtain the illusion of complete control over the natural and human world around him; he could, without labor of his own, endlessly work over the land, take valuable substances out of it, and do what he pleased with the people about him. Of his white women he could make an icy ideal—because by making the female, ultimately his mother, an abstraction, he defended against his sexual guilt, and, covertly but very potently, revenged himself upon her; of his black woman he could make a degraded breeding animal, the perfect warm, helpless, instinctual creature from which to obtain free sexual pleasure; and upon the black man he could visit all the woe that collected onto the biblical Ham—there, in the darktown shanties, was the guilt: blackened, virile yet castrated, childlike, abject, a totally manageable blackened father within a totally contained blackened son. And all this rested upon the stream of abstractification and the mystique of property. Without the sanctity of property, the whole defensive structure would break down: things would become people again, and people would make one guilty, or even fight back.

The culture of American slavery, although in the full Western stream, belonged to an early phase; moreover, its inner contradictions were to bring about stagnation and, eventually, disaster. We are talking now about the first distinctive phase of racism, *dominative racism*. We have described its psychology as it appears today, in the frustrated desires of bigots; and this contemporary form, we further noted, was an anachronism, deriving itself from a backward look to an age of civilization when direct domination was the organizing principle of social life. In the extreme of direct domination entailed in slavery, dominative racism attained its ideal form. But this ideal form, though enticing, had an inner limitation that made it as unsuccessful in historical evolution as the dinosaurs were in biological evolution. Both dinosaurs and American slavers were freaks of a sort, extremists who could not adapt to changing times; and both were supplanted by humbler but more efficient creatures.

The flaw in the psychohistory of American slave society arose from a radically uneven development of its elements. An exceptional degree of abstractification was applied to one group within culture—the blacks—while the dominant group of whites used them to ensure a degree of seigneurial pleasure unheard of in the West since feudal times. One group was pushed ruthlessly into the total dehumanization that is the ultimate threat of the modern Western order, while the other group literally capitalized upon this—but used their power to move, not forward, but back into a mythic dream. Only a new, open continent could afford this kind of opportunity.

But the slaveholders were parasites upon their human commodities, and needed them for every facet of their lives. While enjoying the prerogatives of barons, they were, in one critical but profound sense, participating more deeply in the capitalist order than the Yankee money-grubbers they despised. The only real difference was that the Southerner missed the turnoff into the generalized abstractification of the whole world that bore its fruit in a money-centered economy. Not money, but human bodies were their goal. The Southerner would live in close proximity, in intimacy, with his black bodies: only thereby could he have his baronial splendor. Total power and the lack of restraints gave him liberty to go as far as he pleased in this direction.

The only check on the development of slaveholding culture could have been from inner control—conscience balanced by morality, or cultural superego. But superego cannot grow unless instinctual gratifications are relinquished. This the Southerner was doubly loath to do: first, because his life was so immediately enjoyable, so gallant, so virile; and second, because of the ever-present threat of slave revolts. This menace, the offspring of projected guilt as much as of a real potential for black violence, always hung just beyond the horizon of the bright Southern sky. Any relaxation of the Southerner's headlong course would awaken the threat as much as the slightest degree of actual Negro insubordination. To each of these sources of danger, the Southerner became inordinately sensitive, even paranoid; and well he might have, for as time passed, the entire inner structure of his culture, composed as it was of a bizarre mixture of the primitive and the hyperabstract, became more brittle and thus more fragile.

The system of American slavery was perfected, then, at the price of its petrification. The black man, denied personage, was split symbolically into a thinglike commodity and a warm, amoral body. Both aspects were drawn helplessly into the white man's self-system, and within its less conscious layers an incorporation occurred: the "good nigger," in the world of the dominative racist, is part of the white self; his presence swells that self into a spectacle of phallic pride. This self-aggrandizement, or narcissism, is one of the central issues in the psychology of dominative racism. The dominative racist of today, let us recall, is he whose sense of failure and exclusion from modern life produces a chronically diminished narcissism. Through his desperate identification with the authoritarian, past or present, he hopes to regain that necessary pride. Such a pride was the Southerner's most characteristic trait, and when granted by a whole culture, it became the prize which he would defend at all cost. Any critical comments, even any attempts to rationalize and make his productive system more efficient, were all spurned as unworthy of white pride, gained by the illusion of holding within the self the possessed bodies of black people. The white Southerner would not hear of any guilt, and so guilt was twisted and exteriorized, to return from without, impinging now in the harsh, sin-ridden revivalist religion, now in the dialectical criticism from the North, and, most of all, in the fatalistic ruin, the sloth, inefficiency, wastefulness and torpor of his slave economy. When slaves sat down on the job, "clumsily" destroyed farm implements, or otherwise behaved in the shiftless way their stereotype demanded, they were engaging in an act of passive revenge; but they were also giving their masters what unconscious guilt demanded—punishment and destruction. A crime that had begun in the transformation of a man into an economic commodity was punished by economic failure. Small wonder that the Southerners despised commercial activity. They projected onto the North a worship of commercial abstraction that was in fact the rock upon which their whole society rested; they attacked the North for pushing wider what they had already pushed deeper; and, when demise came, it came from the very rock that had served them so well. If ever a society rushed headlong for ruin, it was the classical South; the very élan with which it entered the war must have been the fruit of the release of unbearable inner tensions, and, more deeply, of a wish for self-destruction. And yet, even at the end, amid smoking ruins, the Southerner retained his fatal pride.

Aversive Racism and the Rise of the North

No matter how hateful partisans of each region found those of the other, there can be no doubt that the ties which united North and South were deeper and stronger than the differences which separated them. Brothers may destroy one another, yet still remain brothers, and, in the final analysis, North and South were brothers, of common background, in the same cultural stream and equally engaged in the heroic undertaking of establishing a new civilization. And the hate between them, though it was to assume greatly complex forms, ultimately derived from one central point of distinction: the differing roles of black people within the two subcultures.

At this point, the unfolding of the symbolic matrix takes on a different aspect in the two regions. Many factors were at work to channel each region into its own path. Varying geography and climate, individual religious and subcultural styles, different institutional patterns, etc.— all worked in concert to select two distinct patterns from among the endless possibilities of Western growth. As time passed, each regional style would further act upon the other to drive the sections further apart. The essence of their differences lay in the pattern of abstraction that each applied to the world. In the South, as we have noted, a few extreme schismatic abstractions were made—black person into thing, and white woman into ideal—not as ends in themselves, but as means to the provision of a directly gratifying, narcissistic feudalism. In the North, on the other hand, abstraction was diffuse and comprehensive: it extended outwardly to the whole world of nature and man and, most decisively, inwardly to the self: it was an end in itself. The Northern system brought fluidity and adaptability to the matrix of culture; it allowed for indirect domination, and, within the loosened, fluid boundaries of its terms, provided the possibility for democracy and political liberty. These could arise, after all, only within a matrix which ensured the individuality of the self while making possible a kind of equivalency between selves. And through its general abstraction, the Northern matrix offered to history for the first time the possibility of realizing the ageless dream of freedom. Unfortunately—and most unfortunately for black people— that possibility would become seriously compromised by certain other terms of the matrix, to be discussed below; nonetheless, it was there, and it presented the most indubitable and precious contribution of the West to civilization.

In evolutionary terms, then, there could be no doubt that the North was more "advanced" than the South; and, since history, like biological evolution, is the survival of the fittest, the success of the North over the South—which had become economically evident long before the Civil War—certified this advancement. And the historical weakness of Southern culture lay exactly where the white masters took their extreme pleasure—in the oppressed bodies of black people.

This powerless yet alive body, with its enduring and seemingly foolproof tag of black skin for identification, was the cardinal creation of the Southern order. It was this body that the Southerner enjoyed and presented to his Northern brother. And although the black body fascinated the Northerner as much as it did the Southerner, the terms of his culture left him unable to obtain the same kind of gratification from it.

There it was—and one puts the matter harshly but accurately, for slavery stamped an "it-ness" upon the black person which became his enduring curse wherever he went within America—there the body was, enticing, alive, helpless, and yet forbidden. The Northerner had made his pact with history; Faustian, he had achieved the potential for freedom and power by renouncing his own body and deadening the world. The temptation was there, and was powerful; but the prohibition was a little bit more powerful, and made of what was desired a taboo, to be obeyed henceforth by aversion. And now we are in a position to begin understanding *aversive racism*, that form most typical of America, and, indeed, of wherever the bourgeois-capitalist style of life prevails.

Consider first the range of temptations offered. Here, in one living, apersonal body, all of the objects of the partial sexual impulses were combined and concentrated: here was phallus, vagina, anus, mouth, breast, all available and ordained to be without inhibition because they were without guiding self. And more, here was the magical excremental body itself, the body-as-a-whole: black, warm, odorous, undifferentiated—the very incarnation of that fecal substance with which the whole world had been smeared by the repressed coprophilia of the bourgeois order. Here was the central forbidden pleasure that had become generalized into the pursuit of world mastery: the playing with, the reincorporation of lost bodily contents, the restoration of the narcissistic body of infancy, the denial of separation and the selfhood that had been painfully wrung from history. Here was the excremental body that had been hated, repressed, spread over the universe, but which was still loved with the infant's wish to fuse with the maternal image. In its own direct pursuit of narcissism, the South had created this body; in its own convoluted, tortuous search for the same goal, the North was confronted with it.

The best that the North could do within the terms of its symbolic matrix was to express hatred and rage against the black body. Buried beneath the rage rested the layers of affinity, repressed incestuous wishes, love of the body lost in childhood, love of body contents—even more deeply buried—held back by the historical search for power. All that surfaced of this iceberg of submerged feeling was the disgust that came last in the series of instinctual developments, and which sealed off all the rest. An obscure yet violent hatred for Negroes arose, puzzling indeed, yet scarcely examined because of its intensity, a violent passion contrary to the external moral principles of the culture, yet congruent with the deeper symbolic sources of that morality. The conflict between ideals and disgust has been a very potent one in our history; in its many forms, it has spread from this core to become the central American dilemma of race relations. Thus the underlying instinctual conflict between love and hatred of the body becomes transmuted with the advance of civilization to higher ground. In its "higher" form, the conflict is between id and superego, or between the disgust, which is the only one of the many layers of instinctual feeling to remain exposed, and the pure ideality of moral principle. Within the terms of the higher-order conflict, aversion becomes the paradigmatic resolution. And the reason for this is that aversion has rich symbolic content of its own.

In itself, aversion is an ego activity, effected as a compromise between the diverse forces pressing in upon the ego. But it is also—for such is the multiple functioning by which we carry out important tasks—a form of gratification, attenuated perhaps, but the best that can be managed under the circumstances. The prototype of aversion is the physical turning away from what is bodily disgusting, and the prototype of the latter is filth. Filth must not touch the body, or, to the magical infantile thinking that persists alongside of the most mature mental function, it will contaminate it, despoil its purity, perhaps get back inside. Needless to add, such an intense repulsion corresponds to, and is the negation of, its contrary desire—to take back in what is lost and hated. Negations affirm their repressed positive contradictions: hatred affirms love, disgust affirms the lost desire for incorporation, aversion affirms lost body narcissism.

Just as the dominative Southerner needed to keep "his" black body powerless, so does the aversive Northerner need a powerless object with which to play out the symbolic game. And not only must this object be powerless; it must be suitable to represent what has to be projected upon it. Thus for the black to fit into the aversive equation, he must be made into the affirmation of the excremental body. He must become the double negative of anality, the fantasy of a fantasy—not cold, pure, clean, efficient, industrious, frugal, rational (that is, not the pantheon of anal-negative ego traits which are the *summum bonum* of the bourgeois order) but rather warm, dirty, sloppy, feckless, lazy, improvident and irrational, all those traits that are associated with blackness, odor, and sensuality to make their bearer worthy of aversion. And so, throughout our history, whites have created the institutions by which black people are forced to live, and which force them to live in a certain way, almost invariably so as to foster just that constellation of unworthy traits. From slavery itself to modern welfare systems, this has been the enduring pattern, reinforced in popular culture and education by a panoply of stereotypes along the same lines.

The result of these cultural manipulations has been to ensure to the black person a preassigned degraded role, no matter where he turned. This has been true, to some extent, of every group subjected to prejudice, but the quantitative differences have been enormous. For here was a people recognizably distinct from others, easily manipulated because of this and because of their initially abysmal state of slavery, and most of all, dragged down by the profundity of the symbolic equations into which they were drawn. The accumulation of negative images forced upon blacks in America amounted to presenting them with one massive and destructive choice: either to hate one's self, as culture so systematically demanded, or to have no self at all, to be nothing. With the passage of time and abstraction, these alternatives amounted to the same thing: the only self available for black people within the increasingly remote and cold cultural matrix of industrial America and its sewer-cities would be nothingness, the final attenuation of abstracted filth.

Thus black people have been the last to be included into the democratic equation. Such participation requires full and equal selfhood; and while American culture provided selfhood to most, it needed some left-over people to degrade so that the majority could rise. Consequently, the nation that pushed the idea of freedom and equality to the highest point yet attained was also the nation that pulled the idea of degradation and dehumanization to the lowest level ever sounded, to pure nothingness.

In Northern culture, the one activity which permitted unlimited gratification was the making of money. The pursuit of money, the purified and abstract residue of the excremental body, paralleled the repulsion felt toward black people. The incorporation of money into a refined self could be allowed, even as aversion from blacks allowed that self to repudiate its body. Again the two processes mutually fed upon each other, driving an increasing wedge into culture and generating power. Thus it was that throughout the era of slavery, Yankee capitalists, by exploiting the remote operations of finance and commerce, extracted more wealth out of black bodies than the Southerners, with all their direct control, could manage to do. And when machine technology entered the culture of the West at the close of the eighteenth century, it was the North that quickly seized upon these remote means of bodily magnification, and employed them for the infinite multiplication of wealth. Machines, especially the cotton gin, rescued slavery from the doldrums and breathed new vitality into an institution that was beginning to sag under mounting moral opprobrium. The same machines now became the executors of the Northern will. Combined with the mystique of property that had become institutionalized in the Constitution, and directed by that abstract impersonal spirit which was steadily in the process of creation, a machine civilization began to arise, generating endless quantities of money and pushing blacks, by the dialectical process we have been describing, into new depths of degradation. This occurred both within the increasingly ruthless, large scale operations of cotton plantations, and, more productively, in the industrial centers of the non-slave North. For the industrial North, the primary object of degradation was labor itself; wherever this degradation occurred, and no matter how bad matters became for white labor, blacks fared worse, and have done so in industrial work until the present day: last to be hired, first to be fired, lowest wages, most onerous work, tool of management to break strikes, scapegoat of the frustrations of labor. Nor was the process one-directional: just as the creation of white wealth pushed blacks down, so must the presence of degraded black bodies have exerted a continual stimulation to the further pursuit of abstracted money. And the more these simultaneous processes advanced, the more would aversion have to be practiced.

Thus we have reached at least a partial explanation to

account for de Tocqueville's observation that the prejudice of race was greatest in areas which had never known slavery. An equivalent rephrasing would be that the (aversive) prejudice of race was forced precisely in fleeing from the temptations of slavery, and out of the resulting creation of higher, more abstract, things. Either aversion, or direct bodily possession: such was the choice for Americans. Those who chose the former, abstracted course would have to contend with the fact that aversion dialectically degrades what it excludes; and that the more pure and refined they were to become, the less tolerable would be the concrete presence of blacks.

Now we can see the psychology of segregation which was forced upon the South when its direct power over black bodies was broken by military defeat. Southern segregation represents a gross and still relatively concrete effort to accommodate Southern culture to the dominant mainstream of the American symbolic matrix. Northern liberals who have execrated the South for the inhuman practice of segregation might have recognized, though they would scarce be expected to forgive, that the South was simply following in their own footsteps, and mixing its old dominative gratifications with the crude form of aversion which the North had long since sublimated, internalized and rationalized. What is true for the psychology of segregation and apartheid also pertains, in a more extreme way, to the psychology of colonization. Here aversion proceeds past the point where any physical presence is needed for its object. Disgust, guilt, and anxiety overwhelm the narcissistic gains and bring about the fantasy of the final solution: deport, expel the blackness, and thereby radically ensure the purity of the white spirit and blood.

Although it would remain unconscious of it, the American conscience received one of its greatest stimulations from the presence of the degraded black people within its midst. The highest, purest, and most valued of what the North—and eventually all of American culture—gained from the aversive flight from blackness, was the purity of its conscience and ideals. Not that the white conscience has been especially helpful to blacks; usually, it has been applied to appease white guilt and foster white virtue, while strangely ignoring the real human being who is its supposed object. Moreover, and this is perhaps more fundamental, the conscience of whites as a historical structure has evolved to guide the abstractive productivity of culture; it thus propels and energizes the very process in history from which black people have derived their suffering.

The functions of the cultural superego continuously grow with the differentiation of the cultural ego; its structure dialectically absorbs and internalizes forms of aggression released at the point of historical repression. And historical repression occurs with every advance of civilization, with every sublimation of Eros that occurs to weld humanity into a larger unit, with every abstractification of the world, with every drawing away of the self, with every purification. And this kind of repression has occurred at each decisive phase of American growth.

Nowhere did historical repression and the growth of cultural superego occur more profoundly than in the American confrontation with blackness and in the racism which ensued. Let us turn to a revealing early example, quoted from Jordan's study of American white-black relations. Robert Pyle of Pennsylvania, an early anti-slavery Quaker, included the following fantasy in his argument against slavery:

> I considered the motion that rose in me to buy off them whether it was not self,—knowing hitherto by my moderate and honest indevors I have not wanted food nor rayment, theyrwith be

content, saith the Apostle; being excercised upon my mind for many dayes considering those things as I was lieng upon my bed as in a sleep I saw myself and a friend going on a road, and by the roadside I saw a black pott. I took it up, the friend said give mee part, I said no, I went a little farther and I saw a great ladder standing exact upright, reaching up to heaven up which I must go to heaven with the pott in my hand intending to carry the black pott with me, but the ladder standing so upright, and seeing no man holding of it up, it seemed that it would fall upon mee; at which I steps down and laid the pott at the foot of the ladder, and said them that will take it might, for I found work enough for both hands to take hold of this ladder.[53]

Jordan continues, "When he awoke this good Quaker considered the matter and declared firmly, in an astonishing phrase, 'self must bee left behind, and to lett black negroes or pots alone.'" Jordan speculates, rightly, I think, that the symbol of pot and the reference to being "left behind" implies that the basic instinctual level here is excremental. Another matter should be noted here, for it expressed the peculiar situation of America. Pyle had to climb the ladder alone, no man helped hold it up; similarly, Americans were alone in their efforts to resolve the problems of life. Having no institutional foundation, they were forced to accentuate self-reliance; with this, much that could have been included in a more traditional framework had to be excluded, radically if necessary.

Pyle's candid fantasy reveals that the white striving for moral purity is fused in the unconscious mind with the flight from the black, excremental body. But here a deep paradox intrudes: since in history the grossest wrongs have been committed upon the people who inhabited these black bodies, then the object of Western conscience, the goal of its reformist activity, must be the same as the object from which the self flees in the formation of its idealistic superego. This was the great problem of aboli-

---

[53] Jordan, *White over Black*, p. 256.

tionism, and it has been the dilemma of much of the reformist movement in America since. And once again abstractive splitting has been used to aid the white Westerner in the resolution of his conflicts.

The good Quaker Pyle, in his ascent of the ladder of virtue, leaves blackness behind. But this is only his conscious wish: what is held by desire in the mind cannot be expelled. It may be repressed, denied, projected, but a trace remains in the unconscious as a forbidden blackness desired by the white to restore his state of infantile narcissism. Since he cannot regain his loss directly, an indirect means is found. He will seek that which is most forbidden through behavior which is most pure, correct and moralistic. This in fact the superego accomplishes: it redirects the person to real objects in the world that, though shadows of the lost infantile objects, still have the trace of satisfaction. Thus, insofar as the white's superego directs him to the aid of the oppressed black, it allows him to bring back into the self a portion of what has been lost: it has restored the self and "saved" the object, in all the senses of that word. And so blacks have periodically been "saved" by the ministrations of white reformism—except that the saving has all too often been motivated by the desire for the restoration of white integrity. The practical outcome of this "saving," as in the debacle of Reconstruction or, today, in paternalistic welfare practices, has been the further loss of black autonomy.

Indeed, the saving has often been ruinous; and perhaps it must always be so, as long as a split is maintained through aversion—that is, as long as the basic symbolic matrix of our culture holds sway over reformism as it does over the generation of material power. Under such terms, the saving of one part of the black object is accompanied by the degradation of another, as the various elements find their respective niches in the symbolic pattern to represent the nuclear fantasy of saving and destroying. This ambiguous quality seems to be appended to all of the aggressive idealism which our culture has generated, most strikingly in recent years in Vietnam, but equally prevalent in most of America's efforts to help the downtrodden. The principle beneficiary of this activity has been the white cultural superego, continuously rising in mastery, power and the direction of the mystique of productivity.

Consider the founding of the nation. The idealistic demands for the abolition of slavery that attended the Revolutionary struggle stirred the conscience of America for a while, only to become officially incorporated into the Constitutional grounding of slavery. As Karl Polanyi noted, this made America into the only nation for whom property attained such heights of legal institutionalization. Shortly afterward, the advent of machine technology stifled antislavery sentiment. Now slavery was not only legally justified, but useful as well: idealistic reform had developed into dehumanized, destructive productivity; the cultural superego had adjusted itself to fit the symbolic matrix. All was well.

A generation later, in the 1830's, a new crisis arose, and with it, a new outburst of moralism. A combination of territorial pressure and institutional weakness lay behind the rising tide of conflict, but antislavery became its principal manifestation.

A restless growth was the rule, carried out by the free-wheeling entrepreneurial spirit that was to become our hallmark, and bringing about a collapse of more traditional guiding structures. New sources of guidance arose in concert with this aggressive liberation: a host of reformist cliques, religious revivalism, and—what was to become historically crucial—abolitionism, and its philosophical ground, transcendentalism.

In a flash of insight that went to the limit of the idealistic potentialities of our symbolic matrix, transcendental-ism proclaimed the triumph of pure spirit over the coarse things of the world. The transcendentalist movement was intensely puritanical, asexual and harshly guilt-ridden—just what would be expected, as Stanley Elkins pointed out in his book, *Slavery*, from the lack of institutional controls which existed in expanding America. And since the expansion tended to make an entrepreneurial capitalist out of everyone—by intensifying and making generally available the fluid, abstract search for money—the con-science attacked, not the prized abstractive pursuit of wealth, but its concrete forebear, the gross, obviously evil, and inhuman pursuit of wealth through slavery. As many observers have pointed out, and as is manifest in their own statements,[54] the abolitionists' attacks were directed not simply at an external source of evil, but also at the appeasement of an inner sense of guilt. We do not ques-tion the real need to attack the evil of slavery. However, a complex phenomenon such as abolitionism must have been more than a simple attack on a gross evil. People are never so singular in their motivation. And it is doubtful whether the attack would ever have gathered any inten-sity if slavery had not been an evil congruent with what was causing the Northerners' inner sense of guilt—a con-gruence revealed in their similar positions in the psycho-historical matrix, in which they are separated only by a degree of abstraction. Nothing suits the resolution of an inner conflict so much as the presence of an outer fac-simile of it, distant enough to spare the self direct guilt, yet close enough to allow a symbolic correspondence.

It may be argued that what made the antislavery move-ment eventually so powerful was not so much the actual efforts of abolitionists—who were, after all, less than pop-

[54] Cf. Elkins, *Slavery*; for example, the sermon by Theodore Parker, quoted on page 27 above.

ular in the North—as it was the hard material issue of sectional expansion. This is undoubtedly so: no historical event of worth springs simply from emotional or intellectual forces. But we are taking an organic view, by which we must see how all significant levels of a culture alter in a coordinated way. We have seen that each facet of the matrix has its particular cultural representative, and so we might observe here that the slaveholder represented the id aspects of the matrix; the Northern capitalist the ego aspects; and the abolitionists the superego. The historical process may be seen as the outcome of the conflict between those elements, a conflict represented *within* each member of society as much as it is represented *between* cultural institutions. Thus, entrepreneurs felt both guilt and desire to go all the way into slavery; slaveholders felt guilt and desire to participate in the rationalized power of bourgeois capitalism; and abolitionists felt temptations from both abstracted and direct forms of bodily possessions. Of course most of this was unconscious, but each acting person, and each group they worked within, acted in concert with the others to play out the historical unfolding of American culture. Although pure abolitionism was sneered at—perhaps because it was too guilt-provoking—by the time the war began, a good deal of fervor had been worked up on both sides around the issue it presented, and this passion was one of the critical determinants of the course that events were to take.

There is also little doubt that moralistic attacks on slavery only stiffened Southern resistance and strengthened the practice which the Northerners so abominated. Naturally, Southern defiance and paranoia only further inflamed the North. Many observers have noted this paradox, and often have concluded that if the regions had "known better," they might have let reason prevail in the adjustment of slavery that was bound to come. But, as we have seen, neither slavery in the South, nor its relative, capitalism in the North, were rational pursuits: both involved the headlong pursuit of impossible fantasies. Reason was neither at stake nor much valued in this confrontation between different phases of Western growth, increasingly hemmed in by continental limitations. Considered in this light, the paradox becomes less surprising, for was not the North unconsciously forcing the South to enact exactly the fantasy which it had to deny itself? Could it not, then, both vicariously enjoy the spectacle of Southern profligacy and at the same time exteriorize and discharge its own sense of guilt? And would not the South, whose narcissism could not tolerate any internal criticism, need some form of external chastisement, and eventually punishment, to balance its own symbolic equations? The antislavery struggles of the second quarter of the nineteenth century had a kind of bizarre symmetry, even a mutuality—for both regions were much closer to one another than either would admit. Each saw in the other some hated portion of itself. Needless to say, this kind of projection is more than casually reminiscent of the basic situation in which the white forces the Negro to act out his own forbidden wishes, and then punishes him for it. On the larger level, however, there was no possible resolution to the tensions so induced other than warfare. The uncontrolled expansiveness of the energies involved bore fruit first in the call for Manifest Destiny, then in a diversion onto Mexico. When this exteriorization dried up, and the two regions had at last to face one another across a shrinking frontier, the final internecine struggle was at hand.

Throughout, the development of the American conscience and ideals charted its characteristic course. First, attack an evil—as abstract as possible; next, yoke the moral energy to a material pursuit, initially as a side-effect, but eventually as a dominating interest; and create thereby new abstractified versions of the cultural superego —and, in their wake, leave the intended beneficiaries of reform either high and dry, or saddled with a new form of distress. Any amount of symbolic manipulation is possible with a sufficiently abstracted entity, and nothing had been more abstracted, more carved up into symbolically useful pieces, than black people in America. The true historical aim of abolitionism became revealed after it had set North and South upon each other—at which point its energies were appropriated by the newborn Republican Party, which, from the beginning, and to an ever-mounting extent, linked the moral energy of reformism with the material power of capitalism. Superficially, these are strange bedfellows indeed, but not to anyone familiar with the deeper workings of Western culture. Thus what began as a struggle over oppressed blackness ended as another intensification of the mystique of productivity, which is only to say that the same nuclear issue became incorporated into more potent—hence more self-protective— systems. The North grew so powerful under this blackness-driven mystique, that it not only overwhelmed the South during the war, but actually increased its own productivity many-fold during the conflict, and launched itself immediately afterward into the golden age of entrepreneurial capitalism. Meanwhile, the actual black man, for whose liberation so much was professed, was progressively ignored and eventually granted a freedom that was *de jure* only, and scarcely an improvement over his previous condition of servitude. We need not be surprised, since the actual aim of the reform movement, so nobly and bravely begun, was not the liberation of the black, but the fortification of the white, conscience and all. The courageous sallies of a few visionaries against a monolithic wrong had become consumed by culture for its own purposes.

The cultural force of conscience reached full flower during the conflict over slavery. For the first time, a President rode to office on a moral issue, and with the war, the mightiness of righteousness was once and for all established. But America had achieved not only rightness, but whiteness as well; for with the cessation of hostilities and the readjustments of Reconstruction, the black bodies who had so haunted the nation were at length put out of sight. For the next fifty years, aversive racism would seal off blackness from whites, while entrepreneurial capitalism held full sway and a white nation pursued the unification that had so long been denied to it by the nightmare of race. With the abolition of slavery, dominative racism began to fade from the forefront, even in the South. It would be activated there to put blacks in their place, or to remind them of that place whenever, either in reality or white fantasy, they strayed from the bottom of the social heap; but once firmly affixed to their place, black people could now be handled through the crude form of aversive racism embodied in segregation. Meanwhile, in the rest of the country, the specter of blackness scarcely existed. Blacks were clowns, jackanapes, grinning simpletons over whom a good laugh could be had, and no more need be made of it. The fierceness and terror had been abstracted away: blacks had been saved from slavery by the morally superior white race, and any other problems they might have were their own fault—not an acquired fault, but something hidden deep in the essence of things, and revealed as it seeped outward through their skin. Profound laws of nature were seen to be immanent in the inherent unworthiness of the dark races. The latter part of the nineteenth century and the first two decades of the twentieth were the high-water years of race ideology. Americans—white Anglo-Saxons, that is—were able to prove to themselves by a whole panoply of ingenious arguments that, by virtue of their extreme whiteness, they were the finest people who had ever lived. And they had an expanding, optimistic society to prove it. By and large, this was an era of successful repressions: aversive racism was a success so seamless that it could not only retain the gaseous arguments of racist ideology, but spread them to so wide an extent that they were endorsed by virtually every American from the most ignorant to the most sophisticated. The tenets of racism became axioms—to replace, for a later stage of civilization, the now unthinkable axioms of slavery. And there were no serious pressures in late nineteenth-century America to make racism unthinkable. Indeed, it had to be thought, for within its terms the sense of individual self that history had given to the dominant groups was guaranteed: they are black, unworthy, subhuman; I, white, am defined by contrast, worthy, perhaps—who knows?—even superhuman. Racism then was what the symbolic matrix allowed in the way of self-cognition at this phase of history.

But history was giving its helix still another turn. Even as black people slid into the despair of those denied membership in the cultural community, and as they struck the bottom of the long arc of their degradation, a societal transformation was beginning that would eventually restore them to the forefront of national attention.

The nadir for black people in postbellum America came at the turn of the century, in the course of numerous explosive developments. North and South had been at length reconciled; a serious agrarian and proletarian revolt that might have upset the whole mystique of capitalism had been stemmed, if but temporarily; and a spate of imperialist adventures was set into motion. All this pointed our story in two directions: for black people, it spelled disaster, since they were among the ever-useful expendable scapegoats upon whom the burden of surplus aggression inherent in these processes could be dumped; for the nation-state, it spelled birth. A new, aggressive and expansive entity had begun to be created out of the mélange of regions and classes that had divided the country. A long course still lay ahead for this process—indeed its end is not yet in sight—but a turning point had been reached, at the price of rendering black people invisible. Our culture was at last able to provide a degree of abstractification within which all white Americans could conceive of sharing a common identity: this meant, of course, that the divisive and embarrassing presence of blacks had to be abstracted away virtually completely.

At the same time, another psychohistorical trend of the greatest import was unfolding. The hectic pace of events all reduced to one element: the nation was growing in size, power and internal complexity. Consequently, it would have to grow—individualistic entrepreneurs notwithstanding—in the power to control its inner events.

The Progressive Movement, and the generations of Deals, Frontiers and Great Society's which followed, are the familiar ideological labels pasted by reformers onto the new type of control. It is by now clear that the successive waves of liberal innovation have served to ensure and rationalize the basic operations of our culture, and not to tamper with them. Despite the original howls from business interests, no radical change was intended; and the same capitalists who once yelped in dismay now eagerly queue up to contribute to and share in the good life of the New Industrial State.

The good life for America is, as ever, a materially expansive one. And the immense material rewards of contemporary society have served to blunt radical protest and insight into the workings of our culture. In retrospect, however, we can see the larger operations obscured behind the screen of material bounty. With the passage of time they have blossomed into a life of their own. Consider, for example, the tone of the great wave of expansion which occurred at the turn of the century. Here was the new nation, having completed its half-century of consolidation, launching outward again to express its "manifest destiny." But now a new tone intrudes. Let us quote Richard Hofstadter,[55] commenting upon Albert Weinberg's book *Manifest Destiny:* "Previously destiny had meant primarily that American expansion, *when we willed it,* could not be resisted *by others* who might wish to stand in our way. During the nineties it came to mean that expansion 'could not be resisted by Americans themselves, caught, willing, or unwilling,' in the coils of fate. A certain reluctance on our part was implied. This was not quite so much what we *wanted* to do; it was what we *had* to do. Our aggression was implicitly defined as compulsory—the product not of our own wills but of objective necessity (or the will of God)."

The "we" no longer wills the act; the act is willed for us. Here is the critical change of contemporary times. And who does the willing? God? This was the reassuring ideology at the turn of the century, but even then it deserved the parenthesis, for it was only a remnant from an earlier epoch, when the idea of God could really sway men. No, objective necessity had begun its rule of the world. But where was the locus of this necessity? Necessity, cultural superego, derives from the source of power, and with the twentieth century, power in America began to leave the hands of individual entrepreneurs and moved to the new entity of the nation-state, now the modern industrial state. Productivity, the real God of the West, now becomes autonomous and beyond the will of men. With it, men attain a new degree of abstraction, and the power

[55] *The Paranoid Style in American Politics* (New York, Vintage Books, 1967), p. 177. Italics Hofstadter's.

of the self, which men had won from history, passes over to machines and the impersonal regulatory forces of industrial society. From that transfer of power, control now returns from the impersonal outside—returns over white and black men alike. And with this, the terms of racism begin to shift and a new order of racism arises.

Metaracism

We have observed that the general direction of American reform has been to paint over an older symptom with a newer one in order to protect the underlying disease. Thus did slavery yield to late-nineteenth-century racism. In terms of the ideal types we have been employing, dominative racism was succeeded by aversive racism as the principal mode employed by our culture to utilize and defend against the darkness within it. Now in modern times, racial distinctions themselves are anachronistic, and culture must choose a different structure to preserve its inner plague. Once again an erotic, life-giving, trend—the assault upon racism—has become infiltrated with the forces of destruction. Let us isolate the pathologic factors in the fight against racism. We shall consider them as another ideal type, and, bearing in mind that they are deeply intermixed with other influences in our actual situation, sum them up under the heading of *Metaracism*.

Racism, which began with the random oppression of another person, and moved from directly dominative, systematic control of his being, into abstracted averted use of his degradation, now passes beyond consciousness, holding only to its inner connections with the symbolic matrix. Metaracism is a distinct and very peculiar modern phenomenon. Racial degradation continues on a different plane, and through a different agency: those who participate in it are not racists—that is, they are not racially prejudiced—but metaracists, because they acquiesce in the larger cultural order which continues the work of racism. Although metaracism is not the only form of modern American racial behavior, nor even the predominant form at present, it is the form which seems in accord with the latest version of the plague of history. Whether or not it will prevail will depend upon history itself—upon whether the matrix will continue its hold upon us, or whether, as we suggested in the previous chapter, its inner weaknesses may signal its forthcoming replacement by a new psychohistorical symbolic order.

A really deep survey of white Americans would doubtlessly reveal a great mixture of racial patterns in everyone, but it might be predicted that the substantial majority continue to reserve their most intense feelings for the hallowed racial patterns of yore; that is, they hold to a mixture of dominative and aversive racist beliefs, according, one would expect, to their authoritarianism and the degree to which their superego has internalized aggression. Certain other Americans—a minority, perhaps—would be revealed as free from racist tinge; not entirely, for no one can escape his culture to that extent, but to a degree so substantial that race thinking plays virtually no significant role in their behavior. It is with this minority, who are in the vanguard of history, that we concern ourselves.

There are several ways to abandon racist belief. A person may pass beyond racism autonomously, by a free and inwardly directed choice; he may, as a result, arrive at a state in which, whatever his other problems in life, he treats and considers another person as he is and without regard for skin color or ethnic origin. He thereby frees himself from the shackles of categories. Admittedly, this kind of behavior is more difficult than the use of simplistic stereotypes. Such stereotypes provide a comforting sense of group continuity; they ground one in a tradition, which is especially valuable in the fragmented modern world; and they spare one the effort of really dealing with another person, of confronting him in his individual richness and complexity. If the result of liberation from racism is a negative opinion of the other person, this will be based not on the automatic reactions of domination or aversion, but on a realistic assessment of him as a whole person. To go beyond racism genuinely means at bottom that the other is considered a human, not a thing; he may be a lovable human, he may be an unlovable human, or he may be, like most humans, an amazing mixture of strengths and weaknesses, assets and deficits, lovable and unlovable traits, all bound up in various conflicts. In a free, nonracist culture, one grants an intrinsic worth to the other person, simply because he is human; this does not mean, however, that one must love him. The essence of love is spontaneity; no "must" can be applied to it without contradiction. The command to Love Thy Neighbor is as contrary to human reality as the converse commands of racism: it is a command rather than a free choice, a denial of the given fact of aggression, and most importantly, it is an adulteration of love, a weakening of its bonds through the fixity of an imperative. "Love Thy Neighbor" is, in fact, the manipulation of love as a defense against the possibility of hate; it implies the inner presence of a crippling rage.

On the other hand, a generally loving attitude toward reality is necessary for any climb out of the abyss of racist thinking. There must be a preponderance within the personality of the forces of Eros—revealed in the capacity for spontaneous affirmation, for enthusiasm, for hope, and, indeed, for love. But Eros is not acquired with a brush; it springs from within, and generates the ability to step out of the seductive ways of racist thinking. Actuated by this affirmative sense, one will spontaneously work against the plague, in concert with others, or alone, in accordance with one's own style and abilities, but ever toward the removal of the endless obstacles set against humanity.

Considerable numbers of blacks and whites live with that affirmative sense today, and it is in their efforts that there is hope for the future liberation of humanity. We will say little about the conditions for such an erotic approach to the world, for our concern is to dissect the pathology of culture. We note it here as an alternative to the metaracist way of going beyond racism. The choice is not, however, whether or not to instill Eros into people. Eros arises spontaneously out of the life force that gave us being. Men do not implant it; all they can do is remove the endless obstacles to its expression. Our choice, then, is whether to side with life or with the plague. It is a dilemma of the greatest dimensions, an ultimately ethical problem whose general answer lies beyond our present scope, although it has been approached by many of the authors whose work forms the underpinning of this book.

Although it enters into all activity, and throughout history, the choice is most exquisitely difficult in modern times because of the infiltration of the forces of Eros by domination—that is, because of the adulteration of desire with the anti-human needs of productivity, because of the global objectification that makes so much that is destructive appear simple, productive, necessary and beyond the power of men to control or even condemn. The rule of objective necessity, the abstract quantification of the basic qualities of living substance, the reduction of the flux of the universe to an endless decimal place—all this is the icy grip of the plague in our time. It is the sense of passivity before the will of Manifest Destiny; it is the sense of remorseless, unsentimental necessity about the manufacture of nuclear weaponry; it is the abject surrender to the mystique of production that permits our bamboozlement by advertisements or our immolation by pollutants; it is the series of banal steps of acquiescence that led to the debacle of Vietnam. It is, in psychohistorical terms, the passage of superego power to the interpenetrated industrial state: to an intrusive, impersonal, technologically brilliant, inhuman system of production and rationalized control. And it is this passage that allows the repressed forms of aggression to return, remote, free from conscious awareness, but vastly more destructive, whether as pollutants, bombs, or the general dying of things—the plasticity of our food, the grotesque barrenness of our popular culture. All this destruction—perhaps no worse absolutely than the havoc of the past, yet much worse relatively, for men should know better by now and not so trick themselves—is the present form of the plague. And, in racial matters, so is metaracism.

Metaracism is, then, the pursuit of consciously non-racist behavior in the interests of furthering the destructive work of culture. Under the terms of racism, the white self was either swollen, as in dominative racism, or pure, as in its aversive form, while the black person was less than a person, less than a self: either a concrete body-thing or, as time went on, a no-thing. In going beyond racism, one can raise both one's self and the other by a free act of mutual affirmation, grounded in a real human relationship in which both self and other are face to face, ends in themselves. Or, as in metaracism, one can reduce one's self: sell part to culture, become a means to *its* ends, and share this fate with people of other races. There is a real appeal to the latter choice, for the degradation blacks suffer in America has reached such proportions that any kind of help is mandatory; and, materially at least, such assistance can most potently come from the modern nation-state. And there is an individually seductive appeal to

metaracism too, exceptionally favored by the conditions
of American culture. It is the two-edged pleasure in acquiescence, in going along with the group: first, the freedom
from freedom, the dropping of the always difficult task
of autonomy; second, the rewards of feeling at one with
peers in a bland and complaisant group, watched over
benignly by the eyes of a materially bounteous system.
The eyes of the Industrial State—which correspond quite
precisely on a cultural scale to the watchdog functions of
the internalized individual superego[56]—are media and advertising, both impersonal apparatuses, powerful in this
electronic age as never before, and embarked upon their
great task of selling racial tolerance to a confused and
anxious populace. For precisely as people awaken, as it
were, from their racial slumbers and seek for ways to
redress the wrongs of the past, they are faced with the
manipulations of the Industrial State which seeks to perfect itself and to remove the threats posed by racial
turmoil in the sensitive modern age. The State, quite
aside from the wishes of the individuals who man its
positions, wishes for itself nothing so much as that the
people within it be perfectly interchangeable nonentities
who can do its differentiated work, buy its differentiated
products, and create as little fuss as possible in the process; it has no use for racial differences, not because it sees
people as worthwhile ends in themselves, but because it
sees them all as means to its own ends, parts in its machines, cells in its body.

The paradigmatic example of metaracism is modern
Army life. Here is a system, immensely powerful and
capable of exercising its will upon individual personalities,
which has elevated the lot of black men within its ranks
to the highest general level that they have enjoyed in

[56] Its potency accounts, for instance, for the modern obsession with
"image."

American history. The top echelons are pure white, to be sure, but in any number of lesser positions, Negroes have done well, are accorded an equality much closer to actuality than that obtainable outside, and indeed are quite frequently in positions of command over white troops. No wonder then that the Moynihan Report proclaimed the military as perhaps the best way to black manhood. Yet what kind of manhood is so fostered by military life? Isn't it simply the mechanized—indeed robotized—reduction of humanity to selfless tools of the will of culture, the grinding of both black and white into gray? Nowhere in our culture is there less freedom, less autonomy, less originality, joy and affirmation; nowhere is there more cold calculation, more mindless regimentation, more dullness, more banality—and more racial equality. And nowhere else is the integrated anal-sadistic wish of the Western matrix raised to such a pitch of perfection, nowhere else is the exteriorized destructivity of our culture so perfectly expressed.

Though we find it here in pure form, metaracism may be said to exist wherever the hand of the modern State reduces people to its own ends, and whenever it finds it expedient—not ethical, but useful—to eliminate race distinctions in the process. Metaracism exists wherever bureaucracies exist to reduce people to numbers—a white number and a black number are, after all, not so different; wherever "demonstration Negroes" are summoned up to improve a corporation's image; or when advertisers need them to sell more synthetic junk to keep the wheels of production turning. Note that no direct oppression occurs, and that certain real gains are made. A few black people are at long last afforded decent employment (though it is hard to conceive of significant numbers being admitted to high executive positions), and the crippling racist stereotypes are at long last dismantled.

And if, in the modern Industrial State, life is made safer, more hygienic, more comfortable, secure and fair, then such boons must be given their due. But just as one would not ignore the beneficial aspects, so must we not overlook the deep pathology. One need not deplore the immense benefits given to mankind by science, for example, nor overlook its beauty, fascination and hope, to recognize that in its full historical role its practice has become infiltrated with an awesome dose of the plague. It is the hopelessly intertwined combination of benevolent and destructive features that gives such historical entities their shadowy nature and makes it so difficult to detect, confront and eliminate the evil fused with the good within them. Thus the greatest contemporary advances in racial justice come from and contribute to the strength of that aspect of our culture where the historical plague now resides. One cannot ignore the real gains, nor forget the abysmal level of Negro life in America that forces upon us the imperative to do whatever possible toward its betterment. And yet, the greatest power our culture has that can be used for this human end, is the set of forces whose underlying ends are the obliteration of Eros and the reduction of people into means to its ends. And so we may say that metaracism—the illusion of non-racism coexisting with the continuation of racism's work—exists wherever, in this subtle balance of human and anti-human forces, destructivity predominates no matter what the gains in "racial equality." Metaracism exists wherever the ends of the large-scale system of the modern Industrial State are considered more important than the human needs of men; it exists whenever production is rationalized, and "order" restored; and it exists wherever we are implored to heal our racial wounds so that, in effect, we can put on a good face to the world.

For who is this "us"? Not the actual selves of people,

but the abstraction of the State—and recent years have demonstrated what this abstraction, eminently powerful, can do to further its own interests under the banner of anti-communism. It is by handing ourselves over to abstractions that we further the plague of history, and it is precisely in racial matters that this transfer of power, control, and self reaches its most ambiguous pitch. For there can be no question as to the most grievous wrong perpetrated by the American people, and no doubt as to where our true national energies should lie. But the most potent influence in straightening out the wrongs—and all agree that only a massive national effort can sort out the disasters suffered by black people because of white repulsion and neglect—is the very same Industrial State, already swollen by history, that seeks to arrogate to itself the rest of the awesome power of the rationalized plague. Are we to add to the military-industrial complex a metaracist-industrial complex? The two may well become one, for nothing in our culture is so free from gross race prejudice as the military-industrial complex; and nothing might involve a more militaristic extroversion of aggression than the large-scale abstracting away of individual selves into a metaracist society.

Consider the depth and intensity of race feelings contained within individuals, and consider the effect if these individuals were to be "integrated" into a larger metaracist unit. As we know, such a transformation would leave unchanged the underlying pattern of fantasies and symbols that nourish our culture. What it would change would be the pattern of control and discharge, by turning outward and performing with large-scale machines what had been done individually. The individuals in such a metaracist system would retain their unconscious id linkages to the outer aggression of the State, and receive from it a pleasure whose symbolic abstraction is balanced by an immense multiplication of technical power. (This equation probably accounts in part for the fact that Vietnam, which is our least fervid, most "objectively necessary" war, has to be the scene of such an oversaturation, such a grotesque superfluity of bombing; it is as if we could not otherwise hear the noise from such a great distance.) And while the will of destruction is done, the voice of conscience—the intense guilt that most sensitive white Americans feel about racial injustice—disappears, leeched out of the self with the rest of the superego power that has passed to the larger unit. This situation of unconscious gratification, forestalled guilt, and impersonal participation is one which will scarcely be questioned by the people within it; indeed, as with the other vicious cycles inherent within our cultural matrix, endless acceleration is its only possible course.

And the spiral points outward, perhaps toward new imperial ventures. The "third world" of dark-skinned countries, fresh from the nineteenth-century version of imperialism, presents a prime object for the exteriorized aggression of the Industrial State. The growing gap between the wealth of the West and the desperate poverty of the "underdeveloped"[57] nations, insures that intense historical conflict will occur between them for at least the remainder of this century. Ample pretext for idealistic conquest will thereby be offered to America, and the struggle of whiteness against blackness will accordingly be enacted on a global scale.

Metaracism continues in the traditional American pattern of reform: a wrong is spotted (when it becomes threatening); efforts are made to redress it; and these efforts lead to a reduction of the threat, a rationalization of the basic power-generating structures, an easing—in-

[57] A wretched word—"overexploited" would be better.

deed a further purification—of the white conscience; and either the neglect of the black victim, or the infliction upon him of a new variety of indignity. Because of their threat to the order of things, sharp protest has been raised against black poverty and oppression. A torrent of words has followed, token changes have been made, racism has been formally and legally repressed out of American culture, and the nation has continued its dehumanization and leapt forward into an unspeakably grotesque idealistic-nihilistic adventure in an obscure Asian country. No one can prove the connection; and yet the timing, the quality of means and aims, the whole conduct of this war, fits into the pattern of exteriorized aggression won by the State through perfection of its inner controls over people and production. And so it is not difficult to venture the hypothesis that the Vietnam war, which, many agree, has inflamed the American racial crisis, has been itself spurred by that crisis. Thus the two crises mutually stimulate one another in yet another vicious cycle, and the perception of this is what gives our times such an anxious and torn quality.

The only conceivable justification for metaracism would be its success in eliminating racial oppression. Perhaps all the costs could be borne if this one aim were achieved. For if it were, if blacks were at last to achieve their goals of dignity and autonomy, then much else would right itself. But here is the critical problem about the approaches America has chosen to deal with its racial dilemma, and why we consider metaracism, though free from prejudiced thinking, a variant of racism. Despite all the efforts of liberal reform, the lot of blacks, though different, is hardly better now in America than it has been at any other time. Although many black people have achieved equality by dint of their own striving, the New Industrial State has also created the black urban masses.

The time is long past when we can lay the blame for their problems upon that benighted whipping boy of liberalism, the Bad South. They arose directly from the basic operations of the industrial order, which metaracism now seeks to defend and rationalize. But we do not rationalize a system such as ours: we only displace its terms from one area to another, and maintain meanwhile the underlying connection. We may exteriorize beyond our shores, or we may—and have—directed the destructive, pulverizing forces of the matrix inward. And the more abstract those forces, the more alienated and dehumanized the objects of their destruction. Thus, the symbolism of dominative racism is an intimately oppressed, narcissistically held body; of aversive racism, a shunned body, fading into excrement; and in metaracism, an inorganic body, fully quantifiable into welfare statistics, brought from farms to concrete abysses of cities, made stone-like, human rubble to merge into the rotting tenements of their ghettos.

A host of specific discriminatory practices converge and prey upon the slums. We see them in the activities of police, unions and employers, and we see them, in different forms, but equally real, in the educational and welfare systems. But whatever their particular structure, all the discriminatory practices meet and join at their cultural root: the worship of production and the material, the impersonal search for gain, the deadening of the world in the interests of that search, the abstracting of the self in the course of that search, and the ultimate visitation upon the deadened world of the anal-sadistic fantasies of our culture, whether by one's own hand, by machine or by computer. And so the black urban masses have been left out of progress, to be reserved instead for the role of objects of the darkness of that progress.

Because no one historical phase of a phenomenon can at once totally replace an earlier phase, today's urban blacks find themselves targets of a mixture of the three ideal types of racism. The black urban slum dweller suffers dominative racism at the hands of the police, aversive racism at the hands of white employers, unions and shopkeepers, and metaracism at the hands—can one use such a concrete metaphor?—of dehumanized welfare agencies. All are "necessary" parts of our culture. The police, after all, only represent that direct domination which culture must keep in reserve if indirect domination is to work properly, and which must be applied from time to time, or all the time, depending on the severity of the case, to elements outside the advanced form of cultural equation. And similarly, the aversive tactics of employers, unionists and shopkeepers only reflect the fact that we are still a bourgeois society, permeated by the attitudes characteristic of this stage of cultural growth. Metaracism differs from the aversive phase of racism's growth, because the individuals who work machines and computers need not be bigoted at all for racist degradation to continue. These workers need only be well-oiled technocrats who may virtuously share in the best intentions: the machines, computers, agencies, corporations and bureaus they man will do the work objectively for them. Of course, they identify with the workings of the institutions they serve, but identification is an unconscious mechanism.

The destructive needs of the matrix are met, then, by its three stages of realization working in concert. And the result has been the creation of a desperate and nihilistic underclass of people. Paradoxically, this is both what the Industrial State wants and what it doesn't want, and it is a paradox that defines both the current race crisis and the failure of our symbolic matrix to deal with it. For the matrix, as expressed by the current stage of the modern Industrial State, wants people who are numbers, but it also needs people who are degraded by its operations. It professes otherwise: that by abstracting people and things it can produce more, and that by producing more, it can save the enumerated people within itself. But these people have already been swallowed and digested by the unconscious terms of the matrix, those anal-sadistic fantasies that get negated yet expressed by the abstraction of the world. And these people happen to have been the ones left over from the previous stage of exploitation; they are the very ones who need "saving," and their skin is black. Thus both abstraction and degradation are suffered by the black urban poor. Their being reduced *both* to a numerical cipher and to a degraded object makes it less possible all the time for them to fit into the productive systems of the State. Worse, the double reduction makes poor blacks more "troublesome"—exactly what the State deplores, and exactly what further stimulates its efforts at rationalization and control.

Such a process has been afoot for the past two decades, a time during which the Industrial State has grown phenomenally in power, but has proven increasingly unable to control its inner workings, or to bring that ease to its people which, according to official ideology, would come from material plenty. Matters began coming to a head in the early sixties, spurred by a series of events: the inability to support the puppet government in Vietnam against an indigenous rebellion; the failure of the ideals of the more moderate elements of the movement for black equality; and possibly the murder of John Kennedy in 1963. By 1964 this unsuccessful process was out of hand on two mutually stimulating fronts. Aggression was then turned outward full scale in Vietnam; and the black masses, long somnolent, struck out at home against the system that degraded them. The presence of their revolutionary potential should hardly have been surprising, though it came as a shock to the eternally complacent average white

American. Indeed, the only questions about it should have been its timing and result—for once started, the black rebellion radically alters our cultural situation.

Never having been granted the elementary humanity that would enable them to be included in moral equations, black people have proven unresponsive to and therefore uncontrollable by the attenuated form of cultural super-ego so useful to the productive needs of the Industrial State. The blackness long imposed upon them has made them invisible; now they will no longer be controlled by white society. They ignore the warnings of American leaders who dredge up ideological restraints, such as religion and respect for law and order. The symbols have a particular meaning for blacks, implanted historically, but it is hardly the meaning our leaders would like them to have: for the God is a Caucasian, supervising the purification of white consciences at the expense of their blackness; while law and order are the conditions of white productivity and black degradation.

With the failure of control comes regression—but it takes place within the terms of the matrix that imposed its negative image upon blacks. And these negatives cancel out in the id; within it, only the wish to include and destroy is expressed. And so the mobs loot the stores of gaudy manufactured things, and burn the filthy tenements in which they have been enclosed, attacking the well-intentioned firemen who, wishing to preserve property, stand flabbergasted at such nihilism.

Also attacked are the police, who have for so long been to black people the direct representatives of white power over them, the foot upon their neck. Whatever the police do in their own right to justify this image, it is plain that they are essentially but the tools—and hence, in a way, the victims as well—of a larger order.

On the other hand, the police, as well as those ranks of

Americans who righteously support them, have gained greatly in power through their physical resistance to the cutting edge of the black rebellion. And herein lies one of the great radical changes brought about in our society by this rebellion, changes that threaten to overturn the whole order of the matrix.

This change, a rise in white reaction, involves the return to authoritarianism and the worship of law and order as ends in themselves, or perhaps—as voiced by some of its extreme adherents who slowly gain power as the center gives way under the strain of violence—even to a new order of fascism. Any further move in this direction would be a calamity, both to the liberal-humanitarian tradition that has been allowed to flourish alongside the growth of our symbolic matrix, and to the power of the modern Industrial State, which leans itself upon abstracted, technically informed, fluid operations, all of which would be seriously compromised under an authoritarian order. Since these cultural elements contain a great deal of aggression, their weakening might induce a turn beyond fascism, into an American version of Nazism—i.e., a vicious cycle of endless regression, an orgiastic return to pure unbridled dominative (and anal-sadistic) racism yoked to dreams of world conquest. This gruesome prospect which, implemented with nuclear weaponry, and met by other totalitarian orders, could mean the quietus of humanity itself, is quite imaginable within the overall terms of our culture. For the aggressive energy of that culture, though patiently abstracted and refined over centuries of Western growth, is quite capable of draining into unbridled form, and might in fact choose exactly some such dynamically charged conduit as racism for its expression. Nazi Germany taught us this lesson.

The other drastic alteration proved by the black rebellion is, of course, that which has occurred in black people themselves. Through open defiance, encouraged by leaders such as Malcolm X and his radical successors, blacks have cleansed the symbol of blackness, stripped it of its accumulated false humility, and have in effect proceeded toward the regeneration of their *own* symbolic matrix based upon a positive concept of blackness. That this return to dignity has been possible at all, is a testimonial to the strength of humanity to resist oppression, and a great sign of hope for black and white alike. That it should have to become real through anger and destruction may seem deplorable, but it is unhappily necessary under the crushing terms of the Western symbolic matrix that would not, could not, itself grant humanity to those who had once been property. Here, in this heroic act, is a real break in the endlessly destructive dialectic of our matrix. But whether the liberation begun with the new sense of black dignity will spread throughout culture, depends in greatest measure upon the responses of white society.

The white response has hardly been positive to date, except for a perhaps saving remnant of youth who can see their way to this goal. But even they arise dialectically, spurred into life by the rising giant of the plague, and awakened to what the culture is about by such monstrosities as Vietnam, or by the headlong growth of the metaracist Industrial State. Meanwhile, the forces of authoritarian reaction also take strength from these frustrations. And so it is that, though many black people have been able both to attain their new dignity and to retain at the same time some glimmer of hope in the American system, the compatibility between these two aspects of their lives grows steadily weaker, to be ever more replaced by the attitude that a positive blackness has no place in the white nightmare of our culture.

Where all this will end is no one's province to predict.

One would hope that our creative people will follow the lead of the vanguard—those who, black and white, have contributed to the beginnings of liberation for black people—into a new dignity, and that we will devise a new inclusive national identity based upon humanity, and not upon color, power and things. Yet even the moderate hope that white Americans will simply admit black people into the present level of bourgeois white society, is unhappily contrary both to the present level of racial passion and to the general drift of our history, which shows us that gains in inclusion or sublimation of differences are accompanied by a freeing up of destructiveness elsewhere. Thus we must consider the possibility of at least two forms of malignant cultural response to the race crisis.

First, there is the possibility that the black rebellion, feeding upon its frustrations, will turn into guerrilla warfare and frank revolution, and bring on in turn the fascist regression that already looms so large. And, second, one might wonder whether the system will find some way—some ingenious Commission, some fruitful "partnership between the public and private sectors," some genuine technological miracle—to muddle through the crisis without undergoing any basic change. This would mean a removal to yet another stage of abstraction and would signal the full triumph of metaracism—a step in which the cultural superego, capitalizing once more on strife, will incorporate strife into itself, make structural what had been dynamic, turn it out again in a new symbolic attenuation, and sublimate the selves of men into still further reaches of technocratic banality. This possibility, scarcely less unhappy than that of fascism, would bear with it even more of that extroverted aggression upon nature and other peoples which we have discussed earlier. It would mean a further distancing of people from each other, a further decline in individual autonomy with a complementary increase in manipulation, and a further increase in the kinds of oral-narcissistic mental disturbances that already are so familiar in clinical practice. The malaise which Freud postulated as the conscious derivative of the repressed guilt—this pervasive sense of pointlessness, ennui and comfortable despair that already haunts our times—is bound to increase with the growth of civilization, and can scarcely be expected to diminish as culture perfects its control over man. Moreover, the result, while bland and smooth, may reach the same endpoint as that attained by fascist regression: the creation, perhaps indeed by 1984, of a totalitarian State. A State in which reduced men will love Big Brother: Brother now, and not Father, signaling the perfection of indirect domination, the full lateral, fraternal intrusion into personality, the usurpation of blind Eros by the will of domination. When the cultural superego reaches full power, it shall take over entirely the function of the individual superego to control the objects of one's love, and shall adapt love to the ends of the State, at last fully rationalized. On the way to this goal, it would complete the distancing between people, and thereby create the essential precondition of totalitarianism—loneliness. "What prepares men for totalitarian domination in the non-totalitarian world," writes Hannah Arendt, "is the fact that loneliness, once a borderline experience usually suffered in certain marginal social conditions like old age, has become an everyday experience of the ever-growing masses of our century."

And finally, if it is true that aggression is displaced outward by a society as it perfects its control over more internal manifestations such as those of racism, then this displacement, paralleled by the development of technology, poses a threat that, though continually predicted by a host of observers, is yet somehow unimaginable—and all the more dangerous for that. For technology is, along with fashion, one of the twin idols of modern culture. It therefore becomes easily invested with magical powers, including the power to discharge the kind of aggression we have been discussing. And by the continual attenuation of symbol, by its never-ending abstraction, awareness of culture's malignancy may disappear from a consciousness that strives to guard against it, and especially from the consciousness of those expert technocrats who, supposedly well-intentioned and rational themselves, blindly discharge the unconscious will of culture. We now number weapons of incalculable violence among our magical machines; and the prospect before us, of a culture increasing its external aggressivity as it abstracts out what has heretofore been bound in racism, is terrifying indeed. The years of certain turmoil ahead, when these several elements wrestle confusedly with each other while enormous reservoirs of previously contained destruction stand ready to be released, may well pose the greatest threat to humanity since the advent of civilization. The darkness sequestered in racism may yet come to rest over black and white alike.

CHAPTER 9
WRETCHED
INFIDEL

Our time itself tends, secretly—or rather anything but secretly; indeed, quite consciously, with a strangely complacent consciousness, which makes one doubt the genuineness and simplicity of life itself and which may perhaps invoke an entirely false, unblest historicity—it tends, I say, to return to those earlier epochs; it enthusiastically re-enacts symbolic deeds of sinister significance, deeds that strike in the face the spirit of the modern age, such, for instance, as the burning of the books and other things of which I prefer not to speak.

Thomas Mann, *Dr. Faustus*

WE HAVE SKETCHED in some of the broad outlines of racism and can now see it for what it is: the systematic exclusion of another from humanity, based superficially upon his color or ethnic origin, and profoundly upon one's own participation in a historical process that degrades him. We have traced in some detail its tangled course in America and have established some ground for understanding the broad extent and deep passion of this delusion. For racism is truly one of the discontents of civilization, and represents its inner attempt to purify itself of the guilt and rage that went into its historical growth. A culture's racism is the reflection of its attempt to introduce spurious boundaries into the otherwise uncontrollable processes of its history. Thus it exists throughout the West and, dialectically, wherever the West has laid its hand; indeed it exists, though in considerably different forms, wherever men have attempted to define themselves within a dominative order. Racism is a disease, a historical ill, a disorder of the historical self, and it reflects the fullness of that self even as it reveals its inadequacies. For wherever the sense of individual self is most highly developed and at the same time most dynamically torn—and where is this more true than in the West, and most of all, in America?—racism is there most instilled into the fabric of culture. We have seen that racism is an organic part of culture, intertwined in its Western form with a constellation of related historical issues: fused most of all with the disjunction of self from body, and with the fabrication of those purified deadened body-surrogates we worship under the term property. It is the outcome of the West's assault upon the living world to create this idolatrous property, of an attempt, existing beneath white rationalizations, to take back from the world what we fancy was taken from us in the process of separation.

And this sense of loss is most intensely organized, for reasons of historical accident, mental fantasy and biological fact, about the perception of body colors.[58] Racism abstracts the color of the living body into non-colors of extreme value, black and white. Within this organization, black represents the shade of evil, the devil's aspect, night, separation, loneliness, sin, dirt, excrement, the inside of the body; and white represents the mark of good, the token of innocence, purity, cleanliness, spirituality, virtue, hope. But is this extreme polarity, the one all bad, the other all good, really so simple? Rather than the symbolic polarity, which is, after all, arbitrary, is it not the activity that generates this polarity which counts—the psychohistorical effort by which blackness and whiteness are generated as

[58] Studies of Rorschach tests have shown that the perception of color is diffuse, emotively charged and, most important, that it precedes more refined discriminations of form and content. Therefore, within symbolic equations, the color term will retain the emotional charge and link together numerous levels of finer meaning.

figments of value and imposed upon the world? And granted this, is it not possible for whiteness to lose the artificial value we give to it, and take on a more sinister aspect? The problem would then reside in that mentality that needs to reduce the world to simple terms, for a world so reduced is a world lost.

Racism, which diminishes its object to non-human status, also diminishes its perpetrator: all are losers by its terms. It does so, in the final analysis, by diminishing life, by reducing it to an abstraction, the better to manage it historically. And racism thereby becomes part of the wider problem of man's compact with the natural world in which he finds himself. And at this level, the psychohistorical problem is best studied through its artistic realization.

Art draws upon the current, historically determined flux of symbolic activity, but it does so only to transform it into something of universal and new meaning. When artistic effort falls short of transcendental purpose, it remains, no matter how well wrought, mannerism, gesture, ideology, even if it is fashionable or greatly successful in its time. An art that is true has a radical content, by which we mean literally that it goes to the symbolic roots of our experience, lays them bare and re-creates them anew for us in their immediate form. The remoteness and attenuation of symbol in the modern age has forced art to become ever more radical in its attempt to bridge the gap between surface and root experience. Today, when atomization and vacuity are the rule, the extreme becomes commonplace: nothing shocks, because nothing matters, for the forms of our symbolic activity have become so remote, so *whitened* by history, as to become anesthetic. This is part of that larger problem of lost sensibility within which we include racism; it merges with racism in the central metaphor of whiteness.

Whiteness, blankness, the attenuation of dynamism into empty form—this is the central structural problem of modern symbolism. We have seen its trace in racism, and how, as in metaracism, abstraction passes beyond even the noncolors of white and black to make men indifferent ciphers within the productive systems of culture. This passage beyond, the final slipping away from the immediate world of experience, is what in a very broad sense makes racism the core problem of contemporary history, and skin color the arena within which men blindly grasp the absurd tags of their concrete differentiation. The older forms of racism represent, then, intermediate stages of this general blankening, stages in which true color has been lost and black and white still remain as intense tokens of value, the stages before black and white alike fade away into a general nothingness.

A great deal of modern art has concerned itself with the implications of this profound symbolic shift, even when its subject is remote from racism. Thus *Moby Dick*, since it is perhaps the greatest American novel, can reveal more about the problem which underlies racism than any other source. Not that *Moby Dick* is a truly modern novel; indeed it is one of those anticipatory works that freshly and naively deal with problems that had not yet reached the full paralytic height in which we see them today. Melville was able to move with the ebullience of his time into the grimness of ours, and so to state what was as yet only latent: the problem of whiteness. And this vision made his work so advanced as to be considered freakish in its own time and to be destined to both critical and commercial failure. By the same terms, an utterly inferior book, *Uncle Tom's Cabin,* written virtually at the same time, became an immense success and influenced the history whose roots Melville exposed.

Both novels derived from the same milieu and the same

time; and both must have been at least partially influenced by the same historical events, most notably the ill-fated compromise of 1850. Rather than abating the controversy over slavery, this measure had but exposed its intransigence and had made all sensitive Americans aware of the destructive immensity of the race problem.

Uncle Tom's Cabin took this dynamic situation and furthered the distortions which white culture had already made. It thereby placed itself squarely in the mainstream of idealistic American reform, and appealed to the destructive falsification inherent in that reform: attack the crime, appease and feed the conscience, and abstract the victim into a new level of degradation. Thus arose the subhuman stereotype of Uncle Tom, the helpless, devoted Negro who would be consumed by the badness in whites if he were not saved by their goodness. And badness reposed exclusively in the rapacious Southerner, goodness exclusively in the Northerners, who were soothed by this and other related works which allowed them to avoid the black man and to further their own abstracted gain. Such a dispensation deserved reward, and Mrs. Stowe became overnight one of America's leading intellects.

Meanwhile, Melville, who had been a successful purveyor of fashionable noble savage fantasies, became reduced in the public mind to an eccentric crank, and died a forgotten failure. Eccentric indeed, for his work strayed all the way from the banal center to the very roots of historical experience.

The themes which are of interest to us in *Moby Dick* deal with the problems of color, of separation, and of man's dealings with his natural world. Melville dissects them out of their tangled unity, and embodies their elementary qualities in discrete people and substances. And the people differentiate themselves into lightness and darkness. Leslie Fiedler has developed this idea most fully, by demonstrating that much of American fiction pairs white, male lead characters with an inseparable dark companion. This device, which reached full bloom in the creation of Cooper's Pathfinder and Chingachgook, or Twain's Huck Finn and Nigger Jim, sustains itself today in a host of popular creations, beginning with the Lone Ranger and Tonto and ending (would it were so!) with any number of television series. We have here another representation of the abstractive splitting characteristic of our culture[59] and essential to its potency. But nowhere is it more systematically turned to the purposes of art than in *Moby Dick*.

As Fiedler observes in the study of *Moby Dick* contained in his *Love and Death in the American Novel,* the "essential themes" of the book are "projected by the dark skinned characters . . . who represent the polar aspects of the id, beneficent and destructive": Queequeg, the Polynesian harpooner who accompanies Ishmael, and the Parsee, Fedallah, whom Ahab smuggles aboard the *Pequod* to be his personal harpooner. (In addition to these, Melville creates the cabin-boy Pip and other dark harpooners, Daggoo the Negro, and Tashtego the Indian, thus rounding out the inventory of "dusky tribes.") All the dark men represent impulse, and all the light ones, intellect and control. Accordingly, the whites need the darkness to execute their will. The polarities—between dark and light, and fundamentally, in Fiedler's terms, between love and death—are not absolute, however, nor are they all congruent; rather they are refractive surfaces of a deeper unity. Queequeg is of all the characters the purest essence of Eros, the one who includes and draws together, and does so both in life—in the moment he hugs Ishmael in homosexual embrace—and in death—when the orphan Ishmael

[59] This is not limited, to be sure, to America, but is an element of Western literature, dating as far back as *Don Quixote*.

floats to the safety of his rescuing mother-ship on the Polynesian's coffin. For Queequeg had slept death-like in this wooden box; and now, the demonic chase done, Eros sleeps in death beneath the shroud of the sea-mother, while Ishmael lives buoyed up by the final sacrifice. Without Eros we die; yet the id is not all Eros, but contains, fused with it, the destructive urges, the wish to death, Thanatos. And Eros, blind, can pull death into itself, as Ahab, under cover of darkness, smuggles the diabolical Parsee who shall execute his revenge onto the *Pequod* and keeps him hidden there in the darkness of the whale-boat.

The dark energy must be hidden, but remains yoked to the mental direction of whiteness. And Melville insists, anticipating Freud, that the unconscious—the hidden dark energy of which he had a very clear and profound notion —is but seemingly controlled by the conscious; and that in reality it drives consciousness along as a wind blows the ship, a horse bears its rider, or as Moby Dick himself lures Ahab to his doom. "The subterranean miner that works in us all, how can one tell whither leads his shaft by the ever shifting, muffled sound of his pick? Who does not feel the irresistible arm drag . . . ?" Thus blackness and whiteness, darkness and lightness were originally one, and remain one in that realm of experience that comes before words, and of which words themselves are but a faint tracing.

The distinction between blackness and whiteness is made by separation, as a child fears the dark upon which he has projected his rage, only after separation from his mother—i.e., only after the event which has generated both rage and fear. And so, for Melville, whiteness and blackness are the diametric arcs of a circle that issues from phenomenal reality, splits apart, and meets behind it. The process that drives the circle away from the screen of reality, and that separates man from his world, is abstraction. It is the peculiar vision of Ahab, for whom "All visible objects, are but as pasteboard masks." And disjunction from reality creates an endless suspicious tension with it. "But in each event—in the living act, the undoubted deed—there, some unknown but still reasoning thing puts forth the mouldings of its features from behind the unreasoning mask. If man will strike, strike through the mask! How can the prisoner reach outside except by thrusting through the wall?" To Ahab's thinking, "the white whale is that wall, shoved near to me." But this is what he *thinks* he knows; actually, the "unknown but still reasoning thing" is himself—his hidden unconscious self, abstracted, separated, capable of being projected outward onto suitable entities, such as a whale or, as with the rest of the Caucasian peoples, upon other, darker races: unknown yet knowing selves to be struck through the mask of abstraction.

In the novel, the great whale is the appropriate symbolic referent. And what is it that makes him so suitable to symbolically represent the inner struggle, what is it about him that brings the demonic to the surface? In part, of course, it is his power and size, corresponding to the grandiosity of human narcissism; in part, certainly, it is his destructiveness, which hints at the havoc wrought by man; but most of all, and beyond these obvious traits, Moby Dick's *whiteness* is the stimulus to the chase. Just as all that is dark in the world comes down to that which is hidden, so does that which is white come down to that which does the hiding, that which acts on reality to segregate it, that which drives the circle away from the screen. And the whiteness of the whale becomes the subject of the most difficult and puzzling chapter of the book, and yet the most important, for, as Melville writes at its beginning (after admitting that "I almost despair of putting it in a comprehensible form"): "explain myself I must, else all these chapters might be naught." Thus Melville's commentary on whiteness, the quality of which gives a "pre-eminence [that] applies to the human race itself, giving the white man ideal mastery over every dusky tribe."

Whiteness brings power and horror alike, the two feeding upon each other across the splitting of the historical ego. Splitting, denial, negation of darkness create within an emptiness which makes the world a pasteboard mask, deadened and suitable to be worked over. The disjunction makes true color suspect and nothing but daubs on the mask: "all deified Nature absolutely paints like the harlot, whose allurements cover nothing but the charnel-house within." And it creates a sense of white, invisible nothingness which the white man perceives in himself and projects onto the Leviathan to be attacked. Thus color is life alone, but black and white both are life-in-death, the one forcibly hidden, the other invisible to a vision for whom what is concretely visible is but a mask. And this is but to restate the racist dilemma: that by oppressing and blackening the dark-skinned races, Caucasians pursue a course that whitens their own self, making it chalky, abstract, separated—eventually blank and invisible. And invisibility is no mere frustration, nor even simply a loss; it becomes for the white man a white, cold flame that endlessly dissolves all before it. Invisibility—which was imposed on blacks but sprang from whites—is the full horror; and, in our time, the ground for totalitarianism. Thus Melville writes: "Though in many of its aspects this visible world seems formed in love, the invisible spheres were formed in fright . . ."; and "whiteness, . . . at once the most meaning symbol of spiritual things, nay, the very veil of the Christian's Deity; and yet should be as it is—the intensifying agent in things the most appalling to mankind."

Black and white are only representations of mankind split within and between itself. The split, conceptualized psychologically in the mental structures of the id, ego and superego, is realized—as it must be—in the historical and racist world created by the ego. An inner split cannot exist without an outer one. Disjoined, separated from men and from nature, the ego sees true, living colors as "but subtle deceits, not actually inherent in substances, but only laid on from without." And deceived substances have no life of their own. Melville here prefigures Whitehead's critique of the Western scientific mentality which deadens the world. But he also goes beyond it to say that such a mentality also hates the world, and seeks to further destroy what it has already abstracted. Nature is a harlot to the abstracted self, which is forced to believe that "the great principle of light, for ever remains white or colorless in itself, and if operating without medium upon matter, would touch all objects, even tulips and roses, with its own blank tinge." Realizing this, for his hostile attacks upon "matter" have separated him from it and given him such a whitened vision, man, "[stabbed] from behind with the thought of annihilation when beholding the white depths of the milky way," terrified by the rage within, the threat of retribution from without and loneliness beyond all, this "wretched infidel gazes himself blind at the monumental white shroud that wraps all the prospect around him. And of all these things the Albino whale was the symbol. Wonder ye then at the fiery hunt?"

The "wretched infidel," who is Ahab—and the Ahab in all of us—projects the blankness of his own whiteness upon the whale and seeks to forestall his own annihilation through annihilating the world. But by doing this, he only retains within himself and stimulates the growth of what has been projected outside, and induces an endlessly accelerating split. Melville states this in a passage which anticipates much that Freud would later develop. In describing Ahab's madness, he writes of

> the eternal, living principle or soul in him; and in sleep, being for the time dissociated from the characterizing mind, which at other times employed it for its outer vehicle or agent, it spontaneously sought escape from the scorching contiguity of the frantic things, of which, for the time, it was no longer an integral. But as the mind does not exist unless leagued with the soul, therefore it must have been that, in Ahab's case, yielding up all his thoughts and fancies to his one supreme purpose; that purpose, by its own sheer inveteracy of will, forced itself against gods and devils into a kind of self-assumed, independent being of its own. Nay, could grimly live and burn, while the common vitality to which it was conjoined, fled horror-stricken from the unbidden and unfathered birth. Therefore, the tormented spirit that glared out of bodily eyes, when what seemed Ahab rushed from his room, was for the time but a vacated thing, a formless somnambulistic being, a ray of living light, to be sure, but without an object to color, and therefore a blankness in itself. God help thee, old man, thy thoughts have created a creature in thee; and he whose intense thinking thus makes him a Prometheus; a vulture feeds upon that heart for ever; that vulture the very creature he creates.[60]

It is this blank living light that finds its object in Moby Dick, whom Ahab seeks to bring down, and to die upon, fused at last to the principle in nature which mankind's separation has made malevolent. The other humans whom we subjugate and segregate into races, the material world which we dedifferentiate and hostilely work over in the name of technology, what are these but projections—external, hated tokens of a self that is spiraling away into blank abstraction? As Shakespeare observed, only thinking —symbolic abstraction—imposes goodness and badness on the world. And imposed badness may return, Frankenstein-like, to turn upon its author and force a new twist of

[60] Herman Melville, *Moby Dick* (New York, Modern Library, 1944), p. 201.

the spiral. Let us remember here the remarks (p. 13, epi-graph, Chapter 2) of a contemporary creative spirit, Mal-colm X, who discerned that the white man in America had created a monstrosity in his midst that would return to haunt him.

In the creation of Ahab, Melville's genius pushed West-ern man's demonic assault upon the natural world to its extreme. It is an extreme point that we ourselves prefigure, in grimmer yet more realistic form, in the nightmare of nuclear holocaust that haunts the modern age. Ahab, of course, is not a realistic character, just as the specter of nuclear holocaust, though potential, may not be realistic. Both are hallucinatory visions of the concentrated destruc-tive wish implanted in us—else we would never sur-vive—checked in actuality by erotic self-interest. But this extreme vision—though terrifying—is an ideological rally-ing point as well. As the whale is Ahab's exteriorization, so is Ahab the exteriorization of the men on the ship; so, indeed, is any leader the embodiment of the ideals of his followers. And Ahab's focused obsession serves to dedicate the *Pequod*'s motley crew, who represent the real men of the world, to their nihilistic chase. This they are all pre-disposed to do. Ishmael himself, an ambiguous figure who represents both the ideal or passively erotic component of man and the actual men of society, admits, before he joins the ship, that amid all his fantasies of whaling, "chief among these motives [being] the overwhelming idea of the great whale himself . . . , [was] one grand hooded phantom, like a snow hill in the air." And if the men on the ship are the ordinary people of the world, what of the men who own the ship and who, as personified by the first mate, Starbuck, would never countenance such insane folly? But let us be fanciful, and, allowing that the *Pequod* and its master represent the repressed unconscious of those of us on the shore, apply the law of association to the passage in which Melville states that whereas the ship-owners "were bent on profitable cruises, the profit to be counted down in dollars from the mint; [Ahab] was intent on an audacious, immitigable and supernatural revenge." By association here, the unconscious purpose of the profit motive is revenge. And, allowing for sublimation and purity of motive, does this wish not correspond to the factual result—not of the *Pequod's* voyage, which goes too far and ends in disaster—but of the "profitable cruises" of the capitalist order? Has not the desire for profit—to count down the world into dollars (and no longer even concretely from the mint)—raped the natural world and brought it to the brink of extinction, no less than the great herds of whales have been destroyed in the headlong vengeful pursuit of profit; no less than the darker races of the world were brought to the edge of doom by the profit that has been wrung from their bodies? And though the whales can do nothing in retribution, the rest of nature, and the races of men as well, have means of exacting their own revenge upon us and our Ahabs. Ahab is then a desublimation of what drives Western culture. There is a part of all of us that leaps up at the insane cry of an Ahab, and will follow him to the end of the universe in search of his immitigable revenge. Indeed, we create Ahabs for this very purpose under the name of statesmen.

But Ishmael, less dramatically interesting than the demonic Ahab, is also a desublimation of what is in us all: Eros reaching out, seeking to rejoin with his dark counterpart and fusing wth his sea-brothers in a baptism of whale sperm—the erotic undoing of the satanic plot against matter. For the astounding episode in which the seamen mutually squeeze the whale sperm, is to be taken for what it literally suggests, and for what, in its intensity, makes it shocking even today: a homoerotic commingling. Homosexual, because the men, whether they be black or white, are all presented as children abandoned by their shore-mother, contained in their ship-mother, and so incapable of an erotic tie that involves more than mutual identification.

The reunion is with the fissioned self, even as, in the Platonic legend, sexes themselves were once one, only to split apart and seek forever after their refusion. And the men relate to each other as children, because they are powerless, not just controlled physically by Ahab's authority, but hypnotized by his maniacal spell. Power, on the *Pequod* and in civilization at large, is the province of the Ahabs of the world.

The powerless self seeks reunion through a love of concrete natural substance, which is not desired for profit or destruction, but accepted in its amorphous givenness: the sperm of the whale. "Those soft, gentle globules ... richly broke to my fingers, and discharged all their opulence, like fully ripe grapes their wine; as I snuffed up that uncontaminated aroma—literally and truly, like the smell of spring violets; ... I forgot all about our horrible oath [to hunt the whale]; in that inexpressible sperm, I washed my hands and my heart of it ... while bathing in that bath, I felt divinely free from all ill-will, or petulance, or malice, of any sort whatsover."

Within the sperm-bath, acting lovingly upon natural matter, the horrid chase recedes and is followed by the creation of an erotic community.

> Squeeze! Squeeze! Squeeze! all the morning long; I squeezed that sperm till I myself almost melted into it; I squeezed that sperm till a strange sort of insanity came over me; and I found myself unwittingly squeezing my co-laborers' hands in it, mistaking their hands for the gentle globules. Such an abounding, affectionate, friendly, loving feeling did this avocation beget; that at last I was continually squeezing their hands, and looking up into their eyes sentimentally; as much as to say,—oh! my dear fellow beings, why, why should we longer cherish any social

acerbities, or know the slightest ill-humor or envy! Come; let us squeeze hands all round; nay let us squeeze ourselves into each other; let us squeeze ourselves universally into the very milk and sperm of kindness.[61]

Why not? Milk and sperm are benign, beloved substances: even the white whale himself, when not in contact with his human symbolizers, presents a "gentle joyousness—a mighty mildness of repose in swiftness." These are natural substances, and the relation to them is not so much homosexual as archaic, for they derive from a stage of human unity which existed even before sexes differentiated themselves—from a ground of infantile wholeness, maternal union.[62] Why not such erotic joyousness; why instead the satanic chase?

The answer lies in the inertia of history. Consider that the route to human community passes back through a concrete grasp of amorphous substance: beloved matter. Consider too the denial in this of the fantasy of filth: hated matter. And compare Ishmael's path with its reversal, the actual path in Western history, in which matter becomes property and dirt: abstracted versions of those feces whose concrete consistency is the same, whose concrete odor and color are the opposite, of whale sperm. Compare then the distinction between Ishmael's "strange sort of insanity" with the "normal" actuality of the anal complex in culture—that sense of imposed horror that can make the world, to us as to Ahab, a "palsied universe [lying] before us a leper." And consider the profound etymological correspondence between matter, matrix, and mother, all transformed by history: matter from milk and

---

[61] *Ibid.*, p. 414.
[62] The very blank whiteness which drives Ahab and Ishmael alike to such paroxysms of revenge, may be also conceptualized as the homogeneous ground of infantile perception, the blank expanse of the mother's breast, termed by the psychoanalyst Bertram Lewin, the dream screen: the backdrop to dream vision.

sperm into shit; the matrix of symbols from vivid life into convulsed dead abstraction; and mother-earth into the province of domination by men who repeat endlessly the fall of Adam from Eden to establish the kingdoms of power, machines and race.

Ahab and Ishmael are both orphans: Ahab, who, we are told, lost his mother at the age of one, lives off the rage of his insults, making the cosmos his goal, the symbol of his lost narcissism; Ishmael conquers loss through brotherhood. If only we could find such brotherhood, some drug as good as whale sperm! But we cannot return, for neither protagonist is whole, each is a split part of the other, and the two combine to represent the eternal struggle between life and death that is the story of evolution, history, and the individual self. Though we would be Ishmaels, there are the Ahabs of the world, and the Ahab within, with which to contend: they grapple within each of us as we leave our infantile fusion and enter civilization; and they contend endlessly as we struggle against the historical plague.

I hope that I have demonstrated why racism has assumed such an agonized and intransigent role in our history. For to state that there is a "gulf between the races," and that there are two "separate but unequal" Americas, is true but superficial. Everyone can see that there is a gulf between the races. What is harder to see, but ultimately more important, is that the gulf is only part of the picture. There are several races in America, but only one American culture; and that culture, the fruit of our history, generates racism for the benefit of a false whiteness. Black Americans have to contend with the awesome problem of living within such a culture. Any sensitive black American who is granted a token of a long-withheld opportunity by one of the great American institutions, soon comes to feel the metaracism implicit in such an advance (as well as the considerable residuum of open racism in the white people he encounters). Accordingly it is not to be expected that blacks of dignity will be as grateful for their boons, as the white conscience demands—and so their struggle will continue.

Whatever the particular black response, the principal task before everyone is to contend with the revolutionary state of our culture. We have learned that this revolutionary situation has resulted neither from chance nor from the plotting of revolutionaries, but from a natural unfolding of cultural forces in the course of our history. And so our struggle with darkness is at last out in the open. Although the sight it presents is grim, its very visibility presents an opportunity, even if, as should be clear by now, the outcome of the struggle is no more than doubtful. Our lot is to be thrown into this struggle, and our only choice is to act as best we can. And, however submerged, we still have Eros on our side, along with its coordinated faculties, a creative intelligence and a free, autonomous ethic. The rest is up to history.

APPENDIX
CULTURAL
PSYCHOLOGY

WHAT FOLLOWS is a theoretical background for the psychological propositions of this study. The presentation is not intended to be complete, but to offer a personal interpretation of a body of theory which is still open to some controversy, while directing the reader's attention to those particular areas which have been stressed in the main portion of the work. It is hoped that it will be neither too simplistic for the expert nor too dense for the newcomer to psychoanalytic thinking.

The following broad questions are to be posed:

1. How does fantasy-based knowledge of the world arise in a person? In particular, are there certain universal aspects of the human situation which lead to universal fantasies? This point must be established if the role of the unconscious mind is to be considered a factor in history. Since the unconscious cannot be known directly, historical evidence of its operation must be inferential. We must therefore at least establish that certain unconscious fantasies about the world have always been part of the human situation—i.e., that the unconscious has been continually available to be put to historical use. The specific uses to which unconscious fantasies have been put are then the province of particular historical studies—such as the history of racism.

2. I hope to demonstrate the existence and general nature of some of these universal fantasies, in particular those centering about the ideas of dirt and power. This

brings us halfway. The second task will be to account for the cultural spread of such ideas, to see how the individual fantasies of an entire population may become organized into a cultural whole. I shall have to discuss the kinds of personality structure that arise to bring about the transformation. This will lead us into a discussion of the adaptive portion of the personality, the ego, and its controlling subunit, the superego. Through the mental operations of these parts of the personality, infantile fantasies become transformed, generalized and put to use in culture.

We will see then that culture contains, traced upon its realistic and rational structure, potent remnants of infantile and bodily experience. We will see also that much of culture presents itself to the unconscious mind and is in a kind of equilibrium with that portion of the mind. In short, personality and culture are parallel organisms, each reflecting the other, the one pertaining to an individual, the other to a society.

Our task is to account for the relations between the two organisms. We know that human behavior is immensely variable, and that it is influenced to a far larger extent than previously imagined by a person's social situation. There are precious few absolutes about behavior; we live in a pervasive and powerful social field which molds our personality into the channels provided by culture—including those which underlie racism.

But the sociocultural field is itself a production of men, and mirrors their desires and needs. Clearly, culture must contain, no matter where or when, derivatives of the absolutes of human life. All cultures must, for instance, come to terms with birth and death, sexuality, and hunger. These are universal human situations which must find a kind of organized symbolic structure within any culture.

Of all universal situations, childhood yields the richest store of culturally meaningful symbols. Along with death, it is the great given of man's experience. But while death can only be imagined, childhood is what all men have actually experienced. Further, childhood is the setting for fantasy thinking. Fantasy arises as the specific mode of thought of the child's mind, and so, if we are to study the existence in culture of a fantasy creation such as racism, it is to the infantile roots of mental experience that we must first turn.

We all were children; and we all went through certain necessary changes during that period which have left a permanent impression upon the rest of our lives. I say *necessary*, because without such changes man could never have made use of his biological capacities—he would scarcely have survived, and certainly not prevailed.

But our strength has been gained at the risk—and often the cost—of our conflict. This dilemma will be explored at some length, for it applies to American culture, and to the situation of every infant born into the world since the beginning of mankind. Indeed, if it is true for a culture, it must also be true for an infant—and *vice versa*—for personality and culture are congruent.

We may now look a little more closely into some of those necessary changes which take place during childhood. Let us consider the hypothetical case of a male infant who might have been born into any social group at any time—not to trace out his development in a systematic way, but to describe his situation so that it resembles the condition of those who have entered into the history of racism (we shall, for example, provide him with a nuclear monogamous and patriarchal family). We have chosen to designate this imaginary child as a male because something peculiar to masculine psychology has by and large enabled men to seize the power of history.

The core of the problem is this: the human personality becomes potent by its ability to adapt to the many possibilities of biology and environment. Such adaptability requires a mental plasticity and refinement, an ability to react in a graded way, and the capacity to sort things out. It requires, in short, a principle of differentiation, a function which keeps things apart. Mentality as used in this essay means nothing less than this: a structured kind of experience, one element of which relates to other elements. These structured elements are what we mean by *symbols*; and so mentality may be defined as a kind of experience that uses symbols, whether the symbols be fixed images, words, or distinct feelings. The condition for the success of the human animal is strictly the wealth of his symbolic experience.

But our human infant is born into nothing like this; he enters life in a state of virtual amorphousness. His mental life is the story of the passage from that amorphousness to a refined and differentiated complexity—a *mind*. He must pass from the state of a helpless, attached infant, to that of a free-living *autonomous* adult. This passage is a dynamic process which leads to certain inevitable conflicts, and infinitely varying results of these conflicts therefore accompany each of us throughout our adult, cultural life. And as the conflicts accompany us, so do their symbolic referents, which find representation in social activity and culture.

But again, our baby has no symbols at his disposal for the first few months of life. All that he experiences (this can, of course, only be inferred) is a sequence of tensions and relaxations, according to whether his bodily needs are unsatisfied or satisfied. At first he cannot relate these conditions to anything else in the universe. We may imagine, therefore, that the infant is born with no idea of the world he is to inhabit and act upon.

He is, then, something of a *tabula rasa*. But the slate, though blank, is not without inborn potential. In fact, it is this potential which, coupled with the baby's profound immaturity, makes the human experiment such a powerful one. Our immaturity is a necessary condition for the increased mental potential of the human species. A head with a fully developed human brain could not, after all, pass through the physiological limitations of the mother's pelvis. And so we may presume that evolution selected out a type of hominoid ape who could be born exceptionally immature so as to become exceptionally brilliant later. Indeed, the greater the immaturity, the greater the potential for mental growth.

However, another consequence of the baby's immaturity is as important as his biological potential. For our hypothetical infant is as *helpless* as he is mentally amorphous. He lacks both the mature human mind and the refined animal instinctive pattern. He cannot cling to his mother, and he cannot find the breast on his own; he must be held and fed and carried about—in short, everything must be done for him, or he will die. Therefore, every human group must organize itself to accommodate the immense and prolonged helplessness of its young.

The mother must be all to her infant. But what is his contribution? Is he totally without resource, an utterly passive recipient of nurture? Obviously not. At the least, the baby is able to root and suck at the beginning of his life and so he will begin to organize his experience of the world through his mouth. He is also able to respond to some stimuli, although in a most unorganized way.

The active stirrings of his developing organism begin to assert themselves in the first months of life. Out of these stirrings, and within the all-encompassing bounds of the mother-infant relationship, the earliest and most basic states of mental organization develop. Although we must always bear in mind that mentality throughout life is an organic whole, let us now break down this whole into logical and discrete functional patterns, by considering some of these discrete functions in the developing mind.

As the baby reaches roughly the age of three months, he begins to organize and respond to his first *perceptual* experiences. The perception is of a human face, and the response is a smile. It is doubtful whether this smile has any specificity to it, since the baby will smile at anything, even a mask, that has two eyes and a mouth. Nonetheless, the smile is the first social response; it gives parents great pleasure, and rewards them for their sacrifices on behalf of their young parasite. In terms of the baby's mental experience, we may say that the face and the smile which responds to it are the first stages of symbolic organization, the first differentiation within the infantile primordium, and the precursors of all later mental differentiations.

During the next few months, the baby expands and refines his symbolic organization. He begins to associate a specific face—that of his mother—with a specific set of inner changes: the rise and fall of tension accompanying the nursing situation. During the closing months of the first year of life, the baby makes this discrimination a firm one: he now responds specifically to a given person, he has some idea of what is not that person, and he is developing a specific set of emotional responses to the presence or absence of his mother. He is by now a recognizable person, albeit a simple one. He has entered the human community, because he relates to another person.

This relationship is of a particularly simple kind, however. The infant is by now *attached* to his mother. By this, we mean that his mind includes a solitary, vivid idea of of another human being whose presence is associated with all the pleasure in the baby's life. This is not to assert that the infant feels only pleasure, for the perception of pleasure would not exist without that of pain. Moreover, pain and frustration are fully as important in development as happiness and pleasure. However, the unpleasure and distress that occur with states of unfilled needs are not mentally organized in the early months of life. They are simply discharged with crying, and presumably do not associate themselves with any symbolic notion in the child's mind. The baby at this age, then, though he may show rage, is essentially *unambivalent* in his personal relationships. If all has gone reasonably well up to now, the mental ground will have been laid for (to use Erikson's term) a basic trust in the goodness of reality. Without this fundamental attitude, none of us could endure life's disillusionments. And with it, the child is at his most simple and lovable.

We must consider now another extremely important functional aspect of the developing mentality. It was stated above that the helpless and immature human infant starts his life as a person in a state of attachment; that he "associates" the perception of his mother with states of pleasure; and that he is unambivalent—i.e., loving without hating—in his attachment to his mother. What of the baby's contribution to those events? Is it a matter of reflex or passive learning, or is there some kind of active principle within the organization of the human personality, some sort of valence which directs a person to those parts of the world where his interest lies. Do humans receive their experience or do they strive for it? In short: are we *driven*?

Such a fundamental question deserves a more thorough answer than the scope of this essay permits. It is my opinion that humans are indeed driven, that their *drives* are innate (i.e., biologically given), although greatly unstructured, and that the structure (including the object of the drive) is provided by development—i.e., through the interaction of the developing person with his family and culture.

The basic evidence for the existence of drives is, in my

opinion, the element of striving, or conation, that pervades human behavior. We may speculate that these drives are biologically grounded, and that they represent the energetic remnants of what had been highly structured instinctive patterns in protohuman species which have, as it were, degenerated with the fetalization of the human infant. Thus the exquisitely adaptive instinct of animals becomes the crude urging of human drive, non-adaptive in itself, indeed forcing the organism into situations of difficulty and danger, but also supplying the raw energy for the brilliant exploits of the human spirit.

I am thus following Freud's conception of drive. The drives are twofold in nature: sexual and aggressive. We have, of course, other instinctive patterns—one thinks of hunger—but none have the organizing influence on mental development and function, and so no other instinctual pattern can properly be called a drive. It is doubtful whether sexuality and aggression are ever fully discrete in human behavior. Since our personality functions as an organic whole, we may presume that the two basic drives always exist in states of greater or lesser fusion with each other.

Each drive has a broad aim and many modes of realization, and each is necessary for healthy development. The sexual drive is experienced throughout life (except in the presymbolic stage, when no object can be said to exist) as an urge to approach and join with an object in the world. We use the word *object* to indicate the great variability of the drive's target. At first, we have seen, the object of sexuality—or, in the broadest sense, Eros—is the nursing mother. Here, sexuality is experienced as a diffuse excitement and satisfaction throughout the skin, along with a particular excitation of the mouth. Hence, this first phase has been called the *oral stage* of development. It should be clear, however, that *oral* is but a metaphor which covers a whole range of attachment behavior. From the standpoint of drives, oral means only that the main area of discharge (and so the main site of pleasure) is through the mouth. The object at this stage will be whatever is *symbolically* organized as linked with this pleasurable discharge. Most important of these objects will be the mother, or part of the mother—such as her face or breast—a bottle, or even a part of the child, such as the thumb he sucks in his mother's absence, which he begins to recognize as something which can provide both perception and sensation—i.e., as something which belongs to his body.

Under normal circumstances, this pattern of erotic activity changes, and is eventually focused upon the genitals and the person of someone of the opposite sex. But we also know that in the course of this development Eros takes a most involved path, investing various parts of the body with sexual significance, and extending its influence to aspects of reality until it binds the whole of life in a network of desires in various forms. In its fullest sense, Eros is whatever binds together aspects of our experience. Indeed, the thoughts and symbols invested by erotic desires become the wishes and fantasies which concern us in this essay.

The case of the aggressive drive is similar, though more problematic, than that of the sexual drive. Aggression has all the elementary qualities of Eros: a raw striving, relatively undifferentiated, able to undergo any number of transmutations, and able to direct itself to any number of objects. In contrast to Eros, whose elemental aim is to *join* with an object, aggression is in the most basic sense an impulsion to *act* upon an object, and to alter the object of its activity. Thus its range of expression extends from a "healthy" sense of mastery to the most unbridled and seemingly gratuitous aim of destruction. Seen in this light, aggression loses its connotation of badness and becomes instead a basic propulsion to act upon the world. What is "bad"—i.e., destructive—is reserved to a particular outcome of aggression, one all too universal, to be sure, but not so much a biological given as it is the consequence of the human situation.

One crucial criterion of a drive is that it be innate, biologically given. We all grant that sexuality is innate, but we feel less certain about aggression. Many students of behavior have maintained that aggression is not a drive at all, but only a response to frustration. Whatever the full answer, it is overwhelmingly likely, judging from the record of human behavior, that either aggression is an innate human quality, or the frustrations that produce aggression are so basic and universal as to raise it to the level of a biological given. This study is grounded in the assumption that aggression is an inevitable part of the human situation, and that it becomes so *both* through biological givens and through the frustrations imposed by life. Thus we maintain that men do have an innate aggression, although it is of an unstructured and greatly modifiable nature. In the course of development, certain frustrations *inevitably* play upon this aggressive propensity. Human aggression is then molded by these inevitable frustrations, and channeled into certain basic conflicts. These conflicts, in turn, generate fantasies in which aggressive (and sexual) wishes are directed toward particular symbolic organizations.

Let us return to our baby. His first symbolic notion is of a nurturing presence, and his initial investment of this is entirely loving. So far he has completed the first great step in the development of his personality: he is attached to the world.

But this is not enough; indeed, if the baby goes no further, he will surely die, for the maternal presence is suitable only to the needs of a helpless creature. Moreover, mothers cannot always be available, and they certainly cannot be as perfect as the all-encompassing wish of the infant makes them. There must be a disillusionment if the baby is ever to grow. After his attachment, he must detach himself. The healthy mother knows this, and gradually but firmly begins separating herself from her infant as he enters the second year of life. And the healthy infant experiences his growth as a thrust away from his mother. Each partner in the mother-infant unity then begins the push.

In mental terms, the outcome of this process is a sense of the baby's *self* as distinct from the rest of the world. We all need this sense of self in order to organize and direct our lives; without it there would be no useful interaction with other people or with any part of the world. And yet we are born with nothing that can be described as a sense of self. The idea is won by the baby through an elaborate process of differentiation. The first idea of a nurturing presence has no gradation between a me and a not-me. The baby experiences only an "it," which gives pleasure and is loved. This "it" includes, of course, both his mother and himself, but he does not know this yet. And he will not know of the difference until he *acts* upon the "it" and separates himself from it.

For this action he can count upon his innate aggressive drive. Whether through biting the nipple or pushing away the breast, or in actively exploring his crib, the baby is propelling himself into selfhood by means of his inborn aggression. Note that no destructiveness is necessarily involved: only a pushing away, a thrust toward mastery. Again, the healthy mother tolerates this and encourages it. So far, neither destructiveness nor grounds for conflict are in evidence. Of course the mother may (and often does) respond to the thrust of her baby with anxiety or counter-aggression. It is plain that such behavior on her part will make matters more difficult for the infant; such a counter-reaction generally provides the nucleus of emotional disorder. In fact, since the mother was once an infant herself, it provides the nucleus for the *perpetuation* of emotional disorder.

But let us forget for our purpose of the moment what we can never forget in reality: that the environment plays a basic role in mental development. We must eventually take this role into account, but here it must be stressed that there are certain inner situations which environment can only influence, but never eliminate. And the most important and universal of these situations is the helplessness of the human infant, his dependence upon a nurturing source, and his need to detach himself from the source upon which he leans. The baby in his attached state demands total care. He can neither control his body nor accurately perceive the outer world. When a need arises he must have the caretaking person there to meet it, and he must have the care he needs at the moment he needs it, for delay is not tolerated. But no mother is good enough to fulfill completely the demands of her tyrannical parasite. And when the mother disappoints the baby—whether by having another child, or simply by being in another room—the infant experiences a state of unbearable and helpless tension. This very unpleasure becomes a stimulus toward a more mature and autonomous development, and it seizes upon the inborn active strivings of the human infant as the means toward healthy growth. But no matter how healthy his development, the gauntlet of conflict must be run, for the old passively erotic strivings toward the mother do not release the infant so easily.

Thus our baby is bound to run into conflict from within, because his active drive for individuation runs against the current driving him toward maternal union. This older, erotic current never dies until the person himself dies.

The experiences charged by Eros are too precious to be let go by the developing baby. Never again will he ever feel as if he were the whole of reality, as if his every wish were omnipotent. The selfhood that is demanded of the baby—that he demands of himself in order to function in the world—is always experienced as a sense of aloneness and privation. Selfhood itself is the great universal experience of frustration. This is the essence of the human paradox: to win mastery at the cost of separation.

The infant can never forget this basic idea. And he can never forgive it as long as the erotic current runs within him—so long, that is, as he remains alive. The very hopefulness that a person sustains himself by is at bottom an impossible illusion, nothing less than the wish to return to maternal fusion, and so to negate all that independent and autonomous living has gained. This wish must then be perpetually frustrated, and the frustration must perpetually generate aggression. Hence, from the stage of separation onward—that is, roughly past the first year of life —the infant becomes ambivalent, hating as well as loving, and will remain so throughout life.

Of course matters are never quite so stark as the outline above implies. A good deal of mental development— which we are unable to further pursue here—consists of coming to terms with the basic conflict. For, since both attachment and separation are necessary, and since each is initially incompatible with the other, some sort of mutual alteration must be made in order to keep peace within the personality and to permit growth.

Our infant at first feels the conflict in all its rawness. He is virtually simultaneously aware of his wish for maternal union, his striving to separate himself, and the impossible frustration imposed by the opposed desires. It is at this point that rage born of frustration enters his life as a real force. Parents commonly note that the baby who had been so adorable during the first year of his life becomes increasingly prone to fits of temper as the second year progresses. This tempestuous behavior can range all the way from tantrums to simple assertiveness. Whatever form it takes, the child becomes more difficult to manage as time wears on. The defiance and willfulness ordinarily peaks (with gross variations) at thirty-six months of age, at which time the separation phase is considered complete, and gradually wanes thereafter as new conflicts arise to goad the developing child. Accordingly, the mental events to be described encompass roughly this period of development. It is a fascinating era, replete with the richness granted by the beginnings of linguistic function, and it is the point of origin of many of our enduring fantasies.

At the beginning of this phase, the baby's symbolic powers of discrimination have matured to the extent of permitting him a somewhat more accurate view of reality. He is, for instance, now able to grasp the fact that he has a body with specific and regular functions, and that his mother is a distinct entity who can come and go. This world view becomes subjected now to the play of forces in the basic conflict.

The baby must at some point experience his rage as threatening. For one thing, severe emotional states have a disorganizing effect upon the immature personality—that is, the more he cries and screams, the less able he is to employ his hard-won mastery, and the more vulnerable he becomes to certain threats. The main such fear is concerned with the central figure, his mother, whom he still needs with such vivid force. The child soon realizes that his rage gets him nowhere. Worse, his mother becomes angry in turn, and to the infantile mind the anger of such an all-powerful and all-important figure is equivalent to impending annihilation.

The child must therefore *defend* himself against such a threatening emotion. By defense, we mean here that he must alter his mental experience so as to avoid the unpleasure, or anxiety, associated with the emotional state surrounding a conflict between opposed wishes. He may do so by changing the way he acts, the way he thinks, or the way he feels; generally speaking, he changes all three modes of behavior. The repertoire of mental defenses is virtually infinite, and becomes as specific for each person as his fingerprints. But all defenses have this in common: they are as universal as the conflicts which underlie them, and they force a certain *distortion* upon a person's mental experience. Thus, at the very time when our infant is forming a picture of the external world (including his body), he is also distorting his experience in the interests of defense. And since the image of the external world needs to be reasonably accurate to permit normal activity, a contradiction arises between the portion of experience directed toward the resolution of the basic conflict and that which seeks to function in reality.

The major way that this incompatibility is side-stepped is through the means of *repression*. What is threatening and contradictory will be blotted out, forcefully forgotten. But it will not disappear, since the basic conflicts which give rise to danger are continued within, and they are unyielding. Thus arises a basic differentiation of the mental life: between conscious and unconscious. The child adapts to reality, and to his conflicts as well, but he does so by splitting his mind and cutting off one realm of functioning from the other. He is defended.

One such defensive pattern is as follows: the child, enraged at the frustration of separation and threatened by his rage, begins to turn the rage onto his own person. The sense of continuity between himself and the rest of the world, which was the first stage of his thinking, enables him to do this. Now, since he needs the world, loves the world, and also fears the world, he chooses to take out his anger on himself rather than on the source of his frustration. The child of two does not, of course, say "I hate myself." Such an idea would be quite impossibly abstract for his stage of mental organization nor is it accurate, for the child (unless crippled by parental neglect or ambivalence) has no reason to hate himself—that is, the totality of what he experiences as his person. He is still loved and protected, and therefore he still, by and large, loves himself. But he does feel anger at separation, and he lacks mature and realistic ways of dealing with the anger. Therefore, he begins to turn it inward, toward his person; and, since he cannot combine loving and hating feelings toward his whole person, *he begins to segregate his person into aspects that can be loved and aspects that can be hated,* into *good parts of the self and bad parts.* Thus at the very inception of the idea of a self distinct from the rest of the world, that self is experienced as split. Such is the control of the past upon the future, that the nature of this split will thereafter influence all the person's judgments of goodness and badness. Just as in embryology, the first splits within a developing organism will cast a trace over all subsequent differentiations.

The child needs a concept to account for these split feelings; his wishes need symbolic objects. And the little child is a shameless opportunist who seizes upon whatever is available to represent his needs. The basic object available is, of course, his own body and its functions. Here is where direct knowledge of the world begins.

Accordingly, the child begins mentally to seize upon a particular body function to represent this nuclear situation. He looks to a function that is regular and reproducible, so that it can serve as a consistent source of knowledge; to one that is suitable to represent separation;

to one which involves strong sensations with which erotic and aggressive wishes can be experienced; and to one that regularly involves the key figure in the world to whom he is attached, and from whom he is separating. He looks, then, to the function of *excretion* as a symbolic currency with which to represent his dilemma.

Nature saw fit to place the anus near the genitals, and to supply the anus with a rich store of nerve endings. The baby's helplessness extends at first to an inability to control his excrements; and, as human social living imposes the need for some such control (with enormous variations, to be sure), the baby's mother has to attend to what the baby cannot do. She must clean his perineum after defecation. In doing so, she stimulates the child and gives him pleasure. Therefore, one aspect of the tie that the baby experiences between himself and his mother is felt in the anal zone. Furthermore, as the baby matures, he will first become able to control his impulses in the function of excretion. Since control of the body is the necessary step in the rise toward individual autonomy, whatever feelings develop in the process of separation and individuation are readily expressed in terms of anal activities. By the same token, that one aspect will become the crucial body region chosen to represent the conflicts about the formation of a self.

In the act of defecation, the person gives a part of himself to the world. True, feces are formed of those substances the body must reject, and are eminently dispensable. But at first the baby has no reason to believe this piece of objective knowledge: what comes from the body belonged to the body; it should be considered as part of the body, and so of the self. In the first stage of knowledge, whatever is known is loved. Therefore, in the beginning (and so, at bottom throughout life), excrement is loved. The smell and touch of it, that later disgust the adult, are sources of infantile delight. Taken away by the mother, it is experienced as the first gift, the beginnings of property.

However, feces are dispensable. They also disgust other people. These data are seized by the infant. Here is a part of the self which can be separated in reality, and so in fantasy as well. Here is something that mother hates. Here, then, is that part of the self which can be cleaved from the rest; here is a piece of badness, the existence of which permits goodness to be ascribed to the rest of the self: here is a piece of shit. And so shit, that most vivid and shameful word, comes by its intensity naturally, for it is that part of the body-self that is hated and given to the world as ransom for the self's autonomy.

The young child is now in his *anal* phase of development. The essential point for us to bear in mind about this most misunderstood stage of life, is that bowel activities become ways of expressing and feeling what is vitally important to the child, and so they also become a source of knowledge. This is the time in which language is beginning to develop, the time of the flowering of human symbolic capacities. But symbols and language cannot as yet be carried out independently of the life of the body. Therefore, the fantasies which are elaborated at this period to account for the child's situation will include body symbolism—specifically, bowel symbolism. Because these fantasies are threatening in themselves, and because they conflict to some extent with the increasingly more exacting demands that reality will make upon the growing child, they too will become distorted and repressed. But it is a fact that the organism never fully abandons prior strivings. Indeed, if *repressed* (i.e., held back by a mental counterforce), the early strivings retain their full force. All that is changed is consciousness; the fantasies become unconscious, although linked at numerous points with conscious, reality-directed activity.

In this way, the original body-based symbols and fantasies serve as organizers for what is to come, and represent turning points and points of departure as well: henceforth, fundamental life situations will be mentally organized along the nuclear symbolic structures of the body. Later developments will layer over the earlier ones; they may hide the former from view, but they will continue to express their inner connection with what has gone before.

The mutual influences of early and later experience are vastly complex. I say mutual, because the person continues to live the life of the body alongside of his life in the social universe. Initially, and as a point of departure, the person splits his feelings of self and begins to hate his excrement. As he grows older, this reaction may well intensify, so that an older child, or an adult, may come to regard his excrement with far greater abhorrence than the two-year-old. The reason is not that the anal phase persists, but rather that other conflicts which have become *associatively linked with anality* are continuing at a more advanced level of adaptation; and these later conflicts are being continually dealt with along earlier modes. Thus, as a person advances through life, becomes more autonomous, more separated and more masterful, he may well achieve resolution of whatever conflicts that might be potentially arresting to his development, by turning his aggressive feelings onto the excrement of his body. In a metaphorical sense, shit—the word symbol we attach to *hated* excrement—bears the accumulated burden of all the rage engendered in the course of a person's separation. Of course a person does not know this consciously. Once the basic repression begins in infancy, the awareness of this connection disappears; indeed, the further the process goes—the more, that is, one heaps rage of separation upon the symbol and substance of shit—the further removed from awareness must the connection become.

In fact the connection becomes so remote as to require some further adjustment. The young child can play with body-contents and express himself freely and directly. But as he grows older, he—that is, his idea of his self— grows more remote from the body which gave him the ground of his being. Eventually, the mature person (unless he is an obsessional neurotic—i.e., unless repression fails, and the return of this particular repressed fantasy plagues him) avoids the whole subject as too alien to the self. In doing so, however, he also loses the opportunity to discharge his feelings directly upon his body. Instead he finds, aided by culture, certain worldly constellations of things which bear a *symbolic* correspondence with the repressed and lost body of infancy. It is exactly culture's province to establish such symbolic correspondences. He now plays out onto the world—where aggression can really be delivered—what had originated with his body when he separated himself from his mother. This point is so basic and essential to our study that it deserves further elaboration.

From another perspective, it may be said that the whole cleavage between body and spirit—which is at root the cleavage between a stage of maternal fusion and a state of separateness—begins at the anal stage, and uses the split between the excremental self and the non-excremental self as its symbolic cornerstone. Accordingly, body becomes identified with the excremental self, and spirit with the non-excremental self.

But this development raises further problems. No one wants the immense estrangement from his body that would result if the course of this split continued unabated. The body keeps making its demands, and keeps affording pleasure; an extreme estrangement is not in the interest of the self. (Unless, of course, we are dealing with psychopathology—but history was by and large not made by neurotics, and so we must keep our eye upon the pattern of normal development.) Therefore a rapprochement is sought.

This is accomplished by another defense. The rage that had been *taken in* in the initial phase of separation, is returned outward in the later phase (which would include, of course, adult life). In this way, what is introjected can later be *projected*. By this means, the body is brought back into the self and once more loved. The child is not aware of his body in any realistic, anatomical sense. Rather, he conceives of it as the concrete and immediate representative of his fantasies. Accordingly, what he can see of himself (and this, of course, amounts essentially to his *skin*) is loved narcissistically. In sharpest contrast, what is hated about the body comes to be that which the body expels—its shit and other effluvia.

The split between a good body, which belongs to the self, and a bad body, which is expelled, becomes generalized to the rest of reality. An enduring polarization between good and bad aspects of the world is built on the foundation of body symbolism. Beyond the body, objects are sought in the outer world as suitable to represent both loved and hated parts of the self. For symbols of what is hated, the developing mind begins to look about to see what can be associated with his own excrement—i.e., what may share certain qualities which may enable the transfer to be made from inner to outer rage. What comes under this category is called *dirt*. Therefore, dirt is the creature of a fantasy; it is what accumulates in the world as a consequence of a person's (or a culture's) separation from the world.

The psychoanalyst Lawrence Kubie described it thus (1938): dirt is "anything which either symbolically or in reality emerges from the body, or which has been sullied by contact with a body aperture." The presence of dirty things indicates a widening of the split within the self which began in the process of separation. The self is to some extent formed in the fleeing from dirt: it must "despite its own uncleanliness shun as dirty everything in the outside world which resembles or represents the body's own 'dirt'; and . . . above all else it must never allow its own relatively 'clean' outsides to become contaminated by contact with the filthy interior of itself or of anyone else."[63] Dirt, then, becomes a metaphor which links the self with the *outside* of the body—i.e., the *skin* and its *color*. Within this fantasy, everything else is dirty: the *inside* of the body, and any part of the rest of the world which is associated with the body's insides. Thus, states Kubie, "quite without questioning it we make the assumption that the insides of the body are in fact a cistern, that all the apertures of the body are dirty avenues of approach, dirty holes leading into dirty spaces, and that everything which comes out of the body . . . is for that reason alone dirty."

And so we see that the fantasy of dirty imposes a kind of value sign upon the world. For the rest of his life, a person will take this enduring infantile notion, incorporate it into his daily activities, and use it in the formation of a world view. Of course this fantasy, like all fantasies, is illogical and unrealistic in terms of the external world. But it corresponds to a mental reality which must have its due. Moreover, the external world is plastic; it can be worked upon by a person and separated into good, clean

[63] Lawrence Kubie, "The Fantasy of Dirt," *Psychoanalytic Quarterly*, Vol. VI (1938), p. 391.

substances and bad, dirty substances, according to the needs of the fantasy.

I have been writing of the origins of the idea of dirt, which we see as stemming from the rage at separation. But rage reflects only the aggressive side of human instinctual life. Eros, the original force of attachment, persists too, and must also have its representation in the outer world. In other words, the child hates what he expels and calls it dirty. But what of those material substances which he loves? His love, too, extends beyond himself and his mother, to include much of the non-human world. And so he wants to take to himself that part of the world which he loves. He wants to *possess* it and to make it his *property*. Insofar as he can no longer have his mother, he wants to own something else, something that can stand for his lost mother. The wars of property begin in the nursery, as two-, three- and four-year-old children begin to displace the intensity of their passions onto toys and other "goods." Thus, according to the eternal ambivalence of the human species, men have always, in all cultures, divided the world up into dirt, suitable to be expelled from the self, and property, suitable to be included into the self. One function of a culture is to designate what is to be dirt in the world, and what is to be property.

Yet beneath this ambivalence lies a former state of unity. In the unconscious, opposites are linked and join at their infantile point of origin. And just as dirt leads back to the idea of hated excrement, so does property lead back to loved excrement. For excrement is also the baby's first gift to the world. Here is something which was indubitably his; and anything else that can once again belong to a person will lead back symbolically to it. And because excrement becomes the symbol of both loved and hated aspects of the non-human world, excremental symbolism will become intensified in those situations where a heightened ambivalence still persists over the conflicts of separation. To such a person, all human relationship may become reduced to questions of property and ownership. His life becomes reduced to the quest for ownership; and since he is looking for what he had to lose and can never regain, no real piece of property can ever satisfy him. Indeed, being ambivalent, he probably will secretly hate that which he owns. Here is where lucre becomes filthy, and its pursuit a tormented frenzy. Eventually he becomes consumed less by the actual ownership of something than by the process of acquisition. He may become concerned only with the power of being able to possess, a sense of potency that was first his when, as an infant, he found himself able to control what came out of his body and discovered that he could use that control to express his ambivalence toward his parents.

The basic human situation is everywhere the same, but there are infinite ways of dealing with it. Each set of ways is the hallmark of a culture, and follows from the specific condition of that culture. Our "generalized" case begins to look more and more like a modern man of the West, a man, that is, driven by the need to acquire material goods. Thus, in studying Western culture, we must account for its tendency to induce in its people such personality traits as outlined above, and describe the ways in which this influence is brought to bear.

The influence of a culture begins to modify the nuclear human situation at birth, so that it is in practice impossible to talk of this situation as free from cultural influence. I have chosen the fiction of doing so up to the present point of discussion in order to demonstrate that some problems—i.e., separation, ambivalence, etc.—have to be represented in *all* cultures, and that body symbolism has to be included in the structure of a culture in order that it communicate with the enduring, infantile core in all humans.

Until this point, we have been focusing on the content of certain conflicts, and the fantasies which arise from them. We have not considered the overall regulation of personality, or the total set of psychic functions—that is, we have not looked into the structure of personality itself, something that must be done if psychology and history are to be related.

There is no need to be systematic here, but a few definitions will be helpful to what follows. We have been talking of the origins of the sense of self, and this sense is only one of a great number of functional mental patterns which develop and mature in the growing child. The total set of such functions has an organic unity of its own, the well-known concept of the *ego*. The ego is what does the work of the personality: adapting to reality, defending itself against unacceptable conflict, regulating itself, and so forth. The goal of healthy personality development is the formation of a strong and autonomous ego. Such an ego will have a well-developed and firm sense of self. A historical group of any potency must structure its culture so as to maximize this kind of ego development among its individuals. Education is one way in which culture carries out this task, but, as the above discussion of conflict suggests, there is much more to the cultural influence on personality than conscious learning.

The ego develops out of the undifferentiated mental state of early infancy. It grows dialectically to a set of instinctual wishes that express the nuclear drives of the organism, but which are both threatening and unrealistic. These we call the *id*, a sea of repressed striving, of fluid, timeless and unconscious wishes pressing for discharge. The id is cut off from reality and cannot act on the world.

The function of activity is, of course, the province of the ego, which contends with the endless pressure of unrealistic id wishes, and, at the same time, keeps the organism operating in reality. The ego must effect compromises to carry out its many tasks, and the maneuvers described above are examples of such compromises. Thus, the primary hatred and love of the body is part of the id. What bubbles to the surface of this cauldron is the work of the ego: i.e., the hatred of excrement and the attitude to those aspects of reality—dirt and property—which are symbolic of hated and loved excrement.

Culture then provides the appropriate symbols as well as the kinds of activity needed to keep the real world in suitable symbolic form for the ego to act upon. What we need to consider now is how culture's forms and symbols influence the ego. In short, how is the ego regulated?

Within each personality is a set of regulatory patterns, of controls, prohibitions, ideals and the like. This set, which we term the *superego*, is a part of the ego, but a part set against the whole, which it regulates and steers through life. The remainder of this essay will be largely devoted to examining the superego. The emphasis is necessary, for the superego is that aspect of personality through which the individual relates himself to his culture, and so to history.

Oedipus Complex and Superego

We are now studying the situation of childhood in which the child has, for all his unconscious and repressed fantasies, created a working system of self and world distinctions. He knows that he is somebody distinct—although with many undefined properties—and he knows that there are distinct others to whom he relates. He has thereby erected an enduring foundation on which to base all his future transactions with the world of real people. He has also readied himself for further complications.

These further problems arise from the same drives, now in a much more differentiated and intricate form, because they are applied to the real people in the child's world. The prime objects of the drives are naturally the parents, but as the child matures the objects and influences of his life will become progressively those of the culture in which he lives, whether they are mediated through that culture's institutions or through the other people who share the life of culture with the developing person. The transition from family world to larger cultural world is progressively graded, with certain well-defined nodal points of accelerated change. These turning points—the entrance into school; the onset of adolescence; the transition from adolescence into the life of work and marriage—are virtually dictated by a closely interrelated set of biological maturations, personality changes and cultural demands, the nature of which we need not pursue further.[64] And, since the child's parents and his family structure are themselves closely shaped by culture, this transition is an orderly one when it is not disrupted by either gross psychopathology or cultural shock.

In the early stage of childhood—roughly from ages two to six years—the child's problems arise because he projects his passionate yet unrealistic drives onto parents and siblings. Human relationships become triangular instead of exclusive. As the relationships differentiate in complexity, so too are other people seen as more differentiated and individual. And the child's emotions also become more subtle and differentiated as his ego develops. Nonetheless, the basic drives persist and endlessly seek objects upon which to gratify themselves. During this period the child

[64] Again, c.f. Erickson's work, especially *Childhood and Society* (New York, W. W. Norton & Company, 1963), for a full discussion.

must master the complex task of establishing these relationships on a more neutral plane. In the process, he comes to control his body ever more fully, becomes aware and, hopefully, reconciled to its sexual identity and limitations, acquires the nuclear mental structures for the inner control of behavior, and develops the ability to sublimate and master the very drives that impel him. It is a large task; I will emphasize only one, central aspect of it: the oedipus complex and its role in the formation of superego.

The small child is a creature of passionate yearnings. These spur his astounding creativity and beauty. But the same strivings, by virtue of their intensity, are also threats. The boy, experiencing sexual excitement in his genitals, wants to obtain pleasure in the body of his mother; the little girl feels similarly toward her father. Moreover, humans appear to have an innate bisexuality, probably the inheritance of our biological unstructuredness. Thus the boy has sexual wishes (of a passive nature) for his father; the girl for her mother.

These wishes and excitations are intense and unrealizable. Out of this situation of frustration, intense feelings of jealousy and envy arise, coupled with the child's awareness of his own impotence which remains keen despite all attempts to deny it in fantasy. Intense feelings of aggression toward the parent-rival ensue. These derive from and add to the never-completely-resolved feelings of anger caused by the demand and need for separation. And once more, this rage is unacceptable to the child, for it cannot be reconciled with his deeply affectionate feelings into a unified view of either his own self or reality. Once again, as with his anger at separation, the child repudiates the anger born of his incestuous frustration and jealousy; and again it becomes turned against the self. This time aggression is translated almost directly into fears of retaliation—fears that the genital, whose excitement is the source of troubled pleasure, will be mutilated: castrated. These fears, along with the forbidden yet present wishes to castrate, come to dominate a boy's mind as the central experience of his whole oedipal problem. And their relief becomes the motive for the resolution of the oedipus complex.

Resolution is accomplished by a change of diverse proportions. Most important is the formation of what Freud termed "a grade in the ego, a differentiation within the ego, which may be called the . . . 'super-ego.'" One portion of the child's ego is now set up to watch over the rest of the ego and to direct its activities. The superego eventually becomes the mental seat of conscience and ideals. In its earliest form these functions are only rudimentary. As it begins its development, the superego is an inner voice which repeats within the child's mind these external commands by which the parents strove to control his behavior.

A set of inner controls now is at last able to "tame" the instinctual drives in the interests of cultural pursuits. What had been intense, passionate and dangerous, both in its erotic and its aggressive implications (and the two are always interrelated), becomes muted and manageable, its aim inhibited, the pressure for its discharge delayed. This is the instinctual essence of the problem of *sublimation*. Sublimations go on before the formation of the superego, but their full swing does not appear until the oedipus complex can be resolved; this is a principal reason for delaying the entrance into school until age five or six. Until instinctual problems are controlled, abstract learning cannot proceed. By this time the mind, though yet to undergo vast changes, has developed a sufficient degree of internal organization to permit the person access to the world of culture. The process is graded, and time is allowed by the institutions of society to make the transition from family world to cultural world manageably smooth; but for the remainder of its course, personal development becomes *directly* influenced by cultural forces, rather than, as had been the case in pre-oedipal years, by culture as indirectly represented in the human influences of the family. From the resolution of the oedipus complex onward, it may be said that culture in itself (as represented by peers, schooling, religion, and later by work and more advanced social functions) exists as an independent influence alongside the biological family.

There are certain dilemmas, however, in this ideal situation, which enter into the structure of personality and drastically affect the reality in which it lives. The problem exists in many forms, all of which focus on the inner structure of that mental system termed the superego.

The human mind is a series of dialectical tensions becoming ever more articulated by the creation of inner structure out of repressing force. This repressing force derives in part from the capacity of the infant to repress itself, and in part from the repressing influence of the family. With the formation of the superego, all these repressing forces are organized internally, from whence they may plague the ego for the rest of its life.

Conscience and ideals—those elements of mentality necessary for civilization—are but conscious traces of the superego. Simple observation will confirm that what goes under the name of conscience-motivated behavior has only a partial relationship to rational ethics. The conscience can be a cruel and sadistic flogger of the self. At its extreme we observe suicidal depression—a death sentence passed by the superego on the ego because of some irrational yet unappeasable sense of sinfulness. But intermediate, "normal," variations are endless. These manifestations reveal a basic fact about the superego: along with the rest of the ego, it contains a substantial zone of enduring unconscious and repressed contents. Indeed its energy, the force of conscience and ideals, is derived from this unconscious zone. But the unconscious zone of the superego consists precisely of all the aggressive fury that the small child dammed up from the experiences of separation and the oedipus complex. Moreover, as Freud pointed out in *Civilization and Its Discontents* (where, in Chapter VII, the still-definitive portrait of the superego was drawn), the necessity to repress these aggressive wishes toward the parents *increases* with the child's love for them; and this love in turn is the *sine qua non* for the life-giving attachment of the infant to his family, the spur to all the higher and valued activities of the human mind, in fact the only condition that keeps life going and makes it worthwhile. If love is necessary, so is the aggression necessary for the propulsion of the infant into individual function, inevitable in the frustrations of infantile love, and generated by our biological apparatus. Thus Freud concluded that the higher the degree of civilized activity, the greater becomes the disposition to internalized aggression—aggression directed at the self.

The superego suffers yet another paradox in its formation, noted by Freud in *The Ego and the Id,* in which his final theory of mental organization was expounded. In saving himself by abandoning his incestuous strivings, the child must also weaken the ties of love with which he had held onto his body and world. The first victim of repression is the strength of human sexuality. Despite the idealistic yearnings of Western culture, love without sexuality is a weaker love. Furthermore, a weakened love is less able to contain relatively unbridled infantile aggression. Thus it comes to pass that the superego, besides controlling the organism's mental activity, has also to deal with a relatively harsher form of aggression. Civilization is obtained then by the loss of a significant portion of infan-

tile happiness and freedom—freedom from the interioriza-
tion of hostile and destructive wishes, freedom from guilt.
Let us sum up these reflections in Freud's own words:

> The super-ego arises, as we know, from an identification with
> the father taken as a model. Every such identification is in the
> nature of a desexualization or even of a sublimation. It now
> seems as though when a transformation of this kind takes place,
> an instinctual defusion occurs at the same time. After sublima-
> tion the erotic component no longer has the power to bind the
> whole of the destructiveness that was combined with it, and
> this is released in the form of an inclination to aggression and
> destruction. This defusion would be the source of the general
> character of harshness and cruelty exhibited by the ideal [i.e.,
> by the superego]—its dictatorial 'Thou shalt.'

> . . . . since the ego's work of sublimation results in a defusion
> and a liberation of the aggressive instincts in the superego, its
> struggle against the libido [i.e., its repression of incestuous fan-
> tasies] exposes it to the danger of maltreatment and death. In
> suffering under the attacks of the super-ego or perhaps even
> succumbing to them [as in suicidal depressions], the ego is
> meeting with a fate like that of the [protozoons] which are
> destroyed by the products of decomposition that they them-
> selves have created. From the economic point of view [i.e., in
> terms of the semiquantitative disposition of mental forces] the
> morality that functions in the super-ego seems to be a similar
> product of decomposition.[65]

Thus the child pays a heavy and painful price for the
abandonment of his oedipal wishes. However harsh it
may be, the transaction is considered worthwhile by the
child if it will ensure him freedom from his intense fears
of abandonment and bodily mutilation. Indeed the harsh-
ness of the superego corresponds in a rough way to the
magnitude of those fears. No amount of idealization of
either childhood or morality can erase the anxiety amidst
the beauty of the former, or the hobbling imposed by the

[65] Sigmund Freud, *The Ego and The Id*, in *Standard Edition*, Vol.
XIX, pp. 54, 56.

latter. The child *cum* superego is a child who has abandoned the vivid beauty of body-erotic feeling for pale mental sublimations: each differentiation of his prior development has entailed some such change; but the formation of superego makes it definitive, for now the repressing and sublimating force is inside and cannot be evaded except by further subliminatory alteration. And on top of this, the superego presents itself immediately as a harsh and self-punitive imperative, the alternative to externally directed aggressive wishes and the fears of mutilation they stimulate, as well as the source of inhibition and suffering of its own. Is it any wonder that men are beset with insoluble dilemmas and certain suffering?

The reader may have observed another paradox revealed in this discussion. The goal, or end result, of human development is the creation of an autonomous ego. This, the substitute for animal instinctive patterns, is the immensely powerful organ of human adaptation. Autonomy in this sense means a self-generated activity that can direct the organism toward its realistic satisfactions, free from inner or external compulsion. Certainly, advanced civilized activity cannot proceed without such autonomy. In a very significant sense, whatever advances civilization has undergone have been both cause and result of increasing ego autonomy. The internalization of parental controls in the superego is the decisive childhood step by which autonomy is made possible. But—and here is the paradox—this autonomy is immediately threatened by the fact that the superego takes into itself, not just parental controls, but also the child's aggressive wishes toward the parents which have been accumulated since infancy. One cannot be autonomous if one's self is continually bombarded from within by an aggressive wish that had been directed outward. Indeed, if Freud's suggestion about instinctual delusion in the process of sublimation is correct, then the formation of the superego, as we have so far described it, appears to be a disaster. Not only has body-Eros been lost, but autonomy has not been gained: the organism is crippled from within and scarcely able to adapt outwardly.

Some such unhappy outcome does in fact occur in severely pathological development. By and large, however, things work out much better than the above theoretical outline would predict. Most people—even most neurotics—achieve enough autonomy to do their work and reproduce themselves in a family; did they not, civilization would perish. This fact has been used to demonstrate that the Freudian theory, with its somber prediction of unhappy tidings flowing from the abiding inner aggression of mankind, is erroneous in this respect. In particular, it is suggested that aggression, appeased by love and tamed by intelligence, will fade away and not trouble the adjusted, normal human being except in certain ritualized (and thereby controlled and pleasurable) expressions, such as athletics. It is argued that whatever surplus aggression exists in men is the result of parental neglect, or derives from the imposition of social ills upon an otherwise benign organism. There are indeed some gaps in the theory presented above, and some addition must be made to account for the normal, adjusted functioning of the average citizen.

But the evidence concerning human aggression, both in its excessive clinical manifestations and in its gross appearance in the record of history, makes it impossible for us to deny its central role in any theory of human nature and culture. The nightmares of history, racism included, did not arise simply from neglect, ignorance, or economic scarcity, as liberal theoreticians would have us believe. They came from some source, and, barring the discovery of a new form of ethereal or diabolic influence, that source is in human nature, and is writ enduringly upon human activities. It is true that aggression is *perpetuated* by malevolent social forces, such as privation, ignorance and neglect. But who made the institutions that serve these sufferings, and who created the culture within which we all reside? And why do the "best" and most favored of people suffer their comfortable despair and perpetuate endlessly the sufferings of others?

If we accept the proposition that human development is saddled with aggression, how are we to account for the kind of autonomy that enables people to become rationalized, sublimated and productive citizens? The answer is in the word adjusted. What is "adjusted" in the adjusted, normal person? "Adjusted" and "normal" are synonymous, and etymology tells us that "normal" means, not "average," but proceeding from norms. Norms are the values of a society, and flow from the total set of its organically related cultural functions. It is to these norms that we are adjusted, and the process of adjustment consists precisely in the gradual shaping of the individual superego to fit the norms of culture.

As an individual becomes adjusted to his culture, he participates in culture's activities and institutions. This participation becomes the means by which he applies to the world the excess aggression deriving from unresolved infantile conflicts. And it is by means of this exteriorization that the personality is spared disorganization and loss of autonomy.

Thus, amidst its more rational structures, culture comes to play a role of immense importance in the stabilization of the human personality. To fulfill its vital role, however, culture must be organized along lines which reflect symbolically the inner splits and drives of personality. The parallel organization of culture and personality is what we mean when we say that the two systems are congruent. One might say that culture is both benefactor and heir to the eternal human dilemmas. By providing a worldly scaffold on which men can erect their inner conflicts, culture becomes the benefactor who grants autonomy and a measure of peace to the ego. But culture also becomes the heir who accumulates over historical time an ever-increasing collection of infantile fantasies, desires and discontents.

Within culture there must exist, therefore, a kind of nuclear representation of what men need in order to lift themselves out of the impossible situation of their infantile conflicts. Culture must provide enough satisfactions to permit the transition. There must be, in short, a common ground within culture and personality. This ground will not be in anything material, but in a pattern of meanings, events and forms of action. The mind must get to know culture through the infantile experience of the body, and as it advances outward into culture from childhood it must retain, amidst all its other activities, a lifeline—albeit unconscious—to the infantile past which gave it life.

And since the turning point, as the individual sets off into culture on his own, is the passage of the oedipus complex, that lifeline must lead back to this last mooring of full infantility. Consequently the forms of cultural activity that will become psychologically decisive and necessary are those processes that match the as yet unfinished business of the oedipus complex. And this consists of the unresolved conflicts that persist within the superego according to the limitations imposed by its unsuccessful attempt to do away with infantile aggression.

At its very least then, society must contain a basic form of activity that provides a functional template to match these strivings. That template we have mentioned before; indeed it served as a red thread through our historical discussion (as it would through any historical discussion):

it is the process of *domination;* its social product is the entity of *power;* and its historical representations are the entire gamut of power-generating institutions—kings and nation-states—and the power structures that emerge from each and every human institution—from the family, from religions, from the most productive forms of economic activity. History, civilization itself, was set going by the emergence in men of power strivings. This probably required a prehistorical maturation of the family structure, so an oedipal constellation could emerge. Its early phases are a matter of speculation and were first delineated, in a fanciful but deeply true form, by Freud in *Totem and Taboo*. His nuclear conception was expanded and elaborated by Herbert Marcuse in *Eros and Civilization*.

Marcuse writes, "The progress from domination by one to domination by several involves a social spread of pleasure and makes repression self-imposed in the ruling group itself: *all* its members have to obey the taboos if they want to maintain their rule. Repression now permeates the life of the oppressors themselves, and part of their instinctual energy becomes available for sublimation in work."[66]

One may isolate those several phenomena for the purposes of study, but in actuality there is no cleavage. A dominative society includes within its culture a dominative family unit which breeds men who want to dominate and need to be dominated; these men then identify with the interests of that culture and perpetuate its basic mode of activity. And each dominative society tends to swallow its less dominative fellows, and induces in them the basic dialectic of power until domination encircles the earth. The oedipus complex, presented in myth and art, discerned by Freud through observation of the mental life

[66] Marcuse, *Eros and Civilization*, p. 59.

of neurotics (within a dominative society), has, while rooted in biological strivings, become the near-universal condition of human society.

One peculiarity of human behavior has been implicit in the foregoing discussion. Wherever one looks in human affairs, whether into psychology, history, or the theory of culture, he will find it impossible to account for any phenomenon by a single cause. Rather, a whole set of causative factors interplay organically in the determination. Any account of motivation that reduces a given specimen of behavior to one cause is erroneous. Human behavior is multi-determined, and each determination, as long as there is evidence to reveal its existence, is equally real. Both historical and psychological study must take account of this principle.

Although such multi-determination is a universal fact of human life, the separate motives are not random. They are an organized set which, in its totality, would reflect the functioning of the person's ego in the event. The ego is, after all, the unit of organismic functioning. It is a set of functions, each of which is operative in any social event. Some of these functions we scarcely need notice in assessing the "meaning" of an event, but all are present and must be contended with by the ego.

The ego may be thought of as that mental organization which reflects the great multiplicity of roles and functions within the personality. It expresses each of them, and responds to each individually, but according to its overall level of organization. And this may be presented in the concept of the synthetic function. The ego ties its own contents together, and creates, by repression and distortion if necessary, a larger whole out of the many elemental qualities acquired by a man in the course of his life. This synthetic function may be thought of as an expression of Eros, the basic drive that brings together what is separate.

The sense of self and the sense of identity are reflections of the synthetic work of the ego. All the elements presented to the individual by his drives, his past development and the needs of the environment in which he finds himself, must be fused together into a coherent self-image and sense of identity. And if there is something unacceptable, a desire, for example, that cannot be integrated into the self-image, then it must be dealt with in other ways, most notably by repression, followed by some kind of secondary defense, for example, projection outward onto the world. Now, if the projected aspect of reality can be forcibly altered to meet these inner demands for self-unity, the individual may proceed safely.

The work of integration, of the synthesis of all the many influences of a personality into a coherent acting unit, is expressed in a prime principle of ego functioning, which the psychoanalyst Robert Waelder called the principle of multiple function. This states that every reality-directed piece of behavior must be, in some proportion, a solution to all the many tasks of the personality. This does not happen automatically, but requires work. How is this effected in the case of functions that had to suffer repression? In particular, how does one come to retain some elements of knowledge of that which has to be repressed because it will not fit in with a coherent self-image, but must find expression because of the multiple function of the ego? Some sense of realization is necessary in order for directed action to be carried out; and without complete directed action, the ego will not be fulfilling its task of multiple function, nor will the organism survive.

The solution devised by the ego for this lies within a special type of symbolism. What is repudiated and repressed, and must therefore remain in the id, will find a symbolic representation by the ego that corresponds with some perception of the world.

Such symbolically guided activity goes on all the time. Our language, our cultural imagery, the whole world is full of symbolic representatives of repressed trends which the ego, in its everlasting need to synthesize, seizes upon for its action. Many examples are curiosities only, such as mannerisms, eccentricities, remnants of some business that only the particular individual had any concern with, and which need not disturb him or anyone else. Some symbolic activity is of considerable importance in the clinical practice of psychiatry, where it presents itself as some kind of crippling neurotic activity. Still other symbolic activity becomes of decisive importance in history. And, from the discussion so far, the common feature of such activity should be clear: that it is any kind of symbolic distortion, in the interests of the ego's synthesis, that becomes involved in power and domination.

Some such symbolic images are well-known and clear derivatives of the oedipus complex, for example, those of king or of God the Father. For millennia men in power have waved these images before the millions and bemused them with their irrational potency. In certain societies—Czarist Russia, for example—these patriarchal symbols were held on to with delusional certainty by suffering millions who died from the oppression of those they worshipped. Even revolutionaries would turn about and love the Czar whose overthrow they had so recently plotted, and who was about to dispatch them summarily.

Moreover, such power symbols do not have to be limited to direct representations of the oedipal complex. The feelings of the superego which crystallize out of the oedipal conflict each contain highly charged remnants of earlier infantile fantasies: the whole history of the individual is condensed into the oedipus complex. Nothing is discarded; all is worked over and fused with other elements, symbolized, resymbolized, projected onto the world, reincorporated into the self . . . the process continues unabated throughout life.

The vision of reality which emerges from each individual ego is like the dispersion of light from a crystal chandelier. Fragments of light, remnants of an older whole, play about the room. And if we conceive of a mass of such chandeliers, and observe the massed rays of dispersed light, we may find that these elemental rays cluster about certain areas. Certain parts of the room will be light; others will be dark, the light that was to have gone their way diffracted elsewhere. The bright portions look very luminous indeed and may, to a sympathetic observer, seem the image of progress.

Bibliographical Note

HERE ARE the main works used in the preparation of this book. I list them in order to orient the reader to my sources and to offer a guide to further study. The list is not meant to be a comprehensive bibliography.

I. HISTORICAL STUDIES IN RACISM

John H. Franklin's study, *From Slavery to Freedom* (New York, Alfred A. Knopf, 1967), provided a broad yet thorough introduction to the subject. Another general study which supplied useful data was E. Franklin Frazier's *The Negro in the United States* (New York, The Macmillan Company, 1957); along with the same author's *Race and Culture Contacts in the Modern World* (New York, Alfred A. Knopf, 1957). As to the history of racism, proper, two works were of extraordinary interest. One, whose frequent citation in the text reflects my opinion of its merit, was Winthrop Jordan's superb *White over Black* (Chapel Hill, University of North Carolina Press, 1968). The other, a broader view of the whole panoply of American racism, was *Race: The History of an Idea in America* by Thomas Gossett (New York, Schocken Books, 1965). Also of general interest was Oscar Handlin's *Race and Nationality in American Life* (Garden City, N.Y., Anchor Books, 1957). More particularly, I found Basil Davidson's study of the slave trade, *Black Mother* (Boston, Little, Brown and Company, 1961), useful. My understanding of the problem of slavery itself was greatly informed by Stanley Elkins' *Slavery* (Chicago, University of Chicago Press, 1959), which, although controversial, provided an important synthesis of psychological, cultural, and historical data; and by Eugene Genovese's *The Political Economy of Slavery* (New York, Pantheon Books, 1966), which decisively demonstrated the economic ruin attendant upon the slaveholding mystique. The vitally important subject of post-Reconstruction, white reunification and black expulsion was covered by Paul H. Buck's *The Road to Reunion* (1937; New York, Vintage Books, 1959), and especially by C. Vann Woodward's classic, *The Strange Career of Jim Crow* (New York, Oxford University Press, 1966); while the imperialism which attended this process was described by Richard Hofstadter in his essay "Cuba, The Philippines and Manifest Destiny," in *The Paranoid Style in American Politics* (New York, Vintage Books, 1967). As to the modern phase, only the barest mention of the great numbers of useful sources can be given. I would include Kenneth Clark's study of the black slums, *Dark Ghetto* (New York, Harper & Row, 1965); Charles Silberman's survey, *Crisis in Black and White* (New York, Random House, 1964); James Killian's gloomy but trenchant analysis, *The Impossible Revolution?* (New York, Random House, 1968); the "Kerner Report," the *Report of the National Advisory Commission on Civil Disorders* (New York, Bantam Books, 1968); and, finally, the one book that best describes the black man's experience in contemporary America, *The Autobiography of Malcolm X* (New York, Grove Press, 1965).

II. *RACIST PSYCHOLOGY*

Here, of course, much overlap with race history occurs, especially in the collection of essays in the two volumes of *Daedalus* devoted to *The Negro American* (Fall 1965, Winter 1966), and in the volume on *Race and Color* (Spring 1967). A most useful and compendious survey was Gordon Allport's *The Nature of Prejudice* (Garden City, N.Y., Anchor Books, 1958, abridged edition). Another valuable insight into the mind of the bigot is given by Jean-Paul Sartre in his 1948 essay, *Anti-Semite and Jew* (New York, Schocken Books, 1965). Several works on the psychology of Southern culture have become classics. These include *The Mind of the South* by W. J. Cash (New York, Vintage Books, 1960); *Killers of the Dream*, by Lillian Smith (Garden City, N.Y., Anchor Books, 1963); and John Dollard's pioneering study in a psychoanalytically informed anthropology, *Caste and Class in a Southern Town* (Garden City, N.Y., Anchor Books, 1957). An outstanding study of how racist concepts become embedded in children is *Race Awareness in Young Children* by Mary E. Goodman (New York, Collier Books, 1964). Although it is written from a European perspective, no book gives a better account of how racism is experienced by a black person than Frantz Fanon's *Black Skin, White*

Masks (New York, Grove Press, 1967). And the basic sexualization of racism is described in Calvin Hernton's impressionistic study, *Sex and Racism in America* (New York, Grove Press, 1965). Turning to more formal psychoanalytic studies, let me list those essays cited in the text: Brian Bird, "A Consideration of the Etiology of Prejudice," *Journal of the American Psychoanalytic Association*, Vol. V (1957) pp. 490–513; James Hamilton, "Some Dynamics of Anti-Negro Prejudice," *Psychoanalytic Review*, Vol. LIII (1966–1967), pp. 5–15; Lawrence Kubie, "The Ontogeny of Racial Prejudice," *Journal of Nervous and Mental Diseases*, Vol. CXLI (1965), p. 265; Terry Rodgers, "The Evolution of an Active Anti-Negro Racist," *The Psychoanalytic Study of Society*, Vol. I (1960); pp. 237–43; Richard Sterba, "Some Psychological Factors in Negro Race Hatred and in Anti-Negro Riots," *Psychoanalysis and the Social Sciences*, Vol. I, (1947), pp. 411–27.

III. PSYCHOANALYTIC THEORY

Only a few basic titles need be listed. Almost anything by Freud would be significant, but especially pertinent for the theoretical position of this essay would be the following (from *The Standard Edition of the Complete Psychological Works of Sigmund Freud*, ed. and trans. James Strachey [London, The Hogarth Press, 1964]): *Formulations on the Two Principles of Mental Functioning* (1911; Standard Ed., Vol. XII, pp. 218–26); *Beyond The Pleasure Principle* (1920; Standard Ed., Vol. XVIII, pp. 7–64); *Group Psychology and the Analysis of the Ego* (1921; Standard Ed., Vol. XVIII, pp. 69–143); *The Ego and the Id* (1923; Standard Ed., Vol. XIX, pp. 12–66); and *Negation* (Standard Ed., Vol. XIX, pp. 235–39. Of particular relevance to some of our themes have been Sandor Ferenczi's "The Ontogenesis of the Interest in Money," in *First Contributions to Psycho-Analysis* (London, The Hogarth Press, 1952), pp. 319–31; Lawrence Kubie's essay, "The Fantasy of Dirt," *Psychoanalytic Quarterly*, Vol. VI (1937), pp. 388–425; and Robert Waelder's theoretical essay, "The Principle of Multiple Function: Observations on Overdetermination," *Psychoanalytic Quarterly*, Vol. V (1936), pp. 45–62. The definitive work on the formation of the self-concept is *The Self and the Object World*, by Edith Jacobson (New York, International Universities Press, 1964); while the general field of ego psychology is best grasped through the work of Heinz Hartmann: see his *Essays On Ego Psychology* (New York, International Universities Press, 1964), and the paper, writen with Ernst Kris and Rudolph M. Loewenstein, "Some Psychoanalytic Comments on 'Culture and Personality,'" in *Papers on Psychoanalytic Psychology* (New York, International Universities Press, 1964), pp. 86–117. Finally, Erik Erikson's *Childhood and Society* (New York, W. W. Norton & Company, 1963), presents a full, culturally relevant view of human development.

IV. CULTURAL STUDIES

Next to Freud, my two principle sources have been Herbert Marcuse and Norman O. Brown. Indeed, this book is a deliberate attempt to apply the view of history initiated by Freud, and elaborated by Marcuse and Brown, to the particular historical problem of racism. Thus my indebtedness to these authors greatly exceeds the occasional direct mention of them in the text. Both Marcuse and Brown have taken Freud's basic propositions about the development of culture, but have tried to go beyond them to find a "way out" of the grim trap that Freud discerned in the human situation. However, despite my profound admiration for their works, I am not convinced that they have succeeded. The wish to find a way out of the trap is attractive enough to obscure from us the fact that reality has no particular interest in our happiness or liberation. We are entitled, perhaps obligated, to strive for these goals, but ethical imperatives are one thing, and objective analysis another, and in the latter pursuit it is Freud's remorseless vision which seems closer to the actuality of our situation than either Marcuse's or Brown's. Thus the view to which I have hewn more than any other is that expressed in *Civilization and Its Discontents* (1930; Standard Ed., Vol. XXI, pp. 64–145), along with Freud's other cultural writings, such as *The Future of an Illusion* (1927; Standard Ed., Vol. XXI, pp. 5–56) and *Moses and Monotheism* (1939; Standard Ed., Vol. XXIII, pp. 7–137). However, Marcuse and Brown each have made fundamental advances in our grasp of the problem, the former by relating Freud to Marx and Hegel, and so bringing psychoanalytic insight into broader historical perspective; the latter by his penetrating exploration of the full historical scope of body symbolism, particularly that of anality. I have therefore drawn heavily on Marcuse's *Eros and Civilization* (New York, Random House, 1955) and *One-Dimensional Man* (Boston, Beacon Press, 1964); and on Brown's *Life Against Death* (New York, Random House, 1959), and, to a somewhat lesser extent, *Love's Body* (New York, Random House, 1966).

There have, of course, been other major explorations into a psychoanalytic history. Many, such as Erikson's classic *Young Man Luther* (New York, W. W. Norton & Company, 1958), have been primarily psychobiographies and so not within the main scope of our essay. But some have gone directly into the history of culture.

See Bruce Mazlish's anthology, *Psychoanalysis and History* (Englewood Cliffs, N.J., Prentice-Hall, 1963), and particularly the essay therein by Géza Róheim, "The Evolution of Culture." Appreciation of Róheim's work has lagged, perhaps because of the obscurity of his style. But his work is a veritable treasure chest of insight into culture. Another pioneer whose analytic explorations into history have been relatively neglected has been Wilhelm Reich. Reich's *Mass Psychology of Fascism* (New York, Orgone Institute Press, 1946) introduced many essential themes about the nature of dominative societies. Finally, H. Stuart Hughes' book, *Consciousness and Society* (New York, Vintage Books, 1961), and his collection of essays, *History as Art and as Science* (New York, Harper & Row, 1964), especially the chapter on "History and Psychoanalysis: The Explanation of Motive," have provided valuable synthesis of these related disciplines.

Aside from these psychoanalytically informed studies, I have relied heavily for my understanding of economic history upon Karl Marx's essay, "Alienated Labor" (in *Man Alone*, edited by Eric and Mary Josephson, New York, Dell Publications, 1962); on Karl Polanyi's *The Great Transformation* (Boston, Beacon Press, 1964); and on Max Weber's *The Protestant Ethic and the Spirit of Capitalism* (New York, Charles Scribner's Sons, 1958). Further study of Weber was obtained from *The Sociology of Max Weber*, by Julien Freund (New York, Pantheon Books, 1968). Johan Huizinga's *Homo Ludens* (Boston, Beacon Press, 1955) and *The Waning of the Middle Ages* (Garden City, N.Y., Anchor Books, 1954), provided valuable insights. Of quite fundamental importance for the whole study, was the work of Alfred North Whitehead, for its grasp of science—*Science and the Modern World* (New York, The Free Press, 1967); of cultural history—*Adventures of Ideas* (New York, The Macmillan Company, 1933); and of symbolism—*Symbolism, Its Meaning and Effect*, in *Alfred N. Whitehead, An Anthology*, edited by F. S. C. Northrop and Mason W. Gross (New York, The Macmillan Company, 1961). And as for the contemporary situation, of all the host of significant sources, I would single out John K. Galbraith's *The New Industrial State* (Boston, Houghton Mifflin Company, 1967) for its lucid economic analysis and Hannah Arendt's *The Origins of Totalitarianism* (New York, Harcourt, Brace & World, 1966) for its vision of what has become of us and what is still latent.

Index

JOEL KOVEL was born in 1936 and was educated at Yale, from which he graduated summa cum laude, and at Columbia University Medical School. At present a resident of New York City, he directs the undergraduate medical education program in psychiatry at the Albert Einstein College of Medicine.

VINTAGE POLITICAL SCIENCE
AND SOCIAL CRITICISM